D1859528

POLITICAL DEVELOPMENT IN MANIPUR 1919–1949

POLITICAL DEVELOPMENT IN MANIPUR 1919–1949

Dr. S.M.A.W. Chishti

Publications

KALPAZ PUBLICATIONS

DELHI - 110052

Political Development in Manipur 1919-1949

Rs. 690
© : Prof. S.M.A.W. Chishti
ISBN : 81-7835-424-1

All Rights Reserved. No Part of this book may be reproduced in any manner without written permission.

Published in 2005 in India by
Kalpaz Publications,
C-30, Satyawati Nagar,
Delhi-110 052
E-mail : kalpaz@hotmail.com

Lasertype Setting by: Tact Computer Graphics, Delhi
Printed at: Salasar Imaging Systems, Delhi

Contents

Appendices

Preface

The thesis deals with the political and constitutional developments in the erstwhile princely state of Manipur from 1919 till its merger with India in 1949. Based on an intensive analysis of the available source-materials and interviews with the surviving members of the power-elite of the era under study, it constitutes, perhaps, the first systematic, objective and critical analysis of the political history of Manipur as well as the genesis, growth and rise of the democratic movement in the region.

Apart from unpublished documents, such as the files of the Foreign and Political Department, I have considerably relied on some of the available published material such as various pamphlets and reports published by the Manipur State Congress. But I have been handicapped in my research by lack of access to certain important Government of India files on deposit with the National Archives of India, and certain files of the All-India Congress Committee on deposit with the Nehru Memorial Library and Museum at New Delhi. The concerned authorities did not allow me to consult such documents, which related to past-1945 events.

The method of analysis is the 'old-fashioned' historical descriptive, as there was no other way for me to present my material and analysis in a coherent manner. I hope this study of Manipur's rise to political democracy coinciding with her merger with the Indian Union constitutes not only an original contribution to the exiting knowledge about the politics of the erstwhile princely states but also ipso facto constitutional history of the Indian Union.

The first chapter introduces the Manipuri society and politics in a historical setting and depicts how Manipur underwent changes under several dynasties through ages.

The second chapter analyses the genesis and growth of political consciousness among the Kuki tribesmen. The Kuki rebellion broke out during 1917-1919 when they were compelled by the local

Government to provide labourers to be sent to Mesopotamia. The rebellion put the state in turmoil throughout a whole year, then, gradually, normalcy was restored.

The third chapter studies the development of the semi-religious, semi-political movement led by Jadonang in 1930s, which aimed at the eventual overthrow of the British Government and annihilation of the Kukis and the Meiteis and, therefore, the establishment of a 'Kabui Naga Raj'. The political cult of Jadonang spread to the far-flung areas of Manipur and the Naga Hills. The movement died away as the leader was killed by the Government before it could get out of control.

The fourth chapter is the continuation of the Kacha-Naga movement led by Jadonang. After him the movement was spear-headed and intensified by Gaidinliu. She popularized the non-cooperation movement among the highlanders. In no time it spread over to the areas inhabited by the Nagas. The movement was soon suppressed by the Government of India. On the whole, it played its role in the politicization of the Naga tribals.

The fifth chapter discusses the problem of Manipur's accession to the erstwhile proposed Indian federation. The Maharaja of Manipur came out with certain reservations and desired to introduce some of his own reforms in the state, which were not in conformity with the Government of India Act, 1935. He was unwilling to join the proposed federation as it entailed the limitation of his own administrative authority.

The sixth chapter focuses on the Women's Bazar Agitation of 1939, caused by the scarcity of foodgrains. As the price of rice rapidly rose, the poor people faced starvation. The consequent agitation soon assumed political overtones. The movement subsided as soon as the price of rice went down and economic condition improved.

The seventh chapter deals with the political activities of the Bengali elites for the creation of a north-east Indian frontier province composed of Manipur, Cachar, Cooch-Behar, Tripura, etc., who were apprehensive of the possible Assamization of the Bengalis in Assam. The movement fizzled out as it could not mobilize the support of the general public; moreover, the Central Government turned down the demand for the creation of the so-called 'Purbachal Pradesh'.

The eighth chapter deals with the political factors which led to the constitutional movement in Manipur during the late 1940. This was the period when the people of Manipur aspired to replace the present autocracy by a limited constitutional monarchy. This resulted in a movement for the establishment of a representative government. Ultimately the Maharaja had to introduce a constitution and establish a nominal Assembly.

The ninth chapter describes the further intensification of the merger of Manipur with the Indian Union. Undoubtedly the Maharaja was not in favour of Manipur's merger with the Indian Union, rather, he preferred to be grouped with Sikkim and Khasi States. Since the political leadership of the Congress Party was in favour of the merger, the Maharaja was obliged to sign the instrument of Manipur's accession to the Indian Union in 1949.

The conclusion provides an overview of the political developments in Manipur during the years 1919-1949, and makes one feel that the process of democratization in British Indian territories had an impact on the people and politics of Manipur, particularly during the thirties and the forties. The accession of Manipur to the Indian Union was a landmark in the political development of the Manipuris and, later on, the granting of full statehood to Manipur gave it a status of equality with other constituents of the Indian Union.

S.M.A.W. Chishti

Acknowledgements

I am profoundly grateful to my supervisor, Professor S.A.H. Haqqi, Head of the Department of Political Science Aligarh Muslim University, for his constant help, guidance and unfailing encouragement to me in the course of my research work. Without his consistent concern with the progress of the work it would not have been possible for me to complete it. I shall forever remember his kind support to me and his large-hearted patience against my encroachment upon his precious time.

I am really indebted to the staff of the National Archives of India, the Nehru Memorial Library and Museum, the National Library, Calcutta, and the Maulana Azad Library, Aligarh, for their invaluable help. I am beholden to the teaching and non-teaching staff of the Department of Political Science for their encouragement.

The University Grants Commission's support is most sincerely acknowledged. The Junior Research Fellowship that the Commission awarded to me made it possible for me to devote four years and six months to this research work. Last but not the least, I am all praise for Mr. M.A. Khan Afridi of the Department of History for his meticulous typing of the manuscript.

S.M.A.W. Chishti

1
The Manipuri Polity in Historical Setting

Introduction

Manipur, with an area of 22,327 sq. kms. and a population of about 1.1 million*, occupies a strategic position in east India. Surrounded by Nagaland in the north, Mizoram in the south and Assam in the west, Manipur has an international boundary with Burma in the east. The territory has had a variety of names in the past. In the memoirs of Rennel it is called 'Meckley'.[1] The Burmese and Shan tribes, knew it as 'Kase' or 'Kathe'.[2] Lord Irwin once compared Manipur to 'Switzerland' because of her scenic beauty and richness in natural resources.[3] Manipur is also referred to as the 'jewel of India'.[4]

Manipur was a princely state of India before 1947. On October 15, 1949, she became a Chief Commissioner's Province. Under the Indian constitution, Manipur was initially placed in category 'C' of States. An Advisory Council was formed in 1950 to advise on its administration.

It was replaced in 1957 by a Territorial Council composed of thirty and two nominated members. Manipur was made a Union Territory on November 1, 1956. Later, under the Government of Union Territories Act, 1963, a Legislative Assembly of thirty elected and three nominated members was established. On December 19, 1969, the chief executive was designated Lieutenant Governor. Manipur became a full-fledged State of the Indian Union on January 21, 1972.

---

* 23,88634 (Source: North East Council)

The Ethnic Structure, Culture and Religion

The population of Manipur mainly consists of hill tribes and plain people. Some of the clans namely Meitei, Khoomal, Looang and Moirang came from different directions and settled in Manipur. The Khoomal clans was initially most powerful. After its decline the Meitei clans dominated all other clans to such an extent that they came to be known as sub-clans of the Meitei.[5] About the origin of tribal structure of Manipur, T.C. Hudson remarks that "... there is far more ground to conclude them to be descendants of the surrounding hill tribes.[6] He highlights similarity in language to prove his contention. R. Boileu Pemberton contends Manipuris "... to be the descendants of a Tartar Colony, which probably migrated from the northwest borders of China during the sanguinary conflicts for supremacy which took place between the different members of the Chinese and Tartar dynasties in the thirteenth and fourteenth centuries."[7]

There is yet another theory about the origin of the Manipur tribes. William Shaw traces the relationship between Manipuris and Thais during 707-717.[8] It may also be of interest to note that the Thais or Twangs of southern part of China had penetrated into Manipur and Burma (now Myanmar) in 1250 A.D. They were more Chinese than Thais. In the frequent skirmishes with the ruler of Manipur, some of them were taken as captives. Gradually they became part of Manipuri society by marrying local women. This introduced elements of Chinese-Thai culture in Manipur. The Chinese influence is evident in the royal insignia of the Manipuris which is winged lion which was the insignia of the Chinese T'sang dynasty.

The complexion of population in the islands on the Eastern Archipelago with adjoining portions of the mainland depicts fusion of cultures and races of the east, the west and the north. Apart from this, there has been vivid manifestation of the fusion of the Austric, the Bodo, the Dravidians, and the Aryans. Due to the situation of Manipur as a route for the migration of various races and cultures, the Manipuris appear to be Mongolians by features, Chinese by culture, Aryans by tradition. Naga by observance and Mithraic by faith.[9]

Among the hill tribes, the Kukis and Nagas are the only important ones. The Kukis largely live in the south hill portion of Manipur. The Nagas are found in the north and north-east hill areas. There are a number of sub-tribes about twenty-nine among the Nagas and Kukis.

Hinduism is claimed to be the oldest religion in Manipur.[10] It was at its highest during the reign of Gopal Singh or Garib Newaz (1714-49) as he was popularly known. When he got converted to Hinduism under the influence of some 'wandering Fakir'.[11] his subjects were made to follow willingly or unwillingly the same faith. Hinduism was declared as official religion and any religious dissent was severely punished. The advent of Hinduism and some of the traditions, which were established under its influence, resulted in a cleavage in Manipur society. The entire social structure of the plains was recant into Kshatriyas, Brahmins and other Hindu varnas. The Brahmins dominated all other castes and intermarriage was strictly prohibited. Untouchability was practiced. The distinction between the hill tribes and the people living in plains also became more apparent. The Marwaris and the Punjabis who were mainly engaged in business, were dubbed by the Manipuris as *Mayang* (foreigners). There is a minority of native Muslims forming about 6.62* percent of the population. Various views have been expressed regarding the arrival of Muslims in Manipur. The origin of Manipuri Muslims could be traced to the reign of Meitei King Khagee-gama (1579-1651),whose brother Shelungba, tired of unjust treatment by his brother fled to Sylhet. With the help of Muslim soldiers, he invaded Manipur. The raid was not successful; for whatever reason might be some of the Muslim Soldiers had stayed behind after the incident. These Muslims soldiers got married to Manipuri women and this was the beginning of a new race, Manipuri Muslims. It was in 1622 that the Mughal Emperor, Aurangzeb, sent three ambassadors to Manipur. This was reciprocated by the Maharaja of Manipur. This indirectly encouraged immigrants from outside.[12] Majority of Muslims came from Bengal and Assam.[13] Some of them also came from the western areas of the sub-continent with the sole purpose of preaching Islam. In the early days, as we have already seen, intermarriages between Meiteis and Muslims were very common. The population of Manipur was affected by the Burmese raids on Manipur. Many of them were taken as captives by the Burmase.[14] At present the Muslim population of Manipur has adopted itself to Manipur culture and they are known as 'Panggans', the corrupt form of 'Bengal'.

Political Evolution

To trace the political history of Manipur is very difficult since ancient records are not fully available. Since the advent of the Christian

Era about forty-seven native kings have reigned till 1714. Only one important happening worth mentioning during all these years is the conquest of Khumbat by the united forces of Pong and Manipur in 1475. This followed the annexation of the Kabaw Valley in the territory of Manipur.[15] It is said that a king named Pakhangba reigned some 300 years before 1714. Edward Gait terms the accounts of this period as 'merely legendary'.[16] The present political history of Manipur started from 1714 with the rule of Garib Newaz (patron of the poor). He has been considered one of the most powerful kings of Manipur. During the years 1725 and 1749, he was able to capture many important towns of Burma. It would not be any exaggeration to say that Manipur owes her present shape to him. His influence in the west extended up to Cachar; to the south, as far as the water-shed flowing seawards; and to the north for about nine days journey from the capital.[17] As has already been mentioned – the remarkable event of his reign was the introduction of Hinduism. He was a peace-loving Raja. He was murdered by his second son, Jit Shai, on the bank of Ningthee river, while returning from the Burmese campaign with his eldest son, Sham Shai who also shared the fate of the father. Jit Shai immediately ascended the throne.

Jit Shai succeeded his father but after a short reign of five years, he was expelled from Manipur by his own brother Barut Shai. Barut Shai was on the throne of Manipur for about two years. After his death, Goura Sham, the eldest son of Sham Shai took over the administration. He being crippled was unable to perform his functions properly and so he took the help of his brother Jai Singh or Chingthungkhamba in ruling the country. Jai Singh took the throne after the death of Goura Sham in 1764.

During these years an active hostility developed between Burma and Manipur. The Burmese were unhappy with the murder of Garib Newaz by his son. In 1755 the Burmese king Alaungpaya attacked Manipur, and took away many captives. It was the 'first devastation' inflicted by the Burmese on the Manipuris. The Burmese could occupy Manipur for not more than nine days, as they were pushed back by the Manipuris. The second invasion, one of the 'worst disasters' in the history of Manipur,[18] resulted in the occupation of Imphal by Alompra in 1758.[19] This could have serious consequences but for the timely intervention by British. An agreement was signed between the Governor of the Bengal Presidency and Manipur. The former agreed to help the latter in expelling the Burmese from Manipur.This agreement, however, was never put into practise. During the reign of Shemhegwen, the Burmese crossed the Hiroke Range and there was a ferocious battle at Tamu. Jai Singh escaped to Cachar. The Burmese put Kalemba, a descendant of the former Moirang Rajas, on the throne of Manipur as a nominal king. He reigned under the protection of Burma for three years. With the help of the Cachar king Jai Singh expelled Kalemba from Manipur. Kalemba immediately fled to Burma.

Between 1770-71, Kalemba's brother tried to recapture the throne of Manipur. This time Jai Singh could not resist their attack, and fled to Cachar. Between 1775 and 1782 Jai Singh repeatedly attempted to regain his throne. But he was always unsuccessful. Following this, there was an interval of political anarchy, during which period many princes, Burmese and Manipuri, would appear to have alternately held Manipur. Meanwhile, the year after 1782, a Manipur price Eremba could bring a peaceful atmosphere for a period of three years. But this state of affairs was not permanent. Once again when Burmese attacked Manipur, but suffered heavy loss. Eremba handed over the administration to Jai after his return from Cachar.

Jai could rule only for one year when suddenly he was forced by the Burmese invasion to leave the country. He was compelled to flee from the country as he was unable to face the powerful Burmese army. There was complete disorder in the country and many important changes took place.[20]

Jai, shortly after he returned in 1798, apparently tired out by his constant wars against Burma, stepped down from the throne in favour of his eldest son Rabino Chandra. After the death of Jai in 1799, Manipur was once again plunged in a state of chaos and confusion. Rivalry among the princes was one of the main sources of political disorder in the country. This continued till 1819. During the regime of Marjit Singh, one of the brothers of the former king Rabino Chandra, a strained relationship developed between his country (Manipur) and Burma. Marjit appeared to have meditated throwing off the yoke of Burmese supremacy at the first opportunity. With change of kings occurring in Burma, the new ruler Bagyidaw (1819-37) sent a message to Marjit, demanding his presence as a feudatory. Marjit refused to obey the order of the Burmese king. This led to another invasion by the Burmese in 1819. The Manipuris strongly resisted for seven days, but were at last overpowered, and Marjit fled to Cachar. During this invasion the Burmese army almost completely devastated the country. The houses of the villagers were extensively demolished, and the walls of the king's enclosures leveled with the ground. G.E. Harvey writes, "... it is now impossible to tell what their social and political conditions were like."[21] The great disaster of 1819, was followed by a period of anarchy and political instability. 'From this period the history of Muneepore (*sic*) presents an unvarying scene of disgusting treachery, between the numerous sons of Jai Singh, who in their contests for supremacy, arrayed the unhappy people of the country in hostile warfare against each other and inflicted miseries upon them..."[22]

During the ascendancy of Chourajit Singh, one of his brothers, Marjit conspired against him. But it was an unsuccessful attempt and he had to flee to Ava. With the help of Burma, Marjit once again attempted to overthrow his brother Chourajit, but he failed to do so. He fled to Cachar. Then he reached Burma. This time the king of Ava helped him with a large and strong force, which could defeat Chourajit who escaped to Cachar. Finally, Marjit was placed on the throne of Manipur in 1813. As a token of friendship, Marjit had given the Kabaw Valley to the Burmese.[23]

Marjit reigned for a period of five years and the Manipuri had a peaceful state of affairs. A problem started when he refused to pay tribute to the Burmese king, a promise he had made during the Burmese help in overthrowing Chourajit. Hpagyidoa, the king of Burma, determined to punish Marjit, sent an army under the command of General Maha Bandula to depose Marjit. Burmese raided Manipur during the rainy season, and defeated Marjit in 1819. The Burmese this time destroyed a number of Manipuri villages. Marjit escaped to Cachar. He was received by his brother there. The Burmese placed Manipur under the rule of Jagu Singh, a son-in-law of Garib Newaz. He was succeeded by a brother of Nar Singh. Both these rulers were never really accepted by Manipuris and were regarded as stooges of Burma.

Before the outbreak of the Anglo-Burmese War in 1822, repeated attempts were made unsuccessfully to free Manipur from the control of Burma. In the meanwhile Gambhir Singh, a prince of Manipur, implored British help for his country. The British were ready to help him as they were opposed to the Burmese policy of expansionism. This resulted in the Anglo-Burmese War. On March 5, 1824 the Burmese invaded Manipur and Cachar simultaneously. After a number of engagements at different places, the Manipur forces repulsed the Burmese from the territory of Manipur. The war was brought to close by the treaty of Yandaboo, in 1826.[24] Manipur was declared as an independent State. Gambhir was installed as the Maharaja. By the treaty of January 25, 1834, between the (British) Government of India and Manipur, Kabaw Valley was transferred by the former to Burma. As a compensation a monthly subsidy of five hundred rupees was granted to Manipur.[25] This continued till the death of Gambhir. Later it was withdrawn, and a Political Agent was appointed for preserving friendly relationship with the State of Manipur.

After the death of Gambhir, the administration passed on to his son, Chandra Kirti. As Chandra Kirti was minor the whole burden of administration was borne by his Senapati, Nar. Chandra Kirti's mother was sceptical about the loyalty of Nar and conspired against him. As she failed to get Nar murdered, she with her son fled from the country. She took shelter in a British camp. In spite of her best endeavours, the Chief Commissioner of Assam refused to give her help in overthrowing the Manipur Regent, Nar.

After the death of Nar in 1850, his brother Debendra Singh ascended the thrones. When Chandra Kirti became major, he successfully revolted against Debendra, who fled to Cachar. During the reign of Chandra Kirti several attempts were made to overthrow him by Debendra's brother and three sons of Nar. But always they were pushed back by the army of Chandra Kirti. And they had to take refuge in Cachar.

Chandra Kirti, the young Raja, assumed the title of Maharaja by virtue of his strength and popularity. He established a strong government. The British also seemed to be satisfied with his rule. Slowly however, some misunderstanding developed over the Maharaja's demand for the resumption of the payment of Kabaw Valley compensation, which had been suspended after the death of Gambhir. He threatened to forcibly take back the Kabaw Valley if they did not fulfill his demand. This was not liked by the British Government. The Political Agent characterized this demand as '... unbecoming from the court of the son of the man who owed his throne to the British

Government.'[26] Analyzing the situation, the Political Agent wrote to the British Government of India, 'I have met with some petty acts of annoyance indicating a bad spirit in the authorities, who (at least many of them) seem to think the presence of the representative of the British Government ought to be no check on them; that by their prowess they gained the throne for the young Raja in spite of the British Government, and now they have got it, they may do exactly as they choose. I trust, however, as they cool down they may understand their positions. The young Raja, I believe, does'.[27] The British Government in India in reply warned the Raja of serious consequences if he did not stop the campaign against the British. This calmed down the Maharaja. The British Government promised to extend all help to him on demand.[28] Thus silenced, as a gesture of goodwill Chandra Kirti helped the British during the outbreak of Indian Mutiny in 1857 by putting his troops at their disposal.[29]For this act the Maharaja was highly honored by the British Government of India.

Chandra Kirti was succeeded by his son Sur Chandra in May 1886. But his ascendency was challenged by Bara Chauba Singh, the eldest son of Nar. He was not successful and Bara Chauba was taken into custody by Sur Chandra. Sur Chandra was a weak ruler. This encouraged rivalries among his eight brothers, which later on resulted in the emergence of two groups[30]—the Maharaja (i.e. Sur Chandra Singh), Pucka Sena, Samoo Hangaba, and the Dolairoi Hangaba formed one side; whilst the Jubraj (i.e. Kula Chandra Singh), Senapati (i.e. Tikendrajit Singh), Angau Sana, and Zilla Singh all combined together. It reached a climax when the group of Tikendrajit attacked the palace in September 1890. The Senapati Tikendrajit and two of his other brothers (i.e. Zilla Singh and Angau Sana) took possession of the palace. Panicked, Sur Chandra abdicated the throne and sought asylum at the residence of the Political Agent whose advice to the contrary he disregarded.

In the meanwhile Jubraj Kula Chandra Bhaja was installed on the throne as the king of Manipur, with the help of the Senapati, Tikendrajit, who was the chief architect of the uprising. The British government recognized the new king. But they developed bitterness against Senapati for his illegal acts against the former king. A small military force was sent to Manipur by the Assam Government, to carry out the decision of the Government of India, including the arrest of Senapati.[31] The party which included Chief Commissioner, Quinton, reached Imphal on

March 22, 1891. The Senapati had sensed the British designs and so he avoided attending the Durbar held in the honour of the British. When the Chief Commissioner decided to arrest the Senapati at his residence, it resulted in serious hostilities in which the Chief Commissioner and his four officers were brutally murdered by the Manipuris. The remaining British officers fled to Silchar (Assam) as they found the situation beyond their control. On 27 April, 1891, a big military force arrived at Imphal to control the Manipuri uprising. The Manipuris were completely overpowered. The Jubraj, Senapati and other brothers who had taken part in the rebellion were arrested. Tikendrajit was convicted of waging war against the Queen Empress, and abetment of the murder of the British officers. He was sentenced to death; Consequently, he (along with General Thangal) was executed by hanging on August 13, 1891. Kula Chandra and his brother with thirteen others were transported for life.

After the sudden political upheaval of 1891, Manipur lost her identity for the time being. In September 1891, plans for future administration were finalized, and Chura Chand Singh, a great grandson of Nar Singh was nominated to be the future king of Manipur. By Sanad No. LXXII, the State of Manipur was made brought under the complete control of the British Government. Manipur was made to pay a subsidy of Rs. 50,000 to the British Government with effect from 21 August, 1891.[32]

Since Chura Chand Singh was a minor, the administration in fact was in the hands of the Political Agent. In May 1907, the State Administration was handed over to Chura Chand Singh. The Lieutenant Governor formally installed him as Raja. A council of six persons was nominated to help him run the affairs of the country. Beside this he was assisted by an officer of Indian Civil Service in his day to day administration. The hereditary title of Maharaja was bestowed on him on 1 January, 1918. The Maharaja, with the help of the British, efficiently ruled the State and abolished the system of slavery and *Pothang*.[33]

References

1. James Rennel, *Memoir of a Map of Hindustan; or the Mogul Empire* (London: W. Bulmer & Co., 1793), p. 295.
2. R.B. Pemberton, *Report on the Eastern Frontier India* (Gauhati: The Government of Assam, 1966), p. 21.

3. *Manipur: A Decade of Progress*, August 15, 1962, p, 46.
   Sir William Birdwood found Manipur to be a place of beauty – 'a Kashmir in miniature'. *The Times* (London), December 24, 1926, p. 9.
   It is also described as a 'little paradise on earth' Sir Geoffrey Evans, Antony Brett-James, *Imphal* (London: Macmilian & Co. Ltd., 1962), p. 6.
4. *Ibid.*, p. 46.
5. Mac Cullock, *Munnipore and the Hill Tribes* (Calcutta: 1859), p. 4.
6. T.C. Hudson, *The Meitheis* (London: David Nutt, 1908), p. 5, Supporting the theories of T.C. Hudson and R. Brown, B.C. Allen shows the close relationship between Nagas and Meiteis, as in the coronation ceremony the kings were dressed in Naga fashion 'rimchaw'.
7. R.B. Pemberton, *Report on the Eastern Frontier India* (Gauhati: The Government of Assam, 1966), p. 37.
8. W. Shaw, "The Manipuris", *Eastern Sentinental*, June 17, 1959, p. 4.
9. R. M. Nath, *The Background of Assamese Culture* (Assam: A.K. Nath, 1948), p. 86.
10. According to Manipuri pundits and authorities, Hinduism can be traced back to the ancient time. They claimed that it existed even before the reign of Garib Newaz. But for some time its popularity seems to have been eclipsed. It was revived only during the reign of Garib Newaz. The proof of the revival is so meager, and the statements in support of the idea that the Hindu religion existed in the country at a very ancient period are so contradictory and unsatisfactory, that there is no hesitation in stating that in all probability, although a spurious and imperfect form of Hinduism may have existed in individual cases previous to the reign of Garib Newaz, about 1750, it was during his reign that the Hindu religion became general, and was adopted by him and by the majority of people.
11. Santidas Goswami, an enterprising Vaishnava of the Chaitanya Mahaprabhu School of Narsingha Akhara of Sylhet (Bangladesh), crossed the hills of Jirighat and reached Manipur and within a short time bewitched as it were, the king including the whole population, with his melodious *Kirtana* bearing on the life story of Lord Krishna and Radha. Thus the Meities gradually converted to Hinduism.
12. R.M. Nath, *The Background of Assamese Culture* (Assam: A.K. Nath, 1948), p. 90.
13. E.W. Dunn says, 'The Mussalman are the descendants of Bengali immigrants, retain a knowledge of Hindustani and Bengali, and are hardly distinguishable in appearence from the Bengali, who have never left Cachar'. Similarly T.C. Hudson writes at one place, 'The Panggans (Muslims-mine) were believed to have originated from Cachar…' R. Brown also infers that Manipuri Muslims are 'chiefly from the districts

of Sylhet and Kachar'. E.W. Dunn (comp), *Gazetteer of Manipur* (Calcutta: Government of India, 1886), p. 14.

14. From great antiquity Muhammadans, have formed part of the population of the Manipur Valley. Naturally, during Burmese invasion, Muslim population was affected considerably, as they chiefly reside to the east of the capital of Manipur.
15. E. Gait, *A History of Assam* (Calcutta: Thacker Spink & Co., 1933), p. 321.
16. *Ibid.*, p. 263.
17. Before the arrival of Britishers in Manipur the roads connected with the neighbouring states were not motorable, rather they were only way ferring by bullock-cart, or on feet or horse, and so the journey could be measured by the time.
18. D.G.E. Hall, *Burma* (London: Hutchinson's University Library, 1950), p. 85.
19. G.E. Harvey, *Outline of Burmese History* (Calcutta: Bose Press, 1925), p. 133.
20. After 1786 there was a rapid succession of rajas in Manipur. There was instability in the country. It led to a state of chaos and confusion. Moreover, during this period, in the reign of one Wankai, a great flood in the valley of Manipur, caused great loss to life and property.
21. G.E. Harvey, *Outline of Burmese History* (Calcutta: Bose Press, 1925), p. 133.
22. R. Boileau Pemberton, *Report on the Eastern Frontier of British India* (Calcutta: Bagchi & Co. 1966), p. 45.

    In 1801 Rabino Chandra was fatally murdered by his step brother, when he was watching a hockey match. The killer faced the same fate when he was killed by his brother Chourajit Singh in a battle in 1806.
23. Arthur P. Phayre, *History of Burma* (London: 7 A High Street, Wanstead, 1967), p. 229.
24. C.U. Aitchison (comp.), *A Collection of Treaties*. Vol. XII (Calcutta: Government of India, 1931), p. 230.
25. *Ibid.*, p. 187.
26. R. Brown, *Statistical Account of the Native State of Manipur* (Calcutta: Office of the Superintendent, Government Printing, 1874), p. 68.
27. *Ibid.*
28. In 1851, 1859, 1862 and between 1864 and 1866 several attempts were made by rival princes to overthrow the Government of Chandra Kirti, but all of them were made unsuccessful with the British help.
29. *Ibid.* p. 69.

30. Ethel St. Clair Crimwood, *My Three Years in Manipur and Escape from the Recent Mutiny* (London: Richard Bentley and Son, 1891), pp. 133-34.
31. Sir Robert Reid, *History of the Frontier Areas Bordering on Assam from 1893-1914* (Shillong: Assam Government Press, 1942), p. 56.
32. C.U. Aitchison, *A Collection of Treaties* ... Vol. XII (Calcutta: Government of India Central Publication Branch, 1931), p. 106.
33. Under this old custom of *Pothang* every village was compelled to repair roads and school buildings and carry the luggage of touring officials within its boundary.

2

Manipur at the End of the Kuki Insurgency: 1917–19

Since the Manipur Uprising of 1891 against the British Government, the Kuki Insurgency during 1917-19 was the first of its kind during the entire period of British rule in Manipur. The Kukis who constitute one of the most powerful tribes of Manipur, revolted against foreign domination. Disturbances in the hills upset the state administration. The British Government felt considerably annoyed with frequent troubles which often resulted in losses of life and property. A number of disobedient villages were burnt down to ashes. Some of the Kuki chiefs were arrested in connection with the uprising and punished after a fair trial.

The British Government could, however, bring the situation under control only in 1919. The experience of the Kuki rebellion made the British Government realise the inadequacy of the rules which were framed for the administration of Manipur State in 1916.

Before we go into the details of the British actions, it would be worthwhile if we briefly probe into the causes of the Kuki Insurgency.

Immediate Causes

The year 1917 marks a landmark in the political history of Manipur tribals. It was in the year of Bolshevik Revolution of Russia, that the Kukis of Manipur revolted against the British Government of India.

The immediate causes of the Kuki Rebellion was the partial recruitment of forced labour from the Kuki tribe for the service of Labour Company in Mesopotamia during the First World War.[1] In the beginning of 1917, the Assam Government was asked to provide labourers for employment with Army in Mesopotamia. The Assam

Government requested the Maharaja of Manipur through the Political Agent. The Maharaja immediately started recruiting labourers with an aim to secure about 4000 labourers.

The British Officers never realised the likely difficulties in the recruiting process. The Kuki tribe strongly opposed the British system of recruitment. The Kuki chiefs or *Pibas* adopted an obstructive attitude.[2]

Regarding the delicacy of the situation the Political Agent of Manipur wisely propose a dialogue between the Government and village chiefs. But the Kuki leaders flatly refused the proposal, and did not turn up for talk with the Political Agent. As the situation became somewhat serious, the Political Agent requested the higher authorities to send force to control the unruly tribals. A small force was sent from Aizawl in the month of March 1917, for the purpose of preventing village heads from interfering with recruitment process.[3] This force was able to bring under control the Tangkhuls – one of the sub-Naga tribes of Manipur and south-western Kuki section.[4] Thereafter, it was reported that Colonel Cole was able to enrol about 736 labourers in the beginning of April. The number increased further and thus a labour corps could proceed to Mesopotamia.[5]

The Maharaja expressed regret for his inability in raising up the wanted number of labourers. When the Chief Commissioner of Assam was asked a second time for raising a Second Labour Corps, the local officers including the Maharaja were confident about doing so.[6] The Chief Commissioner was of the opinion that the Maharaja's proposal of leading a Second Corps to France should be accepted so that the Maharaja himself could have an opportunity to see the outside world. At the same time the Chief Commissioner was doubtful whether the conservative Hindu Brahmins would allow the Maharaja to leave his home state during the war time.[7]

The offer was, however, declined by Chelmsford, the Governor-General of India, who wrote to the Maharaja of Manipur, thanking him for his keen interest in raising the Second Labour Corps. He further added that the Maharaja might be asked if any such corps were needed for service (in France) in the near future.[8] After sometime, however, the British Government changed her policy, and the Assam

Government was asked for raising a Second Labour Corps. A political conference was held in Shillong in August to discuss the matter.[9] The Political Agent of Manipur was confident about raising up a Second Labour Corps from Manipur. With a view to understand the prevailing situation, and to convince the tribals, he arranged some meetings between the Government and the tribals. The tribal chiefs at this conference declined to supply labourers but they offered money.[10] The Political Agent, not fully conscious of the tribal feelings, threatened those defiant Kuki chiefs with punishment if labourers were not supplied within a fixed time. The Political Agent thought that he would be able to get a large number of coolies from the north-east of the Manvum village of Mombi.[11] It was in view of the fact that Ngulkhup, Mombi chief had promised to him to supply the required labourers whenever needed. Subsequently, however, his attitude changed and it was learnt that Ngulkhup had asked the villagers to burn their villages and to kill their women and children, if they were asked to send labourers to the Government.[12] The Political Agent was surprised to find the change in the attitude of Ngulkhup. He decided to teach a lesson to the defiant Kuki chiefs by taking up punitive measure against them.

Before we discuss details about the punitive steps taken by the Government, it would be worthwhile to know why the Kuki chiefs were unwilling to supply labourers on demands from the Government, and how far their objections were justified.

First, the Kukis were afraid of going to an unknown place off their villages.[13] Besides, it was rumoured that following the outbreak of the Great War the Maharaja and Political Agent had been killed in the field. And the British force was defeated in the war. The garrison which was stationed in Manipur was also withdrawn. As Higgins said, 'A garbled version of the retreat from Mons and the substitution of the Darrang Military Police battalion for the regular regiment in Manipur were probably responsible for the stories of disaster and the withdrawal of the garrison'.[14] Probably the ignorant tribals might have been afraid of going to France, and facing dangerous consequences. It was also felt that Kamhaos of the north Chin Hills were planning to attack suddenly the Manipur State. The Kamhao tribe had always been a source of trouble on the border areas of Manipur. This was undoubtedly one of the important reasons for the opposition by tribal chiefs to the proposal for second recruitment. At the same time the Kukis also apprehend that if they left their homes for France at such a critical junture, the Angamis taking the advantage of their long absence would surely kill their women-folk and children.[15]

Another reason for opposition to the recruitment was its resemblance to the old system of forced labour.[16] C.C. Watson, a British Officer, Home Department, expressed similar views when he wrote: 'The requisition to the tribal chiefs to supply coolies looks rather like a revival of the system (force labour).'[17]

Finally, the riotous and superstitious Kuki chiefs became a victim of Chinga Khamba Sana Chaoba Singh. He claimed himself to have supernatural power.[18] He openly incited the Kukis of Manipur to revolt against the regime of Maharaja, Sir Chura Chand Singh. The Charlatan, Chinga Khamba Sana Chaoba Singh, propogated that rule of British Government was going to end very soon, and so, their loyal subject should be annihilated.[19] He went from village to village for this. He was at least to some extent successful in creating a stir among the Kukis.[20]

Chinga Khamba Sana Chaoba Singh was arrested in Burma.[21] The Advisory Committee was of the opinion that he should not be allowed to return to Manipur. The Maharaja held the same view. He was tried by a special tribunal like other Kuki chiefs, and deported under Regulation 111 of 1818 and sentenced to life imprisonment.[22]

Punitive Measures

As the Kuki movement took a serious turn, the local Government felt the need for punitive measures. The disturbances among the Kukis also had an impact on the adjacent areas. In Burma, Chin Hills north of Haka and all other parts except Upper Chindwin, and including unadministered Somra Tract, were affected by the influence of the Kuki unrest in Manipur.[23] The Kukis of Tuzu river or Nantaleik situated east of the Naga Hills, were also agitated.[24] In January 1918, it was quite apparent that Kukis of Burma were ready to help their brethren Kukis of Manipur in their fighting to overthrow the Government. The Kukis of Naga Hills were also prepared to help them. Pachai, an old Kuki leader of Chassad, in the unadministered area of Somra Tract, also pledged to support with men and arms the Kuki insurgents of Manipur.[25]

Encouraged by this in most of the villages, the Kuki rebels in Manipur posed a serious threat to the Government. The Government was alarmed. On October 14, 1917, the Political Agent with an escort of Fifty Rifles of the Darrang Battalion set out for Mombi village with the intention to arrest its leader, Ngulkhup who was the first Kuki chief to commit an offence against the Government. He asked Ngulkhup to meet him. But he failed to come. The Political Agent in anger burnt the Mombi village on October 17, 1917.

The news of the burning of Mombi village alarmed the Kukis. Now onwards they became more aggressive. Finding the situation tense once again, Higgins arranged a meeting with some leaders of Uktal village, situated in the west of Manipur Hills, some twenty-six miles away from Imphal. The discussions did not produce any results. Meanwhile, the Political Agent learnt that twenty-two Kuki chiefs were meeting in order to mobilize opposition against the Government.

The Government of Assam had never contemplated the use of force for the purpose of enlisting labour for the establishment of a Second Labour Corps.[26] The Political Agent, however, argued that in view of the changing attitude of the Kuki chiefs it had become necessary to take a few punitive measures which could teach them a lesson. When the matter came to the notice of the Government of India, it was decided to abandon further recruitment. But at the same time it also passed an order to punish the recalcitrant Kuki chiefs.[27]

Arrangements were made to send out a column in order to arrest the unruly Kuki chiefs, as they did not turn up in compliance with the summons.[28] By this time the Kukis had already prepared to attack the valley of Manipur. Before any action was taken by the Government, the Kukis from Hinglep, Ukha and neighbouring villages, raided and looted the Manipur State Forest Toll Station at Ithai in December 1917.[29] It was learnt that this incident took place at the instigation of Chinga Khamba Sana Chaoba Singh who had also planned with the help of the Kukis an attack on Imphal.[30] This however did not take place since the Assam Rifles had been employed to defend Imphal.

As a precautionary measure several outposts were opened at different hill areas of Manipur, when disturbance was expected.[31] The Government was under the impression that the Kuki trouble would subside as soon as a few of the defiant chiefs were brought to book. But it did not happen. The Kukis became more violent after the military operation.[32] But they had never anticipated the consequences of their armed revolt against a mighty British Empire. The news of the Kuki raids and infiltrations had been very often coming to the Headquarters.

The Government intensified the military operation. During the month of January, Cosgrave, Political Agent, Manipur, with an escort of the Assam Rifles proceeded to Tammu to burn nine hostile villages and destroy their properties.[33] Higgins also destroyed fourteen rebel Kuki villages after fairly continuous fighting. Hutton with the help of the Column of the Naga Hills Rifles conducted an operation in the western hillside of Manipur. There he occupied a Kuki village, Chongjan on February 12, 1918. As a result of this operation, Laipi, chief of the Senting Kuki village, surrendered to Hutton. It was proposed to send further force, from Silchar to Imphal to suppress the Kuki rebellion.

On February 20, 1918, Colonel Cloete led a force from Silchar for Imphal. During the same time Cosgrave with another force had marched on to the south-west of Manipur. Cloete's operation in Maphitel Hills resulted in success.[34] With the exception of one Kuki chief, all surrendered before the British forces. The forces which were operating in the southern hills faced a strong opposition but the party at last emerged victorious. Next they launched attack on Manchangs in the south-hills. On March 14, 1918, Higgins and Cloete left Imphal to join Burmese Column in fighting against Chassad which was supposed to be the strongest, and most disobedient Kuki village. Reaching Kongal Thana they complied nine villages to surrender to them. Sixteen Ayuparel villages situated between the areas of Tammu and Chassad were also ready to surrender.[35] On the Upper Chindwin, Captain Patrick's column had commenced its advance on Chassad in Manipur from the South. The military operations were expected to stop in April, i.e., before the start of rainy season, to be resumed if necessary in the next winter.

In the meanwhile, the British Government was keen to find out why the force was comparatively weak in dealing with the Kuki rebels.[36] One of the factors was to be the lack of modern equipment. Military was also not well organised.[37] There was also lack of efficient trainees in Manipur.[38]

For the next military operation, the Chief Commissioner of Assam felt the need of complete re-armament of the Assam Rifles because in his opinion the integrity and security of the North-East Frontier of

India depended on its success. A Home Department communication dated the 28th May 1918 approved the proposal made by the Assam Chief Commissioner.

As soon as the rainy season ended in Manipur, the military operation again started. There were reports of fresh attacks by the Kukis in several villages. One Kuki leader Khuthinthang of Jampi claimed himself as Maharaja. According to his instructions some of his followers started collecting revenues and guns from weaker villages. In the meantime, it was reported that out of dissatisfaction with the Maharaja of Manipur, Moirang had established some unauthorised courts.[39] The Political Agent said that they were in touch with the Charlaton Chinga Khamba Sana Chaoba Singh.[40]

In June, the Kuki rebels renewed their attack on Khwakta, Khongda and Iringbam villages. Immediately an outpost was established to deal with these rebels. The Kuki insurgents even threatened to attack neighbouring areas beyond Manipur boundary. It was reported that seventy-five Kukis had entered the North Cachar Hills from Manipur side.

The political situation in Manipur became very serious as the Kuki movement could not be fully crushed. The Government decided to stop active military operation since it realized that the military operation in the hills were not as successful as expected. Describing the development in Manipur, in a letter to Secretary of State for India, the Viceroy commented, 'operations against Kukis in Manipur and Burma and Chins have already been a failure and we are considering advisability of putting operations next cold weather under one military control....'[41]

The administration confined itself to protected valley, Imphal. Eight police outposts were established at different places for the security of the valley.

On May 18, 1918, Beatson-Bell, Chief Commissioner of Assam, arrived at Imphal in order to have consultations with the local officers in connection with the suppression of Kuki rebellion and further continuation of military operation in the next winter. Later in July 1918, he visited Simla where he discussed the problem of Kuki rebels in Manipur with the Viceroy and the Commander-in-Chief.[42] Therefore, the Political Agent and Deputy Commissioner, Naga Hills, were summoned to a conference in Shillong to decide further measures pending the renewal of operations next winter under the command of General Keary.[43]

At the close of August General Keary who had to command the military operation in Assam (and Burma), came to Shillong in order to discuss the situation with the Chief Commissioner of Assam, and plan military campaign. It was decided that in accordance with the usual procedure the General Officer Commanding would assume complete political as well as military control of area of operation.[44] He would inform the local Government regarding any development having political implications, so that the Government of India could be posted with the latest developments.

Before the planned military operation in the winter could materialise, the Assam Rifles were badly affected by influenza which spread in Assam.[45] As a result of this, the Government of India even thought of suspension of active military expedition.[46] Yet the military operation started in January and continued up to February 13, 1919. These were undoubtedly among the most active military expeditions against the defiant Kuki rebels of Manipur.[47] During the operation, Longya, the village of the Kuki chief, Ngulbul, was occupied. His brother and fifty-five persons were arrested. His son died during the operation. The Chief of Ukha was also captured. Two hundred persons including women and children of Umdum had also surrendered. Among the captured were Ngulkhup, Chief of Mombi, and Tinthong, Chief of Longya, with his henceman Enjakhup.[48] Lt. Goldsmith, in his operations in the Chassad area, captured Bongmul and his twenty-six men. All the Mombi area chiefs had surrendered with the exception of Loothang of Gobok. In a combined expedition of Broome and Goldsmith led to the capture of five Kuki rebels. South-west and north-west areas became the victim of harassment by the military police.[49] Further surrender of Chiefs of Makan, Phunjong, Asang, Khulen and Malhang was also reported. In the south-east area Loothang of Gobok surrendered at last on February 22, 1919. Semkhupao of Simol followed him.

General Officer Commanding, Kuki punitive measure, Imphal, telegraphed to the Chief of the General Staff, Delhi, on March 1919, that Pachei had submitted to the military force this morning.[50]

Following that, Pachei's lieutenant Nokhao also surrendered on the next day. The last of the special list was completed with the submission of Ngukhuka to Montifiore. During the operation in the

Chassad area Montifiore burnt and destroyed several villages. The submission of Pachei together with the capture of Tinthong and Enjakhup in Jampi area, marked the end of active rebellion.[51] His followers were left without a leader to guide them during the rebellion.

By the middle of 1919, the active military punitive operation was over, as almost all the recalcitrant Kuki chiefs had been either captured or surrendered. They were tried by Special Tribunal, and awarded punishments under.Regulation 111 of 1818.

Gradually, the troops were withdrawn from north-west, south-west, south-east and western areas. The rebels were completely disarmed. Some seventeen permanent posts were established at different places in Manipur (including Assam area). Important roads which were closed during the Kuki insurgency were opened. Demobilization was nearly completed, and civil power was handed over to the local administrations.[52]

The old system of administration to which we would now refer, was found inefficient to deal with the situation and many changes were made in it.

The Nemesis of Local Maladministration

Of the factors responsible for the Kuki rebellion the most important was their accumulated dissatisfaction with the local maladministration. The British officers were mainly responsible for the outbreak of the rebellion. Had they realized the strong feelings of the Kukis on labour enrolment, there would have been possibly no such revolt. Here we would highlight the drawbacks in the administrative machinery which failed to check the rebellion.

First, the method of recruitment was not justified from the point of view of 'fair selection'. The Home Department, Government of India, had already advised the local Government not to use force against the persons who were unwilling to become labourers. It had further warned that action should be taken only if peace and tranquility within the state were threatened. The Political Agent made a mistake by giving warning to the Kukis that they would be punished if they did not enlist themselves in the Labour Corps to be sent to Mesopotamia. With regard to the raising of the Second Labour Corps both the Political Agent and the Maharaja committed a mistake by whole-heartedly enclosing the proposal, even-though they had the previous experience of the Kukis (and Nagas) offering resistance at the time of the first such recruitment. The use of force by the Political Agent ultimately led to the Kuki rebellion. Similar feelings were expressed by S.R. Hignell, Army Department, Government of India, who felt that the recruitment procedures adopted by the local administration officers seemed to have been extra-ordinarly ill-advised.[53]

When the hostilities actually opened the administration further proved itself incompetent for dealing with the situation. It was highly unimaginative to leave the entire administration covering about 7000 sq. miles of tribal area in the hands of the one British Officer designated as 'president' of the Manipur State Durbar. It was more serious particularly, in view of the fact, that the President was busy with the valley administration, and could not devote full time to the affairs of the hills. He was understandably not able to frequent visit the hill areas for administrative purposes. Such visits were highly essential for good administration. Naturally the people of hill areas felt neglected. The Political Agent, who shared the responsibility for the administration of the hills, abstained from action which might have weakened the President's authority.[54] Thus, lack of 'direct contact' aggravated the situation further and made a compromise difficult. The British Administration later admitted the lacunae in the administration before and during the Kuki rebellion.

Lastly, the *lambus* or interpreters employed as intermediaries during the first recruitment of labourers were largely responsible for creating a misunderstanding between the British officers and the Kukis. These *lambus* played a sinister role in inciting the Kukis to revolt against the British Rule.[55] At the same time they took money from those Kukis who did not like to enlist themselves as members of the Labour Corps.[56] It was a crime committed by the *lambus* against the Government. Thus the role of *lambus* 'as most unsatisfactory intermediatory',[57] was one of the factors in the Kuki insurgency.

Ensuring Political and Administrative Reforms

The Maharaja and British Officers, thus, were made fully aware of the drawbacks in the State administration which had led to the Kuki uprising of 1917. It was realized that one officer was not sufficient to look after the hilly areas as well as the valley of Manipur.

Even before the completion of the Kuki punitive action, the British Government in India felt the necessity of reform in the administrative machinery of the Manipur State. The Chief Commissioner of Assam himself went to Manipur, to discuss with the Maharaja and local British officers the arrangements regarding the future administration of the hill tribes.[58] The Maharaja and the Chief Commissioner agreed to establish three sub-divisions in three separate areas of the hills. It was further agreed that each of the sub-divisions would be administered by one European Officer designated as 'Sub-divisional Officer'. The three sub-divisions were as follows:

1. The South-West Area with headquarters at Chura Chandpur.
2. The North-West Area with headquarters at Tamenglong.
3. The North-East Area with headquarters at Ukhrul.[59]

The hill areas in the north of Manipur including the Mao and Maram Naga groups, the whole of the Mombi areas in the south-east, and the various tribes bordering the valley were to be administered directly by the Durbar President.[60]

The new scheme was likely to be a burden on the State economy as it would involve an amount of Rs. 1,25,000 on the hill administration. This was facilitated by the declaration of the President in an open Durbar that the Government of India had offered certain 'financial concession.'[61] The annual subsidy of Rs. 50,000 payable by the State was reduced to Rs. 5,000 for a period of ten years. The Government also announced to forego the annual contribution of Rs. 30,000, which had been paid hitherto towards the upkeep of the Kohima-Imphal road, and deferred the payment of annual instalments towards the repayment of annual instalments of the loan taken by the Durbar from Rs. 60,000 to 30,000.[62]

The question of jurisdiction of the Maharaja on collection of revenue was also taken up and after prolonged discussions the Governor-in-Council agreed to the Maharaja being given the power of revision in the revenue matter, as it was given in the civil and criminal cases under the sub-heading 'Administration of Justice' of the 'Rules for the Management of the State of Manipur.'[63] This was approved by the Government of India.

One more revision was brought in the rules which governed the administration of the Manipur State. The Rule 18 initially described the Maharaja as only a forwarding agent. Regarding this point the

Governor-in-Council proposed with the approval of the Maharaja to abrogate this clause as it sometimes had resulted in causing unnecessary delay. With regard to the interpretation of the rule 9 which allowed the Maharaja to record his own opinion only with reference to any suggestions made by the Durbar for the modification in the President's draft budget; and took away the Maharaja's right to extend his own suggestions, the Maharaja protested because he considered this as curtailment of his authority. The Governor-in-Council agreed to give to the Maharaja the right to place before the Durbar any observations or criticisms on the budget which he thought fit.[64]

The Governor-in-Council also agreed to the proposal of the Maharaja to restore the power of magistrate to him whereby he could punish any one violating the discipline in the police.[65] Recommendations were made to this effect to the Government of India in the following words:

> 'The Commandant of the State Military Police shall exercise powers corresponding to the powers of a Ist Class Magistrate, and an officer temporarily officiating as Commandant shall exercise powers corresponding to the powers of a 2nd-class Magistrate, for the purpose of inquiring into or trying any offence committed by a member of the Military Police Act, 1861 (V of 1861), or Under the Assam Rifles Act (Assam Act 1 of 1920), and any offence committed by a member of the Military Police against the person or property of another member and punishable under any law in force in Manipur.'[66]

The effects of revisions in the 'Rules for the Management of the State of Manipur' could not be felt immediately. It helped in bringing to an end the after-effects of the Kuki rebellion. The travelling British officers were greeted in a friendly manner and extended due hospitality. In May 1920, Sir Nicholas Beatson-Bell made a long trip, unaccompanied by any escort, through the hill areas which had been in rebellion. He visited also the sub-divisions, and was thoroughly satisfied with the manner in which the new system of administration had been introduced in the hill areas.[67]

References

1. Home Department, Political File No. 34, July 1917, National Archives of India, New Delhi.

2. Chengjapao of Aishan village, head of the Thado Kukis, opposed the recruitment of labourers. He informed all the village chiefs not to obey British Orders, and to resist enrolment of labours, if necessary by force. Foreign Department, Political File No. 4-12, NAI, New Delhi.
3. *Ibid.*
4. J.C. Higgins, *Administration Report, Manipur State, 1916-17* (Calcutta: Thacker, Spink & Co., 1917), p. 2.
5. Foreign Department, Political File No. 4-12, 1920, NAI, New Delhi.
6. To Viceroy of India, as Maharaja wrote, 'In view of the size and frequency of the drafts required for the first Corps of hillmen, I regret that I shall be unable to raise a Second Corps of hillmen. But I hope to raise a second Corps, when required, from any valley Manipuri subjects (i.e. Meities-mine), and it is my desire to accompany it on active service.' Foreign Department, Political File No. 54, 1917, NAI, New Delhi.
7. Foreign Department, Political File No. 40, 1918, NAI, New Delhi.
8. Foreign Department, Political File No. 54, 1918, NAI, New Delhi.

   The Army Department of the Government of India, also was of the same opinion because already there were four Manipuri Labour Companies serving in France. Foreign Department, Political File No. 40, 1918, NAI, New Delhi.
9. Foreign Department, Political File No. 320, 1922, NAI, New Delhi.
10. Foreign Department, Political File No. 4-12, 1920, NAI, New Delhi.
11. Office of the Political Agent, Special File No. 388, 1919, Secretariat Library & Record Branch, Manipur.
12. Foreign Department, Political File No. 7-131, 1918, NAI, New Delhi.
13. J.C. Higgins, *Administration Report, Manipur State, 1916-17* (Calcutta: Thacker, Spink & Co., 1917), p. 2.
14. J.C. Higgins, *Administration Report, Manipur State, 1914-15* (Calcutta: Thacker, Spink & Co., 1915), p.2.
15. As to how these rumours spread the Political Agent in Manipur said, 'The sources of the rumours could not be traced. They were probably attributable to the ignorance of the people'. *Ibid*
16. Under the system of forced labour every male citizen above sixteen years of age had to perform the assigned work for ten days in every forty days. They would be given wages for their service. In certain case if any one failed to pay taxes, one had to give labour instead of taxes. E.W. Dunn (Com.), *Abridged Gazetteer of Manipur* (Simla: Government Central Printing Office, 1891), p. 33.
17. Foreign Department, Political File No. 7-131, 1918, NAI, New Delhi.
18. Robert H. Henderson, *Administration Report, Manipur State, 1917-18* (Calcutta: Thacker, Spink & Co., 1918), p. 1.

19. Foreign Department, Political File No. 4-12, 1920, NAI, New Delhi.
20. Most of the Kuki chiefs admitted that they were instigated by Chinga Khamba Sana Chaoba Singh to rise against the British Government and Maharaja. A Government report also stated that Chinga Khamba Sana Chaoba Singh claimed himself as the elder brother of the present Maharaja. The report charged him with the responsibility of incitement of the Kukis and others to make war on the local Government with a selfish motive of establishing himself as the Raja of Manipur. Office of the Political Agent, Special File No. 388, 1919, SLRS, Manipur.
21. Robert H. Henderson, *Administration Report, Manipur State, 1917-1918* (Calcutta: Thacker, Spink & Co., 1918), p.1.
22. G. Cimson, *Administration Report, Manipur State, 1919-20* (Imphal: State Press, 1920), p.1.
23. Foreign Department, Political File No. 7-131, 1918, NAI, New Delhi.
24. *Ibid.*

    In the Upper Chindwin, the trouble was '....due to no local grievance but solely caused by rebellion in Manipur since Kukis on Burma side are off-shoots of Chassads in Manipur'. Home Department, Police File No. 181-184, 1918, NAI, New Delhi.
25. *Ibid.*
26. *Ibid.*
27. Foreign Department, Political File No. 4-12, 1920, NAI, New Delhi.
28. *Ibid.*
29. Office of the Political Agent, Special File No. 388, 1919, SLRB, Manipur.
30. Robert H. Henderson, *Administration Report, Manipur State, 1917-18* (Calcutta: Thacker, Spink & Co, 1918), p.1.
31. Since December 22, 1917, the Column of Assam Rifles and Burma Military Police were on duty. Foreign Department, Political File No. 4-12, 1920, NAI, New Delhi.
32. After the Military Operation, they had expanded their areas of raids. First, they launched raids on friendly and neighbouring Naga villages. Secondly, the plain people became a target to be attacked. Lastly, they did not spare the Government Force.
33. Home Department, Political File No. 40, 1918, NAI, New Delhi.
34. Home Department, Political File No.181-184, 1918, NAI, New Delhi.
35. *Ibid.*
36. Beatson-Bell, Chief Commissioner of Assam, said, 'Our casualties have been heavier than those of the enemy. Of we have inflicted 'Punishment' and a good many chiefs and their villages have 'come in'. Foreign Department, Political File No. 7-131, 1918, NAI, New Delhi.

37. Home Department, Police File No. 134-135, 1918, NAI, New Delhi.
38. Home Department, Police File No. 190-191, 1918, NAI, New Delhi.
39. Home Department, Political File No. 29, 1918, NAI, New Delhi.
40. Foreign Department, Political File No. 7-131, 1918, NAI, New Delhi.
41. Home Department, Political File No. 251, 1918, NAI, New Delhi.
42. Home Department, Political File No. 31, 1918, NAI, New Delhi.
43. Home Department, Political File No. 185, 1918, NAI, New Delhi.
44. Home Department, Political File No. 221, 1918, NAI, New Delhi.
45. Home Department, Political File No. 42, 1919, NAI, New Delhi.
46. Home Department, Police File No. 47, NAI, New Delhi.
47. On January 15, 1919, General Officer Commanding in Manipur summarising the progress report of the operations, informed the Assam Government that forty-four persons were killed and burnt forty-eight villages and destroyed forty mithuns and large quantities of foodgrain. Fifty-four Kuki rebels also surrendered to the Government.
48. Home Department, Police File No. 8, 1919, NAI, New Delhi.
49. Foreign Department, Political File No. 94-161, NAI, New Delhi.
50. Home Department, Police File No. 135, 1919, NAI, New Delhi.
51. Col. L.W. Shakespeare, *History of the Assam Rifles* (London: Macmillan and Co., Ltd., 1929), p. 235.
52. Home Department, Political File No. 47, 1919, NAI, New Delhi.
53. Foreign Department, Political File No. 7-131, 1918, NAI, New Delhi. W.S. Mevar, President of the Central Recruiting Board, held the same view of Hignall. As the method of labour enrolment was 'injudicious', the Kukis of 'Unadministered Area'–Somra Tract–rebelled out of brotherly fellow-feeling. Foreign Department, Political File No. 350, 1922, NAI, New Delhi.
54. Foreign Department, Political File No. 4-12, 1920, NAI, New Delhi.
55. Cole, wife of the late Political Agent in Manipur, having an opportunity to know well about the Kuki uprising, once said, '... the interpreters used when the first endeavours were made to recruit in the Kuki country were to a large extent responsible for the trouble that they themselves did not want to be sent overseas as interpreters. 'Foreign Department, Political File No. 7-131, 1918, NAI, New Delhi.
56. It was a fact that when the Kuki chiefs were against the enrolment of labourers the *lambus* used it unscrupulously as an opportunity to make money for themselves. Robert Reid, *History of the Frontier Areas Bordering on Assam* (Shillong: Assam Government Press, 1942), p. 5.
57. Robert Reid, *op.cit.*, p. 4.
58. Foreign Department, Political File No. 135, 1919, NAI, New Delhi.

59. C. Gimson, *Administration Report, Manipur State, 1919-20*. (Imphal: State Press, 1920), p. 2.
60. *Ibid.*
61. Foreign Department, Political File No. 190, 1919, NAI, New Delhi.
62. Foreign Department, Political File No. 105-107, 1920, NAI, New Delhi.
63. Foreign Department, Political File No. 1011, 1923, NAI, New Delhi.
64. The revised draft Rule 10 was given approval by the Government of India in its letter No. 1089/1011, dated July 5, 1923.
65. Foreign Department, Political File No. 419, 1924, NAI, New Delhi.
66. *Rules for the Management of the State of Manipur*, p. 4.
67. Foreign Department, Political File No. 105-107, 1920, NAI, New Delhi.

3

Naga Unrest: I. Jadonang's Movement

Unrest among the Kacha Nagas and the Kabui Nagas' of the north-west of Manipur during the early 1930's was a turning point in the political history of the tribals of Manipur. Initially, the movement had a religious colouring. Subsequently, it partially assumed political overtones. The progenitor of this movement was one Jadonang, a Rongmai Naga of Puilon (Kambiron) village in Tamenglong sub-division of Manipur. He was an ordinary soldier enlisted during the First World War, who had served in Mesopotamia (Iraq). On his return to his village, he started preaching a new cult from early 1925 onwards. He was arrested in 1928 on orders of the then Sub-Divisional Officer, S.J. Duncan, for prophesying the imminent replacement of the British Raj by a "Kabui Naga Raj"[1] and was imprisoned in Tamenglong.[2]

Jadonang's cult was based on animistic beliefs. It was a form of 'debased Hinduism'.[3] Like Hindus he constructed a temple and installed beside others an image of the Hindu god, Vishnu. The new cult was contrary to the ancient beliefs and customs of the Nagas. He justified it on the ground that he had been ordained in a dream by the god of Bhubon Hills (in Lakhipur) to build a temple for the prosperity and good health for every one.[4] By posing as a medicine-man he got a chance to meet the villagers at large, whenever he went he preached his religion and political cult. His popularity went on increasing day by day and soon people were to regard him as a god.

The movement of Jadonang had two motives—annihilation of the Kukis and overthrow of the British Rule. The Jadonang movement aimed at the suppression of the Kukis who had made the Nagas their staunch enemies from the time of their rebellion in 1917-1919. The origin of the enmity between the Nagas and the Kukis lay in the fact that the Nagas did not join the rebellion, and at the same time they were loyal to the British Government. Jadonang thought that time had come to take the revenge on the Kukis for their wiping out of a considerable number of Kabui Naga village during the Kuki Rebellion of 1917-1919. He reminded the Nagas of the tragic story of two young Naga girls, who had been murdered during the Kuki Rebellion. He knew that this would pinch the hearts of the Nagas. By this story he deliberately incited them for vendetta.[5]

Secondly, Jadonang predicted the end of the British Rule and advent of the Kabui Naga Raj. This was purely political. He whispered to the Nagas that it should be kept very secret from the Kukis and the Government. He threatened that his miraculous powers were such that he could hear from his house everything that was said, and would kill anyone, who gave the secret away to the Government or to the Kukis.[6] He would not allow the Kukis to walk about the earth.[7] He further advised them not to hit the Kukis first unless they committed any hostile act against them, otherwise it would be better to keep peace. A Naga revolt against the Kukis would mean the suppression of the Kukis by force. He wanted the Angami Nagas also to join the Kacha Nagas in their war against the Kukis. He talked of the common origin of the Kacha Nagas and the Angamis even though they lived in different countries and spoke different dialects, and were brothers of the same stock, who drank *pita modhu* or rice beer. It was only a political approach to the Angamis to get cooperation and help from them. He sent word to the Angamis that he would visit them in the form of a bird or snake. There would be war against those persons who were unwilling to join him. The war might begin in 1930-31 or next generation when the rice plant reached a foot in height. All the Kukis would be wiped out within three years.[8] To prove himself possessing supernatural powers Jadonang said that he would reign for three years, and then would become a bird and fly about, and see exactly all the Kacha Nagas were doing. If Kacha Nagas wanted to speak to him, they must come forward without delay.

Jadonang ordered all the Nagas not to cooperate with the British Government in any way. He gave out word that the revenue for that year could be paid to the Government but it should be paid to him in the following year, 1931-32.[9] He further said no cotton should be sold, as he wanted all the cotton available to make an airship with. It was an open challenge to the powerful and mighty British Empire and was soon to bring its nemesis. Referring to an English translation from an Assamese Report (June 5, 1931), J.P. Mills, Deputy Commissioner, Naga Hills (now Nagaland), reported the further development of the political situation to J.C. Higgins, Political Agent in Manipur. Jadonang expressed the intention of all the Nagas who had been desirous of independence from British Rule.[10] It was learnt that all the Kacha Naga villages of the Naga Hills were going to welcome him with many *mithuns* as presents. The report said that Jadonang has secretly told the Nagas that on hearing a sound in the air following a white cloud they should know that the war was on and they should prepare themselves for it. Only then they should be ready for defence.[11] Another report from the Sub-Divisional Officer said that about four hundred Nagas had gathered at Lunkao village and Jinam river (in North Cachar Hills) where they decided that, before attacking the Government, they should first of all raid Saipimol, one of the richest villages of the Kukis. This news had alarmed the Kukis. The State Kuki servants of Tamenglong were not in a position to move out for their census work, road works, vaccination and serving of *parwanas* and summons. The Kukis of Saipimol complained that Jadonang had collected guns with the intention to go to war against the Kukis, and the British Government.[12] They confirmed the contemplated plan of Jadonang of a mass massacre of the Kukis. The Angamis were coming in three batches to fight against the Kukis in the south. This corroborated the information gathered by Higgins and Mills.[13] The Political Agent, received information from a Naga Christian of Taningjam (a Kacha Naga village) reporting that the Nagas planned to murder the Kuki road *Mohurrier* who had been working there.[14] In the meanwhile, Jadonang intentionally spread a rumour of victory of the Kabui Nagas in their war against the Kukis. The Deputy Commissioner had also received as many as fifty letters conveying that Jadonang had threatened to launch a war.

Ramifications of the Jadonang Cult

Jadonang's movement did not remain confined to the north-west of Manipur but soon spread out to the neighbouring Cachar Hills and Naga Hills.[15]

The Government realized the necessity of dispatching a force to control the Naga disturbances and to bring confidence among the Kukis. The Deputy Commissioner sent a small force of three sections of the Assam Rifles to Henima to forestall the possible disorder. He requested the Political Agent of Manipur to arrest Jadonang, who had just left for Bhubon. The Political Agent, J.C. Higgins, employed some *Lam Sabedars* and interpreters as he saw no need of dispatching an expedition for the time being. Duncan was to follow the *Lam Subedars* but Higgins thought an European Officer would not be so much helpful. But the Deputy Commissioner wanted to deal with the Naga unrest with a strong hand. As requested by the Deputy Commissioner, the Political Agent agreed to the sending of a military expedition to the Naga Hills,[16] under the command of one Dallas Smith.

The Political Agent informed the Deputy Commissioner that Jadonang had left for Binnakandi, a Naga village, some days ago with thirty men taking the presents and offering with him. He was well guarded by his followers. Higgins advised the Deputy Commissioner to send an armed force to arrest him immediately.[17] It was reported that Jadonang had been a frequent visitor to Lakhipur. The Political Agent also informed the *Mauzadar* of Jiribam that the Nagas should be warned that their villages would be burnt if any of them created trouble.[18] Higgins was not in favour of the withdrawal of the armed force from the trouble-spots until the Naga unrest was controlled.[19]

Mills reported that all the Kacha Naga villages were affected by the movement of Jadonang with one exception. Dallas Smith reported from Henima that Jadonang's movement had been increasing rapidly. He suspected that his movement had spread over Khonoma or portions of Khonoma. But he could not collect definite information that how they had been affected. The Political Agent was doubtful whether Mao and Maram areas might have been affected. The interpreters seemed to be ignorant of the development. Probably the Kabuis kept everything secret. The Manipuris were also supposed to be blind about the Naga unrest. He wrote to W.A. Cosgrave, Chief Secretary, Government of Assam: 'I shall also send a detachement up to Tamenglong, to occupy the fort there, to reassure the Kukis and Kacha Nagas. It is possible that the trouble may fizzle out if Jadonang a is arrested....'[20] The Kukis were nervous whether they would be attacked by the Nagas. The Nagas had threatened that they would continue the movement even if Jadonang was arrested.[21]

The news of Kabui Naga unrest was brought by Harvey from Kohima relating that with exception to Lakema all the villages of

Kacha Nagas in the Naga Hills were also affected. Jadonang had taken a large number of *mithun* from the villagers as a fee of his treatment of the sicks and ill persons, and for the improvement of crops and keeping off rats. When some of the Khonoma men tried to see him who flatly refused to meet them on the ground they were innately suspicious being as they were pretty traders. However, there was no restriction, when they saw his sisters. The Sub-divisional Officer of North Cachar wrote to the Deputy Commissioner of the Naga Hills informing the Nagas of this area particularly from the villages of Thinge, Hejaichak, Laisong, Lonkai and Asalu were sending deputations to Rangkombe, a Manipuri Naga.[22]

All of a sudden Higgins received a telegram (dated 20.2.31) from J.P. Mills informing him that Jadonang had been captured.[23]

The Deputy Commissioner asked to send a police escort and extradition warrant.[24] Jadonang was captured on February 19, 1931, and kept under the custody of the Cachar authorities until taken over by the Political Agent on March 8. In reply to the telegram (dated 20.2.31), the Political Agent informed that the warrant had already been posted. And a column might reach Jirighat, probably on March 6, to take over Jadonang.[25] On February 24, 1931, Higgins left Imphal with a column consisting of one platoon of the 4th Assam Rifles and one British and one Gurkha officers with a view to bring Jadonang to Imphal.[26] At last, Higgins reached Jirighat and he brought Jadonang to Imphal via Tamenglong on March 29, 1931.[27]

The Kacha Naga unrest did not subside even after the arrest of Jadonang. Several *maibas* (medicine-men) had sprung up in different villages. They poised themselves as villages leaders in their respective villages. One Naga girl named Gaidinliu became the chief follower of Jadonang cult. She continued the Jadonang cult.[28] About this lady we will have to say something in the next chapter. In Cachar after Jadonang's arrest there was considerable alarm for some days as it was believed that the Nagas were coming down to the plains to raid villages and tea gardens. A detachment of the Assam Rifles under the command of Manipur and Cachar so as to watch the Kacha Naga villages close to the Manipur border.[29] The Political Agent received a report from Haflong that the Kacha and Kabui Nagas were collecting arms to attack the Kukis.[30] As a security measure, the Political Agent sent out a contingent to Tamenglong, and going out with the Cachar

Road column of one platoon. He was already well apprised of the rumour that the Kacha Nagas and Angamis were intending to attack the Kukis of Saipimol. As a matter of fact not a single Angami was issued pass for an entrance into the Manipur territory since February 6. The Political Agent, in the meantime, kept in contact with the Maharaja of Manipur about the developments of the Naga movement. The Sub-divisional Officer reported that the Nagas and the Kukis of Hungrum Mauzas and Changsen were in a state of unrest or tension.[31] The Nagas had started moving in a large group. And in the night all the Naga villages were barricaded and the whole night they kept vigil. They seemed to apprehend danger from across the State of Manipur. There were chances of clash between the Nagas and the Kukis. The Sub-divisional Officer took timely action to prevent the two tribes from going in a group with spears and daos or daggers. He ordered them to go to their *jhums*. In order to restore confidence in the Government, he informed the Nagas about the arrest of Jadonang.

By the end of March 1931, the movement of Jadonang seemed to have died down barring some occasional reports of unrest or tension in some affected areas of Manipur and neighbouring hill region of North Cachar and Naga Hills. The Officer Commanding found the Nagas of Mogulong, Impa and Katon villages of Tamenglong area, showing friendly attitude towards the Kukis.[32] The prolonged tour of the Political Agent in Manipur and Deputy Commissioner's in Naga Hills, with escorts of the Assam Rifles through the effected villages immediately resolved tension between the rival tribes.[33]

The Trial and Execution of Jadonang

The Manipur State Government awarded a sum of hundred rupees to the Cachar Police as a record for the arrest of Jadonang. Some charges of serious nature then were framed against Jadonang for the murder of four Manipuri *pan* or betelnut dealers some time in March 1930.[34] The murder took place in the servant quarters of the rest-house in the village of Kambiron, at the instigation of Jadonang. First, the news of murder was brought to the road *Mohori* by Muktikhulen village on March 30, 1931. And later on it was reported to the Sub-Divisional Officer.[35]

Immediately after the arrest of Jadonang, the criminal investigation was begun. In the Court of Political Agent of Manipur, he and his five associates were convicted for the murder of four Manipuri *pan* dealers. All in all there were twenty-four accused persons directly or indirectly involved in the murder case.[36]

Jadonang was ultimately sentenced to death in the Court of Political Agent, Manipur, in the Criminal Case No. 10 of 1931.[37] And his four associates were treated under sections 302, 109, 201, and 202 of the Indian Penal Code. However, Jadonang was allowed to appeal to the Governor-General. He pleaded his innocence and ignorance. He said that he had no personal benefit or motive in killing those four Manipuri *pan* dealers. He said that he was at Nungkao village when the murder took place. He asserted that he had never advised the villagers to murder the four Manipuris. He pleaded that the other accused when they could find no person, who could be held guilty for the offence (as they lost their leader Gaidinliu) they just tried to pass on the guilt to him. He requested the Governor-General to examine the case, apportion the blame to those really guilty and waive the sentence of death awarded to him.[38]

After a detailed study of the petition of Jadonang, the Governor-in-Council did not find any reason to reconsider his case and upheld Jadonang's death sentence. His Order read: '...His Excellency the Governor-in-Council has heard Srijut Rohini Kumar Choudhary, Advocate, on behalf of the six accused sentenced to death and has examined the evidence carefully.

'It is open to the obvious objection that almost entirely the evidence is that of accomplices in the murder, most of the witnesses trying to exculpate themselves. Under the circumstances however no other kind of evidence was available and His Excellency in Council is disposed to accept the Session Judge's findings as to the facts.[39]

Concludingly, the Governor-General-in-Council said: 'The Session Judge, who had the advantage of seeing this witness and hearing him depose regarded his evidence as unreliable and His Excellency sees no reason to differ from this view. But at the same time on the evidence as a whole. His Excellency-in-Council is not prepared to say that various detailed acts of certain individuals can be proved to the extent of justifying such discrimination as would make it right to impose the death sentence, even when they pleased guilty. All took part in the riot. It was a dark night and there must have been confusion. It is true these men have confessed though only admit actual killing.[40] The Governor, therefore, converted the death sentence of other five convicts namely, Luntong, Machungnong, Dulungpau, Mupuongpsu and Siphai, to transportation for life, whereas in the case of Jadonang the former decision was not altered. Moreover, the Governor-General did not like to interfere with the case of condemned prisoner Jadonang. He said that the 'law must take its course.[41] Eventually, Jadonang was executed by hanging on August 29, 1931.

References

1. Foreign Department, Political File No. 144, 1931, NAI, New Delhi.
2. Office of the Political Agent in Manipur, File No. 12, 1931, SLRB, Imphal.
3. R.C. Johnson to the Editor of *The Living Age* (New York).
4. First, Jadonang came forward as a *maiba* (medicine-man). He also claimed to be divinely 'healer'. He went from door to door and from village to village treating the ill. Often people came to him for treatment. He took three rupees for treatment, a bottle of *zu* (wine) for interpreting dreams and four rupees for praying to god for the welfare of the dead. It is noteworthy that he was very considerate towards the patients whom he could not cure and refunded their money. He told the Nagas to sacrifice more *mithuns* (sacrificial animals) to the gods to gain prosperity. Jadonang displayed mystical qualities by performing magical tricks such as water came out whenever he drew his sword from its case, and whosoever drank that water was to receive the blessings of god. He had two pet pythons also under the plinth of his house. He said that these pythons could talk to him. Thus he impressed the Naga villagers that he had supernatural power.
5. Deputy Commissioner of Naga Hills to Commissioner of Surma Valley, 24 March 1931, Foreign Department File No. 144/-P/31-Poll, 1931.
6. Deputy Commissioner of Naga Hills to Commissioner of Surma Valley, 16 March 1931, *Ibid.*
7. Office of the Political Agent in Manipur, File No. 12, 1931, SLRB, Imphal.
8. Deputy Commissioner of Naga Hills to Commissioner of Surma Valley, 18 March 1931, Foreign Department File No. 144/-P/31-Poll, 1931.
9. Chief Secretary to the Governor of Assam, to Political Secretary of Government of India, 25 February 1931.
10. J.P. Mills to Political Agent, 5 June 1931, Office of the Political Agent, File No. 12, 1931, SLRB, Imphal.
11. *Ibid.*
12. Office of the Political Agent in Manipur, File No. 12, 1931, SLRB, Imphal.

13. Chief Secretary to the Governor of Assam, to Political Secretary of Government of India, 31 March, 1931, Foreign Department File No.144-P/31-Poll, 1931.
14. The Political Agent was of the opinion that there would have been mass killings of the Kukis and Nagas if the road *Mohurrier* would have been fatally victimized. *Ibid.*
15. Henima, Sarema, Injoma, Intema, Jawna, Laloi, Dupema, Insung, etc., were some of the affected villages of the Naga Hills.
16. Foreign Department, Political File No. 144, 1931, NAI, New Delhi.
17. Telegram from Political Agent of Manipur to the Deputy Commissioner of Naga Hills, 14 February 1931, Political Agent File No. 12, 1931 (Tel. No. is not mentioned).
18. *Ibid.*
19. Deputy Commissioner of Naga Hills to Political Agent of Manipur, 14 February 1931, *Ibid.*
20. Political Agent of Manipur to Chief Secretary to the Government of Assam, 18 February 1931. *Ibid.*
21. *Ibid.*
22. Sub-Divisional Officer of North Cachar Hills, to Deputy Commissioner of Naga Hills, 17 February 1931, *Ibid.*
23. A Manipuri described the story of Jadonang's arrest, as he narrated to the Sub-Divisional Officer. A large and long procession of the Kabui Nagas and 'Haos' including persons of both sexes went to the temple of Bhubneswar in Cachar. The party was headed by an 'old Kuki', who was regarded as their god. He rode on a pony. On their return way, they were stopped by Cachar sepoys to find out whether Jadonang was among them. Jadonang was arrested on the spot.
24. Telegram from Deputy Commissioner of Naga Hills to Political Agent of Manipur, 20 February 1931, Political Agent File No. 12 (Tel. No. is not mentioned).
25. Telegram from Deputy Commissioner of Naga Hills to Political Agent of Manipur, 20 February 1931, Political Agent File No. 12 (Tel. No. is not mentioned).
26. They marched down hundred miles on the bridle path from Imphal to Cachar visiting on their way several Naga villages. On reaching Kambiron Village the Political Agent found a decorated temple erected by Jadonang. He destroyed the temple and shot the pet python of Jadonang. Village elders did not raise objection to the Political Agent, because it was not a tradition among the Nagas to have a temple. It was his own style to build a temple. Rather they appreciated the Political Agent. A.C. McCall, *Administration Report, Manipur State, 1930-31* (Imphal: State Printing Press, 1931), p. 2.

27. Foreign Department, Political File No. 144, 1931, NAI, New Delhi.
28. C.W.L. Harvey, *Administration Report, Manipur State, 1931-32* (Imphal: State Printing Press, 1931), pp. 3-4.
29. Foreign Department, Political File No. 144, 1931, NAI, New Delhi.
30. Political Agent of Manipur to the Maharaja of Manipur, 23 February 1931, Political Agent File No.12, 1931.
31. It was also reported that there was tension between the Nagas and Kukis in the north-west hill areas of Manipur. The Officer Commanding, Captain W.K. Phillips, Fourth Assam Rifles, communicated with the Political Agent that there was sign of hostilities between the two rival tribes in some areas of Tamenglong and beyond the boundary of Manipuri, i.e., Kohima, Haflong, Silchar boundary and to the south as far as Aegui and Alauba. But the village heads denied such fictitious report. However, it was a fact that the Nagas refused to talk with the Kukis. And they never visited the Kuki villages. Letter from the Political Agent of Manipur to the Maharaja of Manipur, dated 23.2.31, *Ibid.*
32. In some areas of North Cachar Hills the Naga unrest was subsided just after the arrest of their leader, Jadonang. In Manipur, the last meeting of the Nagas, which held at Laishang or Laijang (Tamenglong) was broken up at once because of the information of Jadonang's arrest and demolition of his two temples at Kambiron. Moreover, the Kukis had started jhuming as before the trouble begun. Personal Tour Notes of C. Gimson, Deputy Commissioner, Naga Hills, dated 21.3.31, *Ibid.*
33. A.C. McCall, *Administration Report, Manipur State, 1930-31,* (Imphal: State Printing Press, 1931), p. 2.
34. The names of the deceased *pan* dealers were namely, (1) Thounaojam Mera Singh, (2) Waikhom Thamban Singh, (3) Waikhom Pheijao Singh, and (4) Waikhom Sajau Singh.
35. Foreign Department, Political File No. 18(7), 1931, NAI, New Delhi.
36. Some of the accused were charged with murder under v/s 302 I.P.C. and a few of them were convicted for the abetment of murder under v/s 109/302 I.P.C. and certain person under v/s 201, I.P.C. for causing evidence of the murderer to disappear. C.W.L. Harvey, *Administration Report, Manipur State, 1931-32* (Imphal: State Printing Press, 1932), pp. 3-4.
37. The petition of Jadonang was rejected by the Political Agent on the ground that it did not disclose any new fact which was not before the session and the Governor of Assam when the sentence was confirmed. Moreover, the offence was deliberate and brutal. The petitioner took the main part in the murder and in arranging it. The Political Agent was under the impression that a lesson should be given to put off the tribal traditional head-hunting by giving them punishment. A counsel defended

the petitioner in the proceedings before the Governor. In the prosecution, nineteen persons were produced in the Court. All of them threw blame upon Jadonang. The Governor commented that this seemed to be a clear case for the death penalty or there were no extenuating circumstances. Foreign Department, Political File No. 18(7), 1931, NAI, New Delhi.

38. Jadonang to Governor-General-in-Council, 30 July 1931, *Ibid.*

39. Foreign Department, Political File No. 18 (7), 1931, NAI, New Delhi.

40. Telegram No. 862-1 from Political Secretary to the Governor-General-in-Council, 18 August 1931, *Ibid.*

41. C.W.L. Harvey, *Administration Report, Manipur State, 1931-32* (Imphal: State Printing Press, 1931), pp. 3-4.

4

Naga Unrest: II. Gaidinliu's Movement 1932-33

After the execution of Jadonang, the Government of India thought peace would reign in the tribal areas of Manipur and adjacent areas. But contrary to their expectations, a Naga Joan of Arch by the name of Gaidinliu emerged to revive the Jadonang cult adding to it elements of her own cult.[1] This Jadonang-Gaidinliu cult was confined to the Kacha and the Kabui Nagas. Her pseudo-religion soon assumed political overtones and was to breed unrest again.

The Government, unaware of the implications of the new cult, did not immediately try to arrest the Sorceress who kept alive and continued to nurture the movement of Jadonang even after his death. Had the Government closely followed the activities of Gaidinliu, the 'witch-doctor', and suppressed her in time, the commotion in the hill areas of Manipur (and the Naga Hills) would have gradually subsided. As a matter of fact, the Government of India did not take any notice of the *laisabi* (unmarried girl) before Jadonang's arrest. A British administrator comments, 'Gaidiliu (*sic*),.... here is comparatively small fry: she is a girl, and I am not taking her along. We can get her later, if we want her, without sending an army for her.'[2] She became prominent and popular only after the arrest of her master Jadonang.

She started her pseudo-religious and semi-martial political movement after the death of Jadonang. The political aims of her movement were (i) the subjugation of the Kukis, (ii) the overthrow of the British Government, and (iii) the establishment of the 'Naga Raj'.

She aimed at the subjugation of the Kukis whom the Nagas envied for the last many years. During the Kuki Rebellion of 1917-1919, the Kukis plundered and looted several houses of the Nagas. They also took many heads of the Nagas. Naturally, it developed in the form of hatred and enmity between the Nagas and the Kukis, eventhough they lived side by side in many villages of the north-west hill region of Manipur. She thought that the right time had come to take revenge from the Kukis when her movement was in zenith. On the other hand, the Kukis opposed the Jadonang-Gaidinliu cult.

Secondly, Gaidinliu aimed at the elimination of British administration. The Government was supposed to be a hindrance against achieving her objectives. Her no-tax campaign was the first kind of political disobedience to the British rule. This made it difficult for the British Officials to collect house-taxes from the tribal villages. Lastly, Gaidinliu's aim was to establish a 'Naga Raj' in Manipur. She calculated that this could be fulfilled only when the first three were materialized.

The fulfillment of Gaidinliu's will was not so easy; she had to establish herself as a champion of the Naga cause. And she had to face the might of the British Raj. In order to achieve her plan she practiced the same policy once adopted by her lord, Jadonang. Superstition was the main political weapon which she used to bring the Kacha and the Kabui Nagas under her loyalty. In every village, she took jointly an oath of secrecy and allegiance from the Nagas that they should not reveal her plan to the Kukis and the Government.[3] She threatened the villagers that if anyone disclosed the matter to anyone, she would bring death to them. And those who disobeyed her would meet devastation and ruin in their life-time. But, on the other hand, with her triumph everybody would be blessed and glorified. She claimed herself not only as a goddess but also a magician. This was nothing but a political manouvre to establish herself as a spiritual leaders. Her propaganda of Jadonang's coming back to life was only a device to keep her hold on the movement. It was even rumoured that Jadonang had been traveling among them in spirit, and seeing them what they had been doing. She talked on the impersonation of Jadonang in some person who had been working with her.[4]

At her order, Jadonang's death anniversary was celebrated in the early spring of every year.[5] During the ceremonies, all the Kukis were barred from entering into the villages where the death anniversary of Jadonang was performed. The Deputy Commissioner of Naga Hills reported that there was a fanatical determination to honour and obey Jadonang at all costs, fanaticism is always dangerous, and in this case it is particularly so owing to its definitely anti-Kuki tone'.[6]

Gaidinliu continued the practice of human sacrifices to the god. She told her people to sacrifice more human heads so that they could get happiness. Like Jadonang she constructed some temples at Nungkao and other places, where sacrifices of human heads and *mithuns* were performed. She advised the Nagas to offer more presents to the god for a better rice harvest.

A study of the inner core of the movement of Guidinliu reveals her political ambitions. Her movement coincided with the Indian civil disobedience movement during the 1930s. Her no-tax campaign was a political manifestation of her disobedience of the British Government in India.[7] She advised the villagers not to pay taxes to the government. At the zenith of her movement, she often used to remember the name of Mahatma Gandhi. She asked the villagers to believe in one 'god Gandhi'. She regarded Gandhi as the son of Jadonang.[8] W.A. Cosgrave, Chief Secretary to the Government of Assam says: 'Apparently the common people had been told that the day of the Kacha Nagas was coming, further they were to believe in a god Gandhi, about whom some vague information had filtered through from the outer Hills, to retain their faith in Gaidinliu and to be ready for war in the autumn'[9] If it were not so, the Nagas would not be coming to pay homage to the Congress President (Name is not mentioned).

In the words of Jawaharlal Nehru, '...I heard a story which India ought to know and to cherish. It was the story of a young woman...she was about nineteen about six years ago when civil disobedience blazed over the length and breadth of India. News of Gandhi and the Congress reached her in her hill abode and found echo in her heart. She dreamed of freedom for her people and an ending of the galling restrictions they suffered from, and she raised the banner of independence and called her people to rally round it. Perhaps she thought, rather prematurely, that the British was fading out. But that Empire still functioned effectively and aggressively and it took vengeance on her and her people. Many villages were burnt and destroyed and this heroic girl was captured and sentenced to transportation for life....And India does not even know of this brave child of her hills, with the free spirit of the mountains in her. But her own people remember their *Gindallo Rani* (*sic*) and think of her with love and pride. And a day will come when India also will remember her and cherish her, and bring out of her prison cell.'[10]

Whether Gaidinliu's movement was really political, and for that she was in favour of the Indian National Congress. The answer to the questions is to be found from her interview by Sarabala Devi, Secretary of the Sylhet Mahila Sangha, when Gaidinliu was in the jail. The Secretary wrote: '...At first she declined to talk to me but when I gave her my credentials as a Congress worker her face bleamed with delight...'[11] It was learnt that she had indicated her desire to see Gandhi as soon as she was set free. When Sarabala further enquired Gaidinliu whether she would remain under the custody of the Mahila Sangha if she be released conditionally, she very happily agreed on Sarabala Devi's proposal.[12]

Containment of Gaidinliu's Movement

As soon as Gaidinliu established herself as a Naga leader, her movement spread far and wide in the tribal areas of Manipur and Naga Hills. The tribal areas of the north-west of Manipur were the main centre of her movement. Particularly, the village of Leng was the most disturbed spot, where, generally, religious ceremonies were performed. Gradually, it expanded up to other areas neighbouring Manipur.[13] In Manipur all the Kacha Naga villages in the Barak Valley, west of Barak river and a few localities in the east were affected. The Renglomai and the Khungpung villages were not touched as those were closed to some bigger Kuki villages.

As the movement of Gaidinliu spread, it created a problem for the administrative machineries of the two Governments of Manipur and Naga Hills. The Government decided to take punitive measures to put down the movement. The Government ordered all the army headquarters that 'Every effort should be made to arrest the accused Gaidinliu who is absconding.'[14] Once she was arrested by the *lambus* who left her under the custody of her village elders who helped her to escape easily on the same day.[15] The village elders were severely punished but she could be never traced out. As a result, Gaidinliu's movement spread like anything.

One of the rather disheartening consequences of her reappearance as a leader was that the estrangement between the Nagas and the Kukis became more widespread. On January 19, 1932, it was reported that Nohanrami and Bopungwami villages just north to Henima were in a very excited state. The Sub-Divisional Officer of Haflong informed the Deputy Commissioner of Naga Hills that the Kukis were about to be massacred by the Nagas.[16] The Deputy Commissioner rushed to the spot and warned the Nagas about serious consequence that would follow such an eventuality.

The Deputy Commissioner once again tried to capture Gaidinliu at Henima but she escaped hurriedly to the North Cachar Hills District. On February 16, 1932, a section of the Assam Rifles met with stiff opposition from Gaidinliu's party who took to their heels after opening fire on them.[17] A report received from the North Cachar Hills described the presence of Gaidinliu at Guilong, a Naga village. The Sub-Inspector with two constables and two interpreters hurried up to the spot. The party met with stiff opposition from the villagers. The Nagas attacked them with daggers and spears and wounded three policemen. On receipt of the news, the Sub-Divisional Officer (North Cachar Hills) accompanied by two sections of Assam Rifles marched on to Guilong on February 18, 1932, and seized all the spears and the daggers from the villagers. But they failed to arrest Gaidinliu. The movement of Gaidinliu seemed to be getting out of control. By an order of the Government of India, all authority was centralized in one person designated as Deputy Commissioner who established military outposts in the affected areas of Manipur, Cachar Hills and Naga Hills.[18] As a result, the disturbed Naga villages of Manipur, Cachar Hills and Naga Hills were brought under control very soon. The Nagas were heavily fined and their arms were confiscated. The villages where the Gaidinliu movement was active were burnt down by the Government columns with a view to suppress the movement.[19] The Deputy Commissioner also threatened to punish and burn down all the Naga villages if they failed to produce Gaindinlu.[20]

The Manipur Government offered a reward of Rs. 500 and guns, and any villager, either in the State or in British India, which gave reliable information leading to her capture, would be granted ten years full remission of house tax. But no village turned up as an informer. The Deputy Commissioner was of the opinion that the movement of Gaidinliu could be easily suppressed if she was captured.[21]

The End of the Gaidinliu Myth

On October 17, 1932, Gaidinliu was arrested at Pulomi village in the Naga Hills. C.P. Mills, Deputy Commissioner of the Naga Hills, described Gaidinliu's last action in this way, 'Gaidiliu (*sic*) was at Pulomi for about ten years before she was captured. She was clearly desparate, for she was at the end of the Kacha Naga country and had nowhere to go. She said openly that in the next two months either she or Government would win. All she could do was to stage a theatrical stand. Apparently she hopped that an 'army' would collect round her. Meanwhile she made Pulomi build an amazing Palisade, ...It ran all the way round the village except the ground is precipiteous, and to make it Pulomi worked like slaves and destroyed a great deal of their valuable firewood reserve to provide the thousands of tree trunks required. Four thousand men with rifles behind it would have been formidable, but a few hundred Nagas inside it could either have thrown a spear over it nor wielded a *dao*. It had not been quite completed when she was captured. Her orders on what was to be done when an attacking force were remarkable. She would strike the *Shahibs* dead with her magic and her supporters were then to use daos only, for they would be enough. When Captain Macdonald made his attack at down on information brought to Kohima by a Pulomi *gaonbura* her 'army' melted away and there was no magic. Pulomi shouted and brandished daos according to her orders, but were careful not to go beyond then. No blow was struck and the village was clearly relieved when sepoys ignomirously hauled out of a house the biting, scratching girl whom they had uselessly worked so hard and killed so many cattle though any mistake on the part of the commandant would probably have led to an attack in desperation by her supporters....'[22]

In the court of the Political Agent of Manipur, she was convicted for abetment of murder, and sentenced for transportation for life. Her petition of appeal was also rejected by the Governor-in-Council. The suggestion of transferring her outside British India was brushed aside.

As a first reaction to the capture of Gaidinliu some of her followers from the Leng and the Bopungwemi villages conspired to murder the Kuki *Choukidar* of the Lakema Inspection Bungalow in the Naga Hills. The Chowkidar was suspected by the Naga to be the informer of Gaidinliu's presence at Pulomi which led to her arrest. On December, 1932, the *Choukidar* along with his wife and children were murdered by the followers of Gaidinliu. It was reported that even on the eve of her arrest her followers were so much agitated that they had stopped their daily work.[23]

It was definitely thought that the movement of Gaidinliu might subside soon, but the unrest continued even after her arrest. Numerous fanatic and self-styled *maibas* sprang up as her successors. J.P. Mills once rightly said: 'The capture of Gaidinlieu (*sic*) will not end the agitation...She will be succeeded by one or more 'mediums'. To be 'mediums' is not an offence under any law. Yet they will continue to keep the people in a state of constant excitement, and Nagas will continue to be set over against Government and Kukis. The result from the administrative point of view will be serious.'[24]

During 1933, the movement of Gaidinliu gradually subsided when the Naga ring leaders Dikeo and Ramjo were arrested. Besides, some of the minor *maibas* were also captured. Subsequently, the tension between the Nagas and the Kukis also subsided and disappeared.

Release of Gaidiliu under Political Pressure

There could be no question of releasing Gaidiliu so long as the country was ruled by the British. She was strictly guarded during her detention. For some time even an interview with her was not allowed. A Mac-Donald, President of the Manipur State Durbar, thought that 'The immediate release of Guidallo (*sic*) is both undesired and undesirable, whether the Mahasabha (The Nikhil Manipuri Mahasabha) agrees or not, no amount of agitation will procure the release of Guidallo...'[25] The Political Agent of Manipur was also of the same opinion. Further, the State authorities were apprehensive of another movement breaking and if she were immediately released, and that she was a potential threat to the peace of Manipur and Assam.[26]

The man who was most considerate towards Gaidinliu was Jawaharlal Nehru. He never failed to understand the underlying political core of her. Nehru was apprised of her movement during his tour in Silchar in 1935. He was greatly shocked by the story of her detention. He discussed the matter with Congress leaders. At the Congress Session held at Haripur in 1936, a resolution was adopted for the immediate release of Gaidinliu.[27] The Assam Mahila Samity at the eleventh session of their conference held in Gauhati in January, 1939, also adopted a resolution of the early release of Gaidinliu.[28]

The long silence of the Government of India regarding the release of Gaidiliu made some of the political minded persons more impatient. They started exposing the wretched health condition of her in the

Shillong jail so that it might draw the sympathy of people. But the Indian Government seemed to be indifferent to the request of different political organizations for the release of Gaidinliu. In pursuance of the resolution adopted at the Surma Valley Women's Conference, Saralabala Devi, Secretary of the Sylhet Mahila Sangha, appealed to the Government of Assam to release Gaidinliu unconditionally pending the decision of the Government of India.[29] She further insisted the Assam Government to place Gaidinliu under the custody of the Sylhet Mahila Sangha.

Referring back to the movement of Gaidinliu, Biresh Chandra Misra, Secretary of the Sylhet District Congress Committee and a member of the All India Congress Committee, criticized the repressive military measures adopted by the Provincial Government of Assam to suppress the no-tax compaign of Gaidinliu in the Naga Hills and the North Cachar Hills. Disapproving the policy of the British Government of India towards Gaidinliu, R.C. Johnson, a scholar of the University of Melbourne, wrote: '.....This rather sentimental story (of Gaidinliu) implies that British rule in India is not only tyrannical but also unjust....'[30]

Sometime in 1944, the case of Gaidinliu was reviewed. Thereafter, she was interned in a village in Naga Hills under strict vigilance.[31] Later, leniency was shown to her as she belonged to the weaker sex. Otherwise she would have met the same fate as Jadonang. In 1945, the question of withdrawal of ban on Gaidiliu received active consideration of the Central and Provincial Government.[32] Gaidinliu was released in 1945 after having undergone fourteen years' imprisonment and was then interned in her native village. All in all, she spent fourteen years' imprisonment in the British Government jails: one year at Gauhati, Assam; six years at Shillong, Meghalaya; three year at Aizwl, Mizoram; and four years at Tura, Garo Hills. With the independence of India she was given her full liberty at the behest of Nehru.[33] All restrictions on her residence and movement were also removed.

References

1. Gaidiliu had come into contact with Jadonang at an early age of thirteen. He found her a promising disciple. Around 1930, first, she met him when she went to him for an interpretation of her dreams. At that time she was ill. She once again met him for the same after two or three months. Then she came under the complete influence of her master Jadonang. She then became a *maibi* (medicine-woman). Gradually, she stepped into the shoes of the master.

2. Political Agent to Captain of the Fourth Assam Rifles, 13 March 1931, Political Agent File No. 12, 1931.
3. Foreign Department, Political File No. 189, 1932, NAI, New Delhi.
4. *Ibid.*
5. On the occasion of Jadonang's death anniversary there would be drumming and singing in a state of dilirium. In honour of their god (Jadonang) the Nagas would dig a tank in spite of the warnings of the Deputy Commissioner, at an incident of Bopungwemi village (Naga Hills), that they should be punished. Rangkilang was the chief leader of the Bopungwemi incident. He was a ring leader and sooth-sayer who claimed to be the mouthpiece of Jadonang. He was already arrested by the Naga Hills police force.
6. Foreign Department, Political File No. 189, 1932, NAI, New Delhi. The Deputy Commissioner was afraid of such death anniversary of Jadonang as there had been chances of clash between the Nagas and the Kukis. He further said that ceremonies meant excitement, and, in this case, excitement meant anti-Kuki feelings.
7. Political Prisoners File No. C. 46, 1930, Nehru Memorial Museum and Library, New Delhi.
8. Foreign Department, Political File No. 459, 1933, NAI, New Delhi.
9. Chief Secretary to the Government of Assam, to Political Secretary to the Government of India, 14 July 1933, *Ibid.*
10. *The Amrita Bazar Patrika* (Calcutta), June 2, 1939, p. 16.
11. *The Hindustan Standard* (Calcutta), October 12, 1946, p. 5.
12. But the British authorities never considered Gaidinliu as a political leader. She was regarded as a head-huntress. When she was in the jail she was never considered as a political prisoner and was given a 'C' class. A. MacDonald, President of the Manipur State Durbar said: 'The cult was suppressed because its chief and most essential rite was human sacrifice….' Political Prisoners File No. 46, 1939, NMML, New Delhi.
13. In the Naga Hills, with exception to a few villages, all the Kacha Naga villages were not free from the influence of the Gaidinliu cult. Bopungwemi village was the place where her movement was quite active. In the North Cachar Hills almost all the Kacha Naga villages were affected. Foreign Department, Political File No. 189, 1932, NAI, New Delhi.
14. Foreign Department, Political File No. 18 (7), 1931, NAI, New Delhi.
15. Last year (1931) Gaidinliu came into contact with the Government column which set out in search of Jadonang, the leader of the politico-religious movement, but she was freed after a thorough interrogation as she was not a person to be counted as a trouble suitor. Political Agent to Officer Commanding, 13 March, 1931, Political Agent File No. 12, 1931.

16. Foreign Department, Political File No. 189, 1932, NAI, New Delhi.
17. *Ibid.*
18. C.W.L. Harvey, *Administration Report, Manipur State, 1931-32* (Imphal: State Printing Press, 1932), pp. 3-4.
19. The burnt villages were Yang-Khulen, Hungrum, Guilong, Makui, etc.
20. C.W.L. Harvey, *Administration Report, Manipur State, 1931-32* (Imphal: State Printing Press, 1932), pp. 3-4.
21. Chief Secretary to the Government of Assam, to Chief Secretary to the Government of India, 21 June, 1932, Foreign Department File No. 189-Poll 1932.
22. Sir Robert Ried, *History of the Frontier Areas Bordering on Assam, 1883-1941* (Shillong: Assam Government Press, 1942), p. 171.
23. Gopinath Bordoloi to Jawaharlal Nehru, 22 May, 1939, Jawaharlal Nehru Papers, NMML
24. Foreign Department, Political File No. 189, 1932, NAI, New Delhi.
25. *The National Harold* (New Delhi), 13 June 1939, enclosed in Political Prisoners File No. C. 46, 1939.
26. Gopinath Bordoloi to Jawaharlal Nehru, 4 June, 1939, Political Prisoners File No. C. 46, 1939.
27. *The Hindustan Standard* (Calcutta), August 28, 1949, p.11. Since Nehru learnt about Gaidinliu, he was giving advice to Gopinath Bordoloi, Premier of Assam, in connection with Gaidinliu's release. As suggested by Jawaharlal Nehru, he took interest in finding out records about Gaidinliu. Eventhough he got the chance to go through the Government files, he was not allowed to publish it without further knowledge of the Governor of Assam. Nehru was well apprised of it. But he never failed to publicize about the tragic story of Gaidinliu.
28. A Shillong report dated October 22, 1938, said that a memorandum had been sent by the Shillong District Youth League to the Secretary of State for India through Elen Wilkinson, the Labour representative of House of Commons, urging the early release of Gaidinliu. Further in another meeting held in Shillong on October 21, 1930, decided that an intensive India-wise agitation would be launched until Gaidinliu was released. *The Amrita Bazar Patrika* (Calcutta), October 23, 1938, p. 4.
29. Ibid, June 2, 1939, p. 16.
30. R. C. Johnson to Editor of the *The Living Age* (New York), Political Prisoners File No. C. 46, 1939, (Date is not mentioned).
31. *The Hindustan Standard* (Calcutta), October 18, 1946, p. 5.
32. *The Amrita Bazar Patrika* (Calcutta), July 19, 1949, p. 10.
33. After Gaidinliu's release on July 18, 1949 after rigorous imprisonment, Nehru presented her a sum of Rs. 500 to enable her to build a home

for herself. The Assam Government also sanctioned her a pension for life of Rs. 75/- per month. Ibid, July 19, 1949, p.10.

The author met Gaidinliu in Kohima, on August 30, 1979. She lives in a Nagaland Government quarters. She is about sixty-five years old and gets, at present, a pension of Rs. 800/- excluding allowances and contingent grants.

5

The Problem of Accession to the Proposed Indian Federation 1935-39

During 1934-35, the Government of Lord Willingdon was going ahead with its reactionary policies to suppress completely the civil disobedience movement and revolutionary terrorism in India. Subsequently the Government seemed to have realized that the sheer force of military strength would not low down the patriotic impulse of the people of India, and that no useful purpose would be served by the repressive measures. The British authorities taking advantage of the new situation, but giving the impression that they were interested in the advancement of India towards constitutional and liberal institutions, began to move cautiously in the direction of urgent political reforms, and the result was the Government of India Act, 1935. This Act, for the first time in the constitutional history of India, opened the way for the princely states to be brought into the All India Federation.

The Government of India Act of 1935 contemplated a federation of British Indian provinces and Indian states. The Act provided for provincial autonomy and a federal government at the Centre, which in its outer form presented all the normal characteristics of a federal set-up.

The accession to the federation, in the case of the provinces, would be automatic, but it would be voluntary in the case of the Indian states.[1] An Indian state ruler would accede to the federation by executing an Instrument of Accession which have to be accepted by His Majesty and the federation would be brought into existence by the issue of Royal Proclaimation.[2]

Under the Government of India Act 1935, the special powers were reserved to the governors to declare a state of emergency, and once a governor proclaimed so, he could suspend the constitution and assume all the powers to himself. Actually, in real sense, the provinces whose governments were to drive their powers directly from the Crown; on the other hand, the Crown Representative exercised his functions over the states through the agency of the Political Department, local Residents and Political Agents. The powers of the Crown with respect to the Indian states were divided between two functionaries, the Governor-General and the Crown Representative. While functions of the Crown in relation to the British India and the federation were to be exercised by the Governor-General, its functions relating to the states, including that of Paramountcy, were to be exercised by the Crown.[3] In the field of the legislative, executive, fiscal and judicial authority, the power of the federal government was very wide, uniform and direct with regard to the provinces; however, it was relatively limited and variable in the case of the states, and Paramountcy was the ultimate sanction for the enforcement of the federal authority in the federated states. The existence of federal units with unequal status and power in the federal field as well as the emergence of Paramountcy as the super power so far as the states were concerned was bound to create many discrepancies in the federal form of constitution. This led Lord Meston to think that the scheme was like 'mixing of oil with water'.[4]

The Government of India Act 1935 was conceived in an atmosphere of suspicion and distrust, repression and reaction. It did not obtain the sanction of any section of the Indian people or the princes or even of the conservative element in England. Rejecting the Government of India Act, 1935, Jawaharlal Nehru said that it would only strengthen the hands of the imperialist domination and intensify the exploitation of the masses. In the opinion of Sitaramayya the main objection to the Act ' ... was that it was the product of neither self-determination nor even of joint determination, but of 'other determination'. In addition, the scheme of government labour under the clear disability—want only and deliberately planned—of the body politic being so shaped as to have trunk without a head and therefore of its activities remaining uncontrolled or uncoordinated'.[5] The square reactions against the Government of India Act, 1935, had come from the sides of the princes; eventhough, the federal scheme provided for provincial self-government or autonomy. The Government of India Act 1935, also failed to win the hearts of the princes; in fact, it limited the legislative, executive, judicial and fiscal powers of the rulers in their relationship with the Central Authority. Some of the princes were affaid that their extra-territorial rights and privileges would be restricted; on the other hand, the main object of the rulers was to increase the sphere of their own sovereignty and at the same time compel the Crown to guarantee protection of their rights. In 1932-33, the Chamber of Princes came out with certain conditions and safeguards on which the federal scheme would be acceptable to the states.[6] But the safeguards demanded by the Chamber of Princes were turned down by the Government of India.[7]

Lord Linlithgow's mission to convince the rulers failed. His Special Emissaries reported to him that the rulers appeared to envisage a federation less organic than that embodied in the Government of India Act.[8]

Studying the attitude of the princes towards the All-India federation, the Political Department revised the Draft Instrument of Accession; however, the Committee of the Chamber of Princes headed by Akbar Hydari rejected the same. Ultimately, it was resolved in a meeting of the rulers and ministers held in Bombay on April 13-14, 1939, that the terms on the basis of which accession was offered to them were unacceptable. As the princes came to realize that Britain would not bargain away Paramountcy in return for their cooperation with the federal scheme, and that any all-India federation involved diminution of their sovereignty and the revision of their treaty rights, their reluctance to accede became increasingly manifest. Thus on the eve of the Second World War, their substantial rejection of the federal offer was apparent; consequently, the outbreak of the War in September 1939 made the British Government abandon the idea of issuing such a white-paper, and on September 11, 1939, Lord Linlithgow announced in his address that, while the federation remained, as before, the objective of His Majesty's Government. 'The compulsion of the present internal situation, and the fact that, given the necessity for concentrating on the emergency that confronts us, we have no choice but to hold in suspense the work in connection with preparation for federation while retaining federation as our objective.'[9]

The question of Manipur's accession to the proposed federation under the Government of India Act, 1935, became highly controversial and was hotly debated in the State. The Central Government was anxious to persuade all the 'native states' to join the proposed federation. It was assumed that Manipur would be joining it if the Chamber of Princes hinted to a definite instrument of accession acceptable to the rulers of the states.

The Chamber of Princes had, even after the publication of the white paper on the federation, in 1932, resolved that unless and until some important guarantees were made, the question of accepting the federation would be out of consideration. In April 1932, at a plenary session on Chamber expressed their views on the federal idea. In the following session, next year, after the publication of the white paper on the federation, it stipulated that the entry of the princes into the federation was fundamentally dependent upon the inclusion in the scheme of the constitutional reforms of the essential safeguards for which the states had consistently pressed.[10] The Chamber was of the firm view that some of the indispensable rights of the princely rulers should not be restricted. After the publication of the white paper, it was obvious that their proposed terms and conditions of joining the federation were not acceptable to the paramount power and would not be incorporated in the federal statute. The Chamber of Princes thereupon resolved that the native states were free to decide individually whether to join the federation or not.

In the case of Manipur, the Maharaja was of the view that the Government of India should preserve some of the most essential rights of the ruler. In 1932, the Maharaja visited Shillong to exchange views with Laurie Hammond, the Governor of Assam, on the question of the federation.[11] Like other princes of different states, Sir Chura Chand Singh, the Maharaja of Manipur, was naturally apprehensive that his rights would be curtailed if he joined the federation. The Viceroy wanted a local Political Officer should be employed to convince the Maharaja that the federation scheme would incorporate, as far as practicable, the reservations put forwarded by his Government.[12] The Maharaja complained to the Chancellor of the Chamber of Princes that he would be unwilling to attend the Council of States unless one seat allotted for Manipur. Although he understood that this would not be considered. According to the administrative rules of 1919, Manipur was not qualified, in strict sense, to become a member of the Chamber of Princes, even if her ruler was a possessor of the dynastic salute of eleven guns, as the Maharaja and the Durbar had no full measure of authority and control within the State itself. For instance, the funds of the State were remained in the Government Treasury and the State accounts audited by the Assam Comptroller. Nevertheless, the Deputy Secretary, Political Department, suggested that the Maharaja, if he wished, might exercise his right to attend the inaugural meeting of the Chamber of Princes.[13] This indicated the attitude of Maharaja towards the federal scheme even though he was supposed to be well aware of the impending re-increase of Manipur's tribute to the Central Government from Rs. 5,000 to a huge amount of Rs. 50,000. This was the amount fixed against the Manipuris as a penalty for their rebellion in 1890-1891, against the British. However, it was reduced to Rs. 5000 taking into consideration the poor economic condition of Manipur.[14] The Assam Government was asked to give its opinion whether the Central Government should increase the tribute to Rs. 50,000, when the period of reduction lapsed, if the Maharaja did not accept the proposed federation. The Foreign Department very wisely answered that this was not a threat to force the Maharaja to join the federation. The fact was that the period of reduction was likely to lapse and, therefore, the re-imposition of the full amount would take effect from April 1, 1937. The Foreign Department felt that it would not be able to justify further continuance of reduction as the financial condition of Manipur had improved during the course of the years.[15]

The Majaraja was disinclined to join the proposed federation as he felt, probably rightly, that his powers and privileges would be undermined by the extension of the Government of India Act, 1935, to the Manipur State. But after a thorough consideration, he decided to discuss and negotiate the issues involved with the representatives of the Government of India.

Manipur's Conditions for Accession

At a meeting held in Calcutta, on January 2, 1937, the question of the federation was thoroughly discussed between the State delegation led by the Maharaja and his second son Maharaj Kumar Priyabarta Singh, and the (British) Indian delegation including A.C. Lothian, Additional Secretary, Foreign and Political Department, Government of India, and C. Gimson, Political Agent in Manipur. C. Gimson attended the conference at the request of the Maharaja on behalf of the State as well as at the instance of the Assam Government. In the meeting the Ruler of Manipur agreed that the State would join the federation provided that the Government of India accepted and/ or the following:

1. As regards the administration matters:

(i) The administration of the hill tribes of Manipur should be handed over to the State authority;

(ii) The appointment of the Durbar President should be placed in the hands of the Ruler;

(iii) The British Reserve, with the possible exception of the Residency grounds and an area required for the Assam Rifles (if they remain), should be returned to the State;

(iv) The keeping of the Assam Rifles should be according to the wishes of the Ruler;

(v) The Political Agent's power of control over the hill administration and the financial matters of the State should be restricted. Further, his magisterial justisdiction should be restricted.

(vi) The federal excise staff should not be necessarily maintained;

(vii) The past treaties and *sanads* should not be superceded.

2. In regarded to financial matters, the Maharaja posed a few problems:

(i) Whether the Ruler of the State would be liable to income-tax and the duties in respect of succession to property, and whether a reservation against the income-tax would be accepted by the Government of India;

(ii) Whether the State would be legally unrestricted in the introduction of the import and the export duties. If the Mao-Imphal section of the road is maintained by money, other than the State money, would this in any way restrict the power of the State with regard to the imposition of taxes on goods carried to and from Imphal by road. Further, the State would like to be clarified, if she joined the federation, would the Mao-Imphal road be maintained by the federal government.

(iii) The State authority should not be restricted to the imposition of the forest duties;

(iv) The State authority has been getting Rs. 2,000 per annum by leasing the saltwells. This product was particularly used for the religious purpose. The State Government wanted to know a clear cut about the salt revenue if it came under the federal supervision;

(v) There should be complete remission of the tribute payable by the State, if the State joined the federation.

(vi) With reference to Section 147 of the Government of India Act, 1935, whether His Majesty would consider a complete remission of the tribute payable by the State. If the remission was conditional, the thing should be explained clearly.[16]

Besides concluding the questionnaires and the demands the State Government referred also the issue of Kabaw Valley which was ceded from Manipur and transferred to Burma under the treaty of 1834. However, the matter was dropped as it might be discussed later. In the opinion of A.C. Lothian, Additional Secretary and Special Representative, Foreign Department, the foregoing conditions applied partly for information about the legal position of the State under the federation, and partly for information with regard to the Government of India's intentions. When the matter came to the knowledge of the Assam Governor who, analyzing the ins and out of the stated conditions of the Manipur Government, expressed his opinion mostly in negative.

The plea for the transfer of the hill administration to the State Government was rejected on historical reasons. From the time immemorial the hillsmen were dependent on the administration of the Valley where the Hindu Meiteis were the majority. The British administrators never believed that the Manipuris would do good for the tribals. The boundaries were not fixed at all. There was no cultural unity between the hillsmen and the Manipuris (the plains). Whenever the ruler wanted to extract a tribute from the hillsmen, he did it. If anyone failed to pay the taxes to the State authority, the Ruler used to arm some other village to suppress the defaulters. Sometimes, the Rulers advised the village-men to kill the non-tax payers.[17]

The British Government saw no reason to give up the adminstration of the hill areas in favour of the Maharaja. That would be tentamount to the betrayal of the tribals. It was learnt that the Maharaja had collected a huge amount of money from the hill people till 1891. The hill administration had to be taken over by the Englishmen after the Kuki rebellion of 1917-19, and put under the charge of a British Officer.[18] It was a fact that even after the uprising of 1891, there had been no proper provision for the hills in the State budget. Only one-fourth of the full amount extracted from them was spend on them. The British Government blamed the native State authorities for neglecting them, which, according to the British viewpoint, was the principal cause of the rebellion. As a result of the Kuki rebellion, the Government of India had to cost nearly twenty lakhs of rupees.[19]

Analysing the past history of Manipur's relationship with the tribals, the Governor of Assam decided that the British control of the hills should not in any way be loosened. 'It is fact, if a regrettable one, that neither His Highness nor his Durbar is interested in the good government of the hill tribes, while they grudge the expenditure of money on them'.[20] On the other hand, the warlike hill people would not tolerate the re-imposition of the old system of the Manipuri domination by a method of periodical massaere. Therefore, the question of relaxation on the administration should be dropped at present.

Once, when the hill sub-divisions were abolished a problem of open clash between the Nagas and the Kukis arose. Afterwards it led to the turmoil of 1930s in the hill areas of Manipur (and the Naga Hills). However, the timely tackling of the situation by the State Governments saved Manipur from a disastrous fate. As a matter of fact, 'History shows that the Manipuri cannot and will not give the hills an administration of the standard to which they are both entitled and now accustomed and that it can only be maintained by the control now exercised. We (Englishmen) are under an obligation to the hills tribes to maintain to them a decent administration.'[21]

Secondly, the Governor took the question of the authority of the appointment of the Durbar President. It was in the hands of the Governor of Assam on behalf of the Governor-General. The Durbar President was always a British Officer from the Indian Civil Service cadre. The Maharaja desired that he should be a Manipuri from Manipur, prima facie, the Governor of Assam pointed out that this might be practicable provided that the valley administration was confined to the Durbar, and the hill administration to the Political Agent appointed by the Government of Assam and approved by the Government of India.

Thirdly, it concerned with the British Reserved Area in Imphal. The Government of India's opinion was to maintain the status quo, as recommended by Sir Michael Keane.[22] The withdrawal of the Assam

Rifles stationed in Imphal in the near future would be too risky. The tribals were wild by nature, so, in anytime they might revolt against the Government. The British officers doubted that any considerable relaxation of their control would inevitably lead to the head-hunting. Above all the past history of Manipur was turbulent and the treacherous murder of the Assam Chief Commissioner in 1891 was still afresh in the memory of the British administrators.[23] Besides, according to the *sanad* the Maharaja and his heirs were really supposed to be safeguarded by the British Government. And the Assam Rifles' first duty was to represent the Government in order to ensure the safety of the Political Agent, which was important, and secondly to help the Government in case of trouble in the hill areas.[24] The removal of the force would be justifiable only when the new lines were provided elsewhere after the abandonment of the old ones. Moreover, it would not be advisable on the geographical grounds. The Governor thought over the matter and decided that '...in the event of His Highness joining the Federation, mention of the British Reserve should be made in the Instrument of Accession as an area to which it is expedient that the provisions of Sub-section (i) of Section 294 of the Act should apply.'[25]

The Governor of Assam recognized that the desire of the Maharaja and his Durbar for the return of the site of the old palace and fort was a genuine and natural one, and he would readily accede to it but for the consequences entailed.

Fourthly, the financial control of the State was in the hands of the British Officers since the advent of the British rule in Manipur. When the Maharaja was a minor, the whole administration was in charge of a Superintendent. The Governor considered that a right time had come to relax the financial control over the Manipur administration. But he was of the opinion that all the financial authority be taken over if there was a threat of financial disorder. This policy could ensure a sound monetary condition in relation to the hill administration, salaries of the officers lent to the State, etc.

Previously, considerable financial control was exercised by the British Authority. The budget of the State was prepared by the prepared by the President of the Durbar and the Maharaja. Then it was forwarded to the Political Agent for submission to the Governor of Assam, who would approve the budget after minute scrutiny and with some slight modifications, if desirable. After his approval, the Durbar would make reappropriations only with the sanction of the Political Agent.[26] Any appointment to a post which carried an amount of one hundred rupee per month as salary would necessarily require the previous sanction of the Governor of Assam, as in the case of reappropriations. And for major changes, the sanction of the Governor was essential.

Fifthly, the Maharaja was in favour of strict control on the entry of the non-State subjects in his State. The power of issuing entry pass was exercised by the Political Agent with the approval of the Maharaja. He never favoured the relaxation in the prevailing system. From the side of the Governor also, nothing short of the relaxation was recommended.

Sixthly, the Governor advocated that the control of the arms and ammunition in the State should not be relaxed as there was a potential possibility of a sudden political uprising which would disturb the peaceful atmosphere of the State. The Manipuris were disarmed after the rebellion of 1891. The arms licenses were not even issued to the relatives of the Maharaja and the members of the Durbar. The Political Agent granted licenses whereas the Durbar President controlled the issuing of licenses to the hill people. The British Officers were doubtful if licenses were issued freely to the Manipuris, the arms might be passed on to the hill people or Assamese, or Burmese for business sake, as the high price of a muzzle might tempt the Manipuri licence holders. The British administrators were well aware of the Angamis' attitude towards them and intertribal conflicts that used to take place till *pax Britannica* was extended to the region. The Angamis ravaged many times their weaker neighbours, and on several occasions they stiffly opposed them with arms which they obtained from the Manipuris.[27]

It also reminded that the Manipuris had passed on many guns to the hill people, when they were disarmed after 1891. The same arms were used against the British during the Kuki rebellion. Understandably, it was held that there should be no relaxation of the control of the arms, otherwise the State might be faced with similar problems of law and order, even anarchy.[28]

It was thus unmistakably clear that the Assam Government wse not in favour of further relaxing control over the administration of the State except in minor matters. However, the Assam Government favourably considered the suggestion for relaxation of financial control, and the appointment of the Durbar President by the Maharaja. The Governor assured the Maharaja that these two suggestions might be given effect to without further delay. But, to the Maharaja, the two concessions were nothing but too inconsequential to satisfy his ambition to be a real Ruler of the State.

In a separated letter, in reply of the Political Agent's letter, the Maharaja further communicated with him explaining the final terms and the conditions on which he wished to join the federal scheme. But he asserted: '... I write to say that before finally deciding whether I shall accede to the Federation, I shall prefer to wait until the results of the present deliberations conducted by the Chamber of Princes are known.'[29] To increase his importance and safeguard his status he put forth the following conditions (including the previous ones):

With regard to the Federal Legislative List:

(a) Item 12 (Federal agencies and institution, etc.): The establishment of such agencies and institutions should be left to the Maharaja's discretion;

(b) Item 29 (Arms): The power now exercised by the Political Agent over the arms and ammunitions should be entrusted to a State officer;

(c) Item 42 (Offences against laws under the federal legislative list): The items to the extent to which such were accepted in the instrument of accession should come under the federal laws through the courts of the Manipur State;

(d) Item 47 (Salt): The Local salt-wells should be reserved. If the Government of India accepted such reservation, it would mean that an immunity to be set off against the proposed remission of the tribute, would be calculated on the figure of the production with regard to the federal rate of tax;

(e) Item 48 (State lotteries): The Maharaja wanted a complete reservation in the local lotteries;

(f) Item 50 (Migration): In the matter of migration, there should be sole reservation. However, it might affect the entry rules for the non-state subjects;

(g) Item 54 (Income-Tax): This item should be wholly reserved;

(h) Item 55 (Taxes on the Capital values, etc.): This item should be reserved completely;

(i) Item 56 (Succession duties): It should be reserved wholly.[30]

Negotiation Cut Short by World War II

The British apprehended that the Maharaja by setting forth conditions of all sort, was using delaying tactice to evade joining the federation. His attitude was incompatible with the aims of the Government of India. The Government of India did not see any reason in meeting all the demands and the reservations put forth by the Maharaja. The question of immediate concern was whether to ask Manipur formally to join the federation. The higher officials, after considering the Maharaja's demands and reservations, were of the view that he should be invited to join the federation.

Most importantly, the Maharaja demanded complete reservation on arms and ammunition. The British Administration was not disposed to accede to this demand which conformed to Entries 29-30 of the Federal List I, which provided that no federal law could prohibit or restrict the possession of swords, spears, axes, bows and arrows, or muzzle-loading shot guns, and black gun powder, percussion caps and shot.[31] Unrestricted possession and movement of arms in the State would be potentially dangerous and might lead to troubles in the border areas. Therefore, strict control over the issue of arms and ammunition both to the Manipuris of plain and to the hill tribes in the State was essential.

The Political Department suggested that Entries 29 and 30 of the Federal Legislative List 1 should not be shown to the Manipur Government at the first stage of the first schedule of the Draft Instrument of Accession.[32] And it suggested that before taking up a definite step, the Governor should be consulted. This was accepted by the Governor-General of India.

In the meantime, a controversy arose as to whether the Manipur State would only be confined to the valley under Section 311(1) of the Government of India Act, 1935, as an Indian State.[33] The Political Agent did not consider the hill areas as an integral part of the Manipur State although this was never declared view of the Raj.

The separation of the hill areas from the valley was not at all acceptable to the Maharaja of Manipur, who did not see any compelling reason for seperating the surrounding hilly area of 7000 square miles from the total area of 8000 square miles, although he conceded that this might lead to better administration in the hills.[34] Whether the case of Manipur represented in different ways the result of the goal should not be a division of the hill areas from the valley itself. But the Secretary of State was not of the opinion that a line of division should be drawn between the valley and the hills. The control of the Political Agent and the Durbar President over the hill administration would in any case be affected by the federal scheme. The Governor of Assam pointed out that the maintenance of law and order both in the valley and the hills was necessary owing to the peculiar circumstances of the State as the bulk of which consisted of the hill areas sparsely inhabited by the uncivilized tribes.[35] Therefore, the administration of Manipur which was in practice controlled by the British local officers should not in any case be lessened at the cost of Entries 29 and 30 of the Government of India Act, 1935. The Governor-General was also afraid that the peace and tranquility of the State might be threatened at any time, and states neighbouring Manipur might also be affected. This may also once again result in the domination of the plains over the hill people and lead to conflicts. He added that 'past history and existing conditions convince me that any considerable degree of surrender of control to Ruler and his own officers would mean neglecting hill tribes punctuated with occasional assertion of Durbar's authority over them by violent methods with result that peace which at present exists in this wild frontier area would be endangered with further possibilities of serious repercussions in Assam and Burma'.[36] Further, with reference to Entries 29-30 the Federal Legislative List, a strict control over the plains and the tribals in the matter of arms would be highly essential.

On the other hand, according to Section 125 of the administrative agreement the question of using arm, licences would fall in the hands of the Ruler, or officers designated by the Ruler, so, the paramount power however would naturally be debarred by Section 294 (2) from interference with the State administration. However, the Governor-General felt that Manipur's accession to the proposed federation should not be foreclosed on the ground that the Ruler was adamant in claiming control over arms and ammunition in accordance with the Entries of the Federal List.

The Governor of Assam and the British officers in Manipur could not arrive at the conclusion on the Manipur question. The matter was eventually referred to the Secretary of State. Here, the Government of India again raised the issue whether the case of Manipur was not similar to that of other Indian states under British Suzerainty, for instances, the Eastern States Agency in which a large proportion of the primitive people would make the control of the paramount power over the supply of the fire-arms and the explosive essential in the public interest.[37] Ultimately, the Secretary of States dismissing the argument of the British Indian Officers approved that Manipur should be invited to accede to the federation without full freedom in accordance with Entries 29 and 30 of the Federal Legislative List.[38]

The dream of the Government of India to bring the Manipur State within the Federal Union under the Act, 1935, was, however, not realized. But the hopes of the Viceroy that federation would be established by 1938, i.e., as year after the inauguration of the Provincial Autonomy were never fulfilled because of the stiff opposition from all the quarters. The Government of India Act, 1935 failed to attract the people of India. The Indian National Congress, at its Manipur session in 1938, resolved that the 'imposition of the Federation will do grave injury towards India, as it excluded from the sphere of responsibility vital functions of government'[39] The federal scheme was also denounced by the Muslim League.

A fresh problem was brought by the Government of India Act, 1935. The Central Government was keen to bring all the Indian princely states still in relations with the local Government of India. But a number of difficulties were found, in the case of Manipur, to stand in the way that it was decided that when the new Act came into force relations with the State should be conducted by the Assam Governor in his personal capacity as Agent of the Crown Representative. In fact this had led to no practical change in the procedure. The scheme of federation in terms of Part II of the Government of India Act, 1935 and all the complicated questions connected with it, was the subject of prolonged correspondence and political discussions between 1936 and 1939 and one of the principal issues of the controversy was, of course, the administration of the hill areas. Though they cover some 7,000 square miles out of the State's total areas of 8,000 square miles with a population of about 1,50,000, it had never been adjudged safe to leave the hill administration in the hands of the Manipuri ruler. In the words of A.C. Lothian of the Political Department, the Maharaja's only concern with the federation was to regain his direct control over the hill affairs. A.C. Lothian who was in 1936-37 on special duty in connection with the federal scheme, added that the Maharaj's struggle was to free himself from the political domination of the British officers.

In this respect the Government of India accepted the views of the Governor that the hill administration should not be necessarily handed over to the Maharaja.[40] After a gap of two years the Maharaja raised once again the question of the hills when the details of the federation were being framed. This time he agreed to federate on the terms which included the exclusion of the hill administration from his direct control.

With the outbreak of the Second World War in September 1939 the question of the federation was relegated to the background. The Women's Bazar Agitation added to the confusion created by the war. The question of Manipur's accession was not taken up before India became independent in August, 1947.

References

1. V.P. Menon, *The Transfer of Power, in India* (Delhi: Orient Longmans, 1957), p. 51.
2. *The Government of India Act, 1935* (Delhi: Government of India Press, 1939), Saction 6(3).
3. *Ibid.*, Section 3.
4. *White Paper on Indian States* (Delhi: Government of India Press, 1950), p. 25
5. Sitaramayya, *The History of the Indian National Congress, 1885-1935*, Vol. II. (Bombay: 1948), p. 12.
6. *Report of the Constitutional Committee of the Chamber of Princes* (Delhi: Hindustan Times Press, n.d.), pp. 1-2.
7. Foreign Department, Political File No. 91, 1934, NAI, New Delhi.
8. V.P. Menon, *The Story of the Integration of the Indian States* (New Delhi: Orient Longmans, 1956), p. 36.
9. Linlithgow, Marques of, *Speeches and Statements* (Delhi: Bureau of Public Information, 1945), p. 23.
10. Foreign Department, Political File No. 91, 1934, NAI, New Delhi.
11. Foreign Department, Political File No. 235, 1932, NAI, New Delhi.
12. Home Department, Political File No. 359, 1936, NAI, New Delhi.
13. Home Department, Political File No. 221, 1936, NAI, New Delhi.
14. Foreign Department, Political File No. 62, 1930, NAI, New Delhi. The question of reduction was taken after the Kuki Rebellion of 1917-19, on the condition that the remaining Rs. 45,000 out of the total amount of Rs. 50,000 would be fully utilized by the State Government for the

development of hill administration. Foreign Department, Political File No. 191-196, 1919, NAI, New Delhi.

15. Home Department, Political File No. 359, 1936, NAI, New Delhi
16. *Ibid.*
17. *Ibid.*
18. *Ibid.*
19. Foreign Department, Political File No. 535-556, NAI, New Delhi.
20. Home Department, Political File No. 359, NAI, New Delhi.
21. *Ibid.*
22. Foreign Department, Political File No. 198, 1934, NAI, New Delhi.
23. Foreign Department, Political File No. 13, 1936, NAI, New Delhi.
24. Foreign Department, Political File No. 7, 1936, NAI, New Delhi.
25. Home Department, Political File No. 359, 1936, NAI, New Delhi.
26. *Rules for the Management of the State of Manipur* (Imphal), pp. 2-3.
27. In one incident of 1879, Khonoma men admitted that those were the guns received from the Manipuris, with which they shot the Deputy Commissioner of the Naga Hills and almost plundered his force.
28. Home Department, Political File No. 359, 1936. NAI, New Delhi.
29. *Ibid.*
30. Home Department, Political File No. 226, 1937, NAI, New Delhi.
31. Foreign Department, Political File No. 218, 1936, NAI, New Delhi.
32. Home Department, Political File No. 143, 1938, NAI, New Delhi.
33. According to Section 311(1) of the Government of India Act, 1935, the Indian State meant any territory not being part of British India and whether described as a State, an Estate, a Jagir or otherwise which His Majesty recognized as being such a state. Home Department, Political File No. 24, 1938, NAI, New Delhi.
34. Home Department, Political File No. 359, 1936, NAI, New Delhi.
35. Home Department, Political File No. 24, 1938, NAI, New Delhi.
36. Telegram No. 1654 from Secretary to the Governor of Assam, to Secretary of State, 15 December 1938, Home Department File No. 143/38-Poll and Fed. 1938.
37. Telegram No. 2164 from Secretary of State, to Secretary to the Government of Assam, 29 December 1938, Home Department File No. 143/38-Poll and Fed. 1938.
38. Secretary of State, to Secretary to the Governor of Assam, 23 December 1938, Home Department File No. 24/38-Poll and Fed. 1938.
39. A.C. Benerjee, *Indian Constitutional Documents*. Vol. II (1949), p. 327. In the words of Krishnamurti, 'The Government of India Act was conceived in an atmosphere of suspicion and destruct, repression and

reaction. It is acknowledgedly imperfect and has not obtained the sanction of any section of the Indian peoples or the princes or even of the conservative elements in England. From the British Indian point of view, it has been attacked because it makes the representatives of the states privileged members of the legislatures with semi-contractual rights, with power to delay the future constitutional development.

'The units which compose the federation are unequal in status and power and the motive of the British Government in introducing such an anomalous constitution is obviously to strengthen the reactionary and conservative elements in order to postpone the grant of responsible government's Y.C. Krishnamurti, *Indian States and the Federal Plan* (Bombay: Ratanscy Parker & Co., 1939), p. 75.

40. Home Department, Political File No. 359, 1936, NAI, New Delhi.

6
The Women's Bazar Agitation, 1939-41

The Background

The month of December is the harvest season in Manipur. Although the State was liable to the vagaries of nature and severe famines like the rest of India, shortage of food was never a usual phenomenon and self-sufficiency was rather the norm. The rice produced in Manipur was just sufficient for local consumption. However, 1939 was the year of scarcity of food-grains. A severe famine threatened the eastern-most area and Manipuris became restless anticipating the impending tragedy.

That year heavy rains caused great damage to crops. The same happened in the Garo Hills and other areas. The harvest was not up to the expectation. Because of the fall in the production of rice, which was the only staple food of the Manipuris, the local populace came to the point of starvation. The price of rice shot up and the poor people, particularly, were badly affected. Moreover the women-folk earning their livelihood from hand-pounding of the paddy were rendered unemployed.[1] The Manipuri women were adversely affected and had to face starvation due to loss of work. The women's bazaar had to be closed down until the situation improved.[2]

Before the trouble started, the price of rice was only one *siccee* (equivalent of four annas of that time) per *shangbai* (about thirty-two kilograms). Later, it rose to two rupees. As the burden of the price-rise increased day by day, the women-folk became more and more agitated. On the other hand, the Manipur State Government did not ban the export of rice. The rice business was mainly run by the outsiders designated as 'Foreign Merchants.' These traders were

Marwaris, who monopolized the rice purchases in the State and became its sole exporters. These same people operated as money-lenders in Assam[3]. As these Marwaris possessed big commercial capital, they naturally controlled and monopolized the whole food-grain business. They purchased all available quantities of paddy at cheap rates in the market and sold rice in turn at higher rates in the neighbouring states. In this way they made fabulous profits. They never sympathized with the cause of the women wage-earners. They were guided solely by self-interest and profiteering. They were thus opposed to the demands of the country people and the labour.

The Government of Manipur took no action against the Marwaris. On the other hand, in November 1939, the export of rice from Manipur was permitted, and the Marwari merchants who had recently started some rice mills in the State bought up large quantities of rice for milling and export.[4] Had the Government banned the export of rice promptly, it could have forestalled the crisis. Neither the Maharaja nor the Durbar took any interest. On December 12, 1939, the women-folk openly agitated against the Government policy and the Marwari business community.[5] A large group of women went to the length of lying down on the roads to stop the movement of rice-carrying trucks which were about to take loads of rice to the Manipur Road. In this way the situation became worse.

On the other hand, the Durbar could not evolve a unanimous policy on rice export as the members had different opinions. The Durbar Prsident T. Sharpe and a member, R.K. Bhaskor Singh, voted in favour of rice export. S. Somorendra Singh, I.M. Ibungohal Singh and S. Nadia Chand Singh, other members, advocated a total ban on the export of rice from the State including civil supplies to Kohima. Maharaj Kumar Priyabrata Singh opined that rice should be exported after thorough checking of the State paddy stocks.[6] The President expressed Durbar's inability to bring about a consensus regarding the suspension of rice export. It was his opinion that the decision of the Maharaja would be highly needed at this critical juncture. The excited women, thousands in number, who had been waiting eagerly outside the Durbar Hall with a view to hearing the decision, being unable to console themselves pressurized the President to send immediately a telegram to the Maharaja, who was at Navadip (in Bengal). Urged by the crowd, the President accordingly wired to the Maharaja.[7] Until the reply came from the Maharaja, Sharpe was not allowed by the crowd to go out of the telegraph office.[8] The furious crowd besieged the telegraph office till 11 O'clock in the night. The Civil Surgeon, Major P.H. Cummins, who was with Sharpe was also detained. It seemed that even the flies were not allowed to fly off the telegraph office. Cummins, however, managed to slip a note to his driver, who was allowed to pass unmolested. The note, besides requesting coffee and sandwiches, also summoned military help.

The arrival of Colonel Bulfield, the Commandant of the Assam Rifles, on the spot saved the British officers who were held up there by the crowd. During the rescue operation, a number of women agitators were injured. For lack of conclusive evidence, it is difficult to affirm that the women were bayonetted with intent to injure and wound. Some twenty persons, however, received wounds from bayonets and five severe wounds.[9] On 11.3.1940, The *Amrita Bazar Patrika*, carried the news that the women agitators were injured following a clash between a group of women and the State Civil Police. In that incident, the women surrounded the Durbar Hall with the Durbar members and President, Sharpe inside, demanding immediate disposal of a case in which an Inspector of Police of Imphal was charged with assaulting a women. The newspaper further mentioned that the women demonstrators kept the members confined in the Durbar Hall for several hours in spite of repeated warnings from the State police, who subsequently dispersed them with a mild charge.

Eventually, the crowd in the telegraph office of the British Reserve compound was shoved away by a detachment of Assam Rifles. However, the tempo of the women's movement was kept up for a few days, then the tempers cooled down.

On the next day of the Durbar Hall incident, the Political Agent in Manipur received a reply from the Maharaja. He instantly issued an order suspending the export of rice. But this could not normalize the situation, and the agitators turned their attention towards the rice mill-owners, who had assured them to close down their mills with immediate effect. In spite of one mill-owner secretly soaked and boiled some paddy for the purpose of making par-boiled rice; then in this way, he would be able to export rice after converting it into the form of thumped-rice. This uncooperative attitude had fanned the movement rapidly. As a result, an angry mob of nearly 10,000 women proceeded to one of the principal mills in order to stop the mill running.[10] At the same time a deputation went to see C. Gimson, Political Agent in Manipur, who was on tour, when he heard about the women movement.

A massive demonstrating crowd of nearly 15,000 threatened to burn down all the rice-mills, if the authorities failed to stop milling. The women agitators gave a slogan that the only way the Political Agent could stop this milling by the Marwaris was to have switches taken out. And this was what the Political Agent eventually had to do before the angry throng would disperse. Seeing no alternative, the Political Agent personally went to, and ordered the removal of electric switches of the mills. Then Gimson took chance of persuading the women agitators to go back home. But it did not pacify the women.

One serious incident took place in the last week of December 1939, when certain bullock-carts carrying rice were thrown into the gutter. At the same time women traders had started to boycott the main women market. It continued a month long. However, some of the women traders, violating the understanding among themselves attempted to sit in the bazaar. But their piece goods were snatched from them and torn into pieces by the group of women agitators, who were in favour of the bazaar economic boycott. Nobody even dared to complain.

On March 20, 1940, hundreds of women took out a long procession along the main roads of the Imphal town. A woman was arrested, but she was rescued from the police by the demonstrators. The matter came to the notice of the Political Agent, who rushed to the scene with armed policemen. The State Police arrested two more women leaders named Shabi Devi and Kabokhi Devi in connection with picketing foreign cloth. As they failed to furnish bond and securities against their charges, they were sentenced for nine months imprisonment by an order of the Manipur State Durbar. The local market observed complete *hartal* as a sequel to the conviction of the women leaders.[11] Further, the general mass including men and women put forward the following demands to the Political Agent and the Maharaja:

1. To stop the export of rice till the next harvest as there is every fear of having a famine due to want of stock.
2. To stop the rice-milling system which has 'eaten up' the earnings of the women of paddy-huskings.
3. To remove the present Durbar members who have proved unworthy for the administration and replace them by new members through elections.

4. To remove the present State servants in the Police Department who are all untrained and also found unfit for administration.
5. To establish a Legislative Council as already claimed by the Nikhil Manipuri Mahasabha and a scheme for which had been submitted to the Maharaja as asked for through his Private Secretary.
6. To decide the case of one Shabi Devi, who was assaulted by the Inspector of Police, by snatching her from the crowd and giving two slaps with a kick of boot on the chest.
7. To decide the case of ten women who were imprisoned for one month on the charge of picketing, by the Durbar.
8. To decide the case of one Oinam Ibemhan Devi who was assaulted in an inhuman manner by a police officer causing bleeding for several days. She remained in the Imphal Civil Hospital for several days under the treatment of the civil surgeon.
9. To decide the case of causing unnecessary assault to the innocent crowd on 14.1.40 and thereby causing injuries to forty women and some men.
10. To decide the case of nine leaders of the Praja Sanmilani, who were arrested out of the processionists, on 28.1.40 and detained in the police custody more than twenty hours, without informing the charge on which they were arrested.
11. To decide the cause of the bayonet charge and thereby causing severe wounds to twenty women including a woman of more than seventy years.[12]

Besides, the demonstrators remined that if the local authorities did not look into the matter, they would continue the bazaar boycott. The Political Agent, instead of sympathizing the cause of women, felt very much satisfied with the dutiful service rendered by the Assistant Sub-Inspector.[13] The women were also unhappy with the order of the Durbar for the withdrawal of ban on rice export which was promulgated about a year ago. The Political Agent openly refused to do anything until he could get orders from the Viceroy. The Governor General of India and the Governor of Assam, had been approached for favour of causing a prompt inquiry by a tribunal and thereby decide the cases; but no action was taken.[14]

Sooner or later, no one seemed to be any longer enthusiastic to the cause of the economic boycott. Gradually the market place was reoccupied by the women-sellers. By the beginning of February 1940, some four or five hundred were sitting regularly. But a fresh problem was created on the issue of allotment of seats to the new and the old occupiers of the market. The Political Agent only to avoid further complication notified that as the seats had been vacated by the old sitters for a long period, he would allot to any one who chose. He announced that if any one of the former sitter wished to return to her respective seat, she should file an application to him within one month. This naturally disappointed the old sitters. They thought that they should be given first preference. The Maharaja was asked by the Political Agent if he had desired to raise any objection on this issue. But the Maharaja was silent. By and by many applications both new and old poured into the Political Agent's office. And for a few days there was a vigorous scramble with many tussls between the parties. However, there was no serious incident. In continuation of the previous notice dated 23.8.1940, the Political Agent wisely issued another notice on September 28, 1940. He cancelled the settlement of old seats for new arrangements. Those who had filed applications for retaining their old seats would be given first preference. It appeared that the Political Agent did not like to do injustice to those old sitters. He was sure if he had allotted seats to other new-comers, that would have a year long ill-feeling and resentment among themselves.

The women's year long movement gradually died down. The economic distress or the political excitement might lead them to take up other form of agitation, as they had in the past, but this time they had learnt that their best interests lay inside and not outside the *Khwairamband Keithal* or bazaar. The majority of them were economically backward. There might have been serious ill-economic consequences if the movement would have continued. On the other hand, there were no prominent leaders who could guide the demoralized women agitators, as most of them had been locked up. The petty leaders failed to revive the dying spirit of the movement. The women also could not complain as the price of paddy had gone down.[15]

The split in the Working Committee of the Nikhil Manipuri Mahasabha took place in 1939, when some of its members came under the influence that the women agitation should be suspended immediately, which was vehemently opposed by a section of members. The split in the Working Committee of the Nikhil Manipuri Mahasabha had disheartened the agitators. This was the only political party which had been fighting for the cause of the women. The defection in the party itself helped to strengthen the hands of the Government. In this way, the lack of political and moral guidance to the women, this economic pressure, defection in the Nikhil Manipuri Mahasabha and with the resumption of their business brought the close of the year long agitation.

Political Repercussions

There was considerable controversy whether the women's uprising was politically motivated. Some observers commented that the scenario had nothing to do with politics. Others said that the women were 'hungry' so they demanded rice only to fill up their bellies. The price index had risen up very high. They wanted rice at a cheaper rate. They sought for this with no exception. The agitation was stopped when the export of rice was suspended. They came to the market and sat as usually and regularly. There was no organization in the movement. That was the reason why the struggle did not last long.

The view that the agitation had economic rather than political causes appears to be partially right. But we cannot overlook the political fact that women-folk resorted to direct action for the redress of their grievances. The shortage of rice caused from the heavy export of rice from Manipur to other neighbouring districts was not only the problem which kept the movement going for about ten years. If we study in details we would be able to see the underlying political trends in the movement. It was the party of Hijam Irabot Singh, which aroused and stirred up the feeling and sentiments of the women. Irabot was the arhitect of this movement. The Nikhil Manipuri Mahasabha used to give instructions to women leaders from time to time.[16] Accordingly, the women sticked to the policies and programmes which were chalked out by the party. The women also received encouragements from Indian political leaders during the movement. 'If I may advise, you should not lose heart and at the same time not indulge in any kind of violence which would give the authorities a pretext to crush your movement. Organise yourselves peacefully and quietly insist on your demands. Do not give in or be frightened by the power of the State. Big changes are coming all over India and your State cannot left out of them',[17] advised Jawaharlal Nehru in a letter to the Working committee of the Nikhil Manipuri Mahasabha. He expressed his inability to approach the Viceroy or Government in the matter, but assured the Working Committee that all those who learned about their difficulties sympathized with them. Nehru recorded his personal admiration for the way in which the women of Manipur had been carrying the agitation, and wished them success.

The Kamrup Mahila Samity recorded with price of fight of the Manipuri ladies against injustice done to them by the State authorities. They congratulated them on their stand for justice, patriotism, selfless service, organizing capacity and moral courage. The Samity wished that the ladies of Manipur would further continue their movement with complete non-violence and unanimity. It further urged the Government of India and the Maharaja to devise ways and means to meet the demands of the Manipuri females and see that peace and order was restored in the State.[18]

The link between the Nikhil Manipuri Mahasabha and the women's bazaar agitation could be seen from the very beginning. When the women's movement started in full swing in the early part of December 1939, they felt the lack of leadership of Irabot, President of the Nikhil Manipuri Mahasabha, who had just gone to Cachar some days back for attending a political conference. Informing him of the women's agitation in Imphal, he was asked by the women leaders to return and lead the movement.

In a massively organised meeting held at Police Bazar, Irabot was pointing out the Government's inefficiency in tackling the situation. He repeatedly condemned the policies of the Government for their carelessness to redress the grievances of the women. As a result of his violent speech, a clash took place between the civilians and the police at the spot.[19]

As the area was already under Section 144 IPC, Irabot was arrested on January 9, 1940, on the charge of giving a seditious speech, and sentenced for three years imprisonment under Section 1, u/s 124A, I.P.C. by the Manipur State Durbar.[20]

It was the Nikhil Manipuri Mahasabha which popularized the women's movement in Manipur and other parts of India. The Political Agent firmly believed that some of the agitating women leaders were playing in the hands of the Nikhil Manipuri Mahasabha. He further asserted that the women's agitation, which was started by the bazaar women of Imphal against the Government policy of rice export, was gradually taken over by the Mahasabha. E.F. Lydall, the President of the Manipur State Durbar, observed that '...the agitation, which is said to have been fanned by an old prophesy that the appointment time had come for the arrival of a new Maharaja riding on the white elephant. The Mahasabha, a local body with congress affiliations, also took advantage of the unrest suggested that their leader (Irabot) was rider of the prophecy.'[21]

A Central Intelligence report showed the role of the Congress in the movement of the Manipuri women and a direct link with the leaders of the Nikhil Manipuri Mahasabha, like Irabot and later Magho Singh with the All India States Peoples' Conference, which helped them in making out plans and direct tactics to be applied in the agitations.[22] In a letter from Purnendu Sen, a Congress worker of Sylhet, who had former revolutionary connections, to Labanya Lata Chandra, a leader of the Congress women's movment in Bengal and a member of the women's sub-committee of the Bengal Provincial Committee, that it was clearly indicated that the writer was trying to gather news about the women's agitation in Manipur for the purpose of its publication in the press. He further persuaded Labanya Lata Chandra that if she could prepare to meet the expense, he would like to send some agents to Manipur. Purnendu Sen also suggested Amrit Kaur, a freedom fighter, should go to Manipur and study the political situation. On account of her ill-health the matter was dropped later on.[23]

It was quite apparent that the leaders of the Nikhil Manipuri Mahasabha also received regular instructions from the Sylhet and Gauhati Congresses. Irabot occasionally visited Gauhati and Sylhet to see the President of the Assam Provincial Committee with a view to receive instructions. When Irabot was in the Sylhet Jail, his lieutenant Magho Singh assumed the party leadership and tried to keep the movement alive. He used to correspond with Kamala Chatterji, a member of the Jugantar Party, who was working with the Communist Party of India in the Bengal Provincial Student's Federation, in connection with the women's agitation in Imphal.[24]

The Manipur Government was quite aware of the political developments in the State. The Government was ready to prevent any sort of activities which might lead to commotion and anarchy in the State. Every incident was vigilantly observed. The State administration prohibited meetings of political character in Manipur without prior permission from the same.[25] As a precautionary measure, the Government also adopted a policy of prohibiting the entry of unauthorized persons into the State. A strict vigilance was kept to prevent the Congress propagandists from entering Manipur. As suggested by D.A. Brayden, the Central Intelligence Officer, the Political Agent accepted the establishment of Agency at Dimapur.[26] This was with a view to prevent the flowing of the Congress political elements and influence over into Manipur. Undoubtedly this was to check the political fomentation of the Manipuri women's agitation by political elements from outside the State.

Administrative Remedies and Reforms

The idea of reforms brought a lot of complications and made it more difficult to follow a line of agreement. The Maharaja, Durbar members and President of the Durbar had different proposals with diverse justifications. Besides, the Nikhil Manipuri Mahasabha had its own demands.

The Political Agent first of all thought that a radical constitutional reform was not so necessary as the Manipuris never had a tradition of democracy. Though certain elements of it would be found in the Mahasabha and Congress adherents. The women were neither interested in constitutional reforms nor setting up a constituent assembly.[27] The Maharaja was also of the opinion that there would be no need of administrative changes. He remarked that the women's disturbance had no direct bearing with the introduction of reforms in the State.[28] It was aggravated by the Nikhil Manipur Mahasabha. However, he felt the need of certain administrative changes. In June 1940, he ordered the members of the Durbar to devise a plan to deal with the problem of agitation and give specific suggestions which could remedy the existing administrative defects. The following were the proposals put forth by the individual Durbar members:

1. Establishment of three or four posts of sub-divisional officers with a police station at every sub-divisional headquarters,
2. A chief court separate from the administrative Durbar,
3. A municipal committee for the capital,
4. A local Manipuri President of Durbar,

5. A legislative assembly composed of twelve elected, and ten nominated members,
6. Abolition of separate administrative branch for the hills,
7. Admission of pleaders into the State Courts,
8. Creation of a Manipuri Civil Service with senior and junior divisions,
9. Replacement of *cherap* and sadar panchayat courts members and the hill sub-divisional officers,
10. Cancellation of village *choukidars* and establishment of ten police stations in the valley and seven in the hills,
11. Restriction on the Maharaja's civil list to ten per cent of the revenue of the State,
12. Opening of a department of excise,
13. Introduction of examination system for the candidates for States services,
14. Revision of pay-scale of State Government servants,
15. Mineralogical survey in the State,
16. Expansion of Durbar by increasing its members and inclusion of elderly statesman.
17. Promotion by efficiency, not by seniority,
18. Starting of an agricultural department and co-operative societies,
19. Opening of more hospitals and veterinary dispensaries outside Imphal, and
20. Introduction of the British administrative system in toto, including trial by jury.[29]

The President of the Durbar was doubtful about the successful implementation of such reforms as the State was lacking in honest, capable and efficient persons who could be employed to implement the reforms.

Secondly, the Nikhil Manipuri Mahasabha weighed in with a demand for a unicameral legislature of 100 members, eighty to be elected and twenty to be nominated by the Maharaja. The other suggestions were for voting by ballot, no communal electorate, electors to be literate or tax-payers or both, a bill to become law if passed by the Maharaja who would otherwise refer it back to the legislature, the legislature to pass the budget, the civil list to be in a fixed proportion to the State's revenues, the Maharaja to ask the leader of the largest party in the legislature to be prime minister and to choose three cabinet ministers who with him would have joint responsibility to the legislature, the Maharaja appointing more ministers whose responsibility would be individual, the Maharaja to set up a constituent assembly and no body to vote twice over. But the reforms proposed by the Nikhil Manipuri Mahasabha were never considered by the Government. The Political Agent was under the impression that as there had never been any form of democratic government in the State, not even municipal or local boards, this proposal seemed to be too wild to consider seriously.[30]

Lastly, the Maharaja also submitted a draft of reforms to the Political Agent.[31] He wanted his reforms should be introduced in his State. The constitutional proposals for reforms submitted by the Maharaja (to the Political Agent) may be studied under the following heads:

The State Executive

1. The Executive authority of the State shall be exercised by the Maharaja either directly or through ministers to be chosen from amongst the members of the State Legislative Assembly.
2. There shall be a council of ministers of limited number to aid and advise the Maharaja in the exercise of his functions.
3. If any question arises whether any matter is or is not a matter as respects which the Maharaja is to act in his discretion will be final.
4. The Prime Minister will be chosen by the Maharaja in consultation with the Prime Minister of the State who will be a lent Indian Civil Service (I.C.S.) officer or a retired officer from British India and shall hold office during the Maharaja's pleasure.
5. The Prime Minister will be responsible to the Maharaja for the proper administration of the finance and revenue departments and will on behalf of the Maharaja exercise general supervision over the working of all departments. The Maharaja in consultation with the prime minister will arrange for the distribution of work between the prime minister and other ministers.

6. The salaries of ministers shall be such as the State legislature may determine, and until the State legislature so determine, shall be determined by the Maharaja provided that the salary of a minister shall not be varied during his terms of office.
7. The question whether any, and if so, what advice was tendered by the ministers to the Maharaja, shall not be enquired into, in any State court.
8. In the exercise of his functions the Maharaja shall have three special responsibilities, i.e., (a) the prevention of any grave menace to the peace and tranquility of the State, (b) the safeguarding of legitimate interests of the subjects, (c) and the securing of the peace and good government of the State.

   If and in so far as any special responsibility of the Maharaja is involved, the Maharaja shall, in exercise of his functions, exercise his individual judgment as to the action to be taken.
9. If it appears to the Maharaja that the peace or tranquility of the State is endangered by the operations of any persons committing, preparing or attempting to commit, crimes of violence which, in Maharaja's opinion, are intended to overthrow the State Government, the Maharaja may, he thinks that the circumstances of the case require him so to do for combating those operations, direct that his functions shall to such extent as may be specified in that direction, be exercised by the Maharaja in his discretion and, until otherwise provided by a subsequent direction of the Maharaja, those functions to that extent shall be exercised by the Maharaja accordingly.
10. (a) All executive actions of the State Government shall be expressed to be taken in the name of the Maharaja.

    (b) Orders and other instructions made and executed in the name of the Maharaja shall be authenticated in such manner as to be suggested by the prime minister and approved by the Maharaja.

    (c) The prime minister, the ministers and the heads of the departments shall transmit to the Maharaja all informations with respect to the business of the State Government.

The State Legislature

1. There shall be a State legislature which will consist of the Maharaja and a chamber to be known as the State Legislative Assembly.

2. The State Legislative Assembly will consist of a lent I.C.S. officer or some retired officer from British India and twenty-seven members. Out of twenty-seven members eighteen will be elected—two each from the four *panas* of *Ahallup*; *Naharup*, *Khabam* and *Laipham*; eight will be elected—two each from the four *leikais* of Kwai, Yaiskul, Khurai and Wangkhai and two will be elected from the Muslim community; nine will be nominated out of which five will be officials and four non-officials.
3. The State Legislative Assembly unless sooner dissolved shall continue for five years from the date appointed for their first meeting and expiration of five years shall operate as dissolution of the Assembly.
4. (a) The Assembly shall be summoned to meet at least four times a year.
   (b) The Maharaja may in his discretion from time to time summon the Assembly to meet at such time and place as he thinks fit and prorogue it.
   (c) The Maharaja may in his discretion send any matter to the Assembly for discussion.
5. The Prime Minister will provide the meetings of the Assembly and manage its workings.
   (a) All the questions in the Assembly shall be determined by a majority of votes of the members present. In cases of equality of votes the prime minister shall have a casting vote.
   (b) The Assembly shall have power to discuss any matter of the State including the budget.
   (c) The State budget will be drafted by the prime minister, and will be laid by him before the State Assembly for examination. After the Assembly has recorded its suggestions, if any, for modifications in the prime minister's draft budget, the Maharaja will record his opinion. If The Maharaja desires any modifications in the budget proposed by the Assembly, the Maharaja will communicate his opinion to the Assembly in order to give them an opportunity or reconsidering their views and submitting a further minute to the Maharaja. The Maharaja will then record his own

final opinion indicating clearly the form in which he desires that the budget shall be accepted by the Government of Assam and will forward all the papers to the Political Agent for submission to the Government of Assam. The Government of Assam after giving due consideration to the wishes of the Maharaja and the Assembly, will finally approve the budget with such modifications as it thinks fit. When once approved by the Government of Assam the budget must be adhered to subject the such modifications as are allowed by the rules sanctioned by the Government of Assam for the keep of the State accounts.

(d) It shall be the duty of the prime minister to adjourn the meetings of the Assembly until more than half of the total number of the members are present.

(e) The Assembly and the council of ministers will submit copies of their proceedings to the Maharaja who may (i) approve thereof, (ii) refer any matter back to the assembly or to the council of ministers as the case may be for further consideration, (iii) veto any resolution and issue what orders he sees fit, stating his reasons in writings. This power of veto will be exercised in very rare cases. After the Maharaja passed his orders, copies of the proceedings and the order passed thereon will be submitted to the Political Agent.

(f) If a member be absent without permission of the Assembly for thirty days from all meetings of the Assembly, the Assembly may declare his seat vacant. Provided that in computing this period of thirty days, no account shall be taken of any period during which the Assembly is prorogued, or is adjourned for more than three consecutive days.

6. The Armed Police shall be under the control of the Maharaja.

7. Qualifications of membership in the Assembly have to be decided later.

8. Members of the State Legislative Assembly shall be entitled to receive such allowances (not salaries) as may be fixed from time to time by the Assembly.

9. No State court shall have power to enquire into the proceedings of the State Assembly.

The Maharaja's Legislative Powers

1. (a) If at any time when the State Assembly is not in sitting the Maharaja is satisfied that there exist circumstances in the State which render it necessary for the Maharaja to take immediate action, the Maharaja may promulgate such ordinance as the circumstances appear to require.

   (b) Such ordinances shall have the same force and effect as resolutions of the assembly approved by the Maharaja.

   (c) But the ordinance shall be laid before the assembly and shall cease to operate after the expiration of three weeks from the day on which they are so laid, or if a resolution disapproving them is passed by the assembly and approved of by the Maharaja upon the passing of the resolutions.

   (d) The Maharaja may withdraw the ordinances at any time.

   (e) The ordinances shall be void if they relate to matters concerning which the State Assembly has no power to make legislation.

2. (a) If at any time the Maharaja is satisfied that circumstances exist which render it necessary for the Maharaja to take immediate action for the purpose of enabling his satisfactorily to discharge his functions in so far as the Maharaja is required to act in his discretion or to exercise his individual judgment, the Maharaja may promulgate such ordinances as in his opinion the circumstances of the case enquire.

   (b) The ordinance thus promulgated shall continue in operation for such period not exceeding four months as may be specified therein, but a subsequent ordinance may be extended for a further period not exceeding four months.

   (c) The ordinance shall have the same effect and force as a resolution of the assembly approved of by the Maharaja.

   (d) The Maharaja may withdraw the ordinance at any time.

   (e) If it is an ordinance extending a previous ordinance for a further period, it shall be communicated to the Government through the Political Agent.

   (f) The Maharaja shall exercise this power with the concurrence of the Government; provided that, if it appears to the

Maharaja that it is impracticable to obtain in time the concurrence of the Government. The Maharaja may promulgate an ordinance without its concurrence, but in that case the Government may in its discretion advise the Maharaja to withdraw the ordinance and the ordinance shall be withdrawn accordingly.

Provisions in Case of Failure of Constitutional Machinery

1. If at any time the Maharaja is satisfied that a situation has arisen in which the State Government cannot be carried on properly the Maharaja may by proclamation-
   - (a) Declare that the Maharaja's functions shall, to such extent, as may be satisfied in the proclamation, be exercised by him in his discretion;
   - (b) Assume to himself all or any of the powers vested in or exercisable by any State constitutional body or authority;
   - (c) Any such proclamation may contain such incidental and consequential provisions as may appear to the Maharaja to be necessary or desirable for giving effect to the objects of the proclamation, including provisions of the State constitution relating to any State constitutional body or authority;
   - (d) Provided nothing in the foregoing provisions shall authorize the Maharaja to assume to himself any of the powers vested in or exercisable by the State chief court, or to suspend either in whole or in part the operations of any provisions of the judiciary relating to the State courts.
2. Any such proclamation may be revoked or varied by a subsequent proclamation.
3. (a) A proclamation thus made shall be communicated forthwith to the Government.
   - (b) A proclamation unless it is a proclamation revoking a previous one shall cease to operate at the expiration of four months.

Provided that, if the Government approves of the proclamations continuing in force, the proclamation, shall, unless revoked, continue in force for a further period of eight months from the date on which it would otherwise have ceased to operate, but no such proclamation shall in any case remain in force for more than two years.

4. If the Maharaja by a proclamation assumes to himself any power of the State legislature to make laws, any law made by the Maharaja in the exercise of that power shall subject to the terms thereof, continue to have effect until two years have elapsed from its date on which its proclamation ceases to have effect, unless sooner repeated or enacted by an appropriate State legislature.

The State Judicature

1. The judicial Durbar under some suitable name (like the chief court of justice) shall continue to exercise the highest original or appellate jurisdiction in the State both civil and criminal cases.
2. The personnel of this court may to some extent be decreased by some gradual process.
3. The Maharaja shall continue to exercise revisional jurisdiction as at present.
4. The State will better borrow a European Officer of the Imperial Police to act as superintendent of the State police for three or five years. He will train the State police work in technical and the force of the present State police is untrained.[32]

The Political Agent remarked that the Maharaja did not mention that how a prime minister would be appointed, and removed from the office. The Maharaja wanted that out of nine members of the State Assembly five should be State officials. The Political Agent suggested that there should be at least some elected members otherwise the ministers would be responsible to him only and not to the Assembly. The age limit at thirty for the members was also unduly high. With reference to the power of the State Assembly, it was not clearly defined that what would be the role of ministers in initiating resolutions, and whether the proceedings of the assembly would go direct to the Maharaja from the assembly or through his council of ministers. The procedure proposed for the budget seemed unduly cumbrous, when dealing with a body of twenty-eight members.

As in the case of judicature, the Political Agent remarked that the intention of the Maharaja was to reduce the Durbar to a purely judicial body. The Maharaja had also overlooked the need of reforming the administration of courts. The Political Agent suggested that these courts should be thoroughly reorganized as they had been the centre of deep-rooted corruption. Further, he said that if the Durbar members had only judicial work, then they should have enough time to supervise the work and duties of the lower courts. It might lead to a better administration of justice.

The Political Agent was certain that the State would not be able to restore and maintain order with the existing police force. He agreed with the Maharaja on his proposal of borrowing a European Police Officers to re-organise and train the police. But he criticized the Maharaja for his unwillingness to allow the control of the State Military police to pass them his own hands.

To the Political Agent, there appeared to be some confusion of the prime minister, who was also to be president of the assembly. The leader of the assembly would take over most of the duties of the President of the Durbar, who did preside over Durbar meetings. The Political Agent presumed that the prime minister would preside over the council of ministers, but not over the assembly. The confusion might have arisen from the use of the term 'President' of the Durbar.

The Political Agent pointed out that the Maharaja's proposals did not touch the hill tribes. He thought that it would be impossible for the prime minister to be responsible for the administration of the hill tribes in addition to his other duties. It would be necessary to consider a new arrangement for the hills.

Finally, the Political Agent rejected the Maharaja's suggestion that any extra expenditure incurred on account of his proposed reforms might be met by a cut in the pay of the State servants. In his opinion the Maharaja had under-estimated the cost and more important had not realized what an unfavourable starts his reforms would receive, if they were depended on a reduction in salaries, which were already very small. He remarked that the State military police and the civil list were two heads under which the economies might be effected. On the other hand, the Maharaja wished to increase the expenditure under both.[33]

Pointing out all the defects and irregularities of the draft proposals of reforms by the Maharaja, C. Gimson, the Political Agent asked him to review it once again. Instead of admitting the validity of the comments by the Political Agent, he rather upheld his reforms. He further observed that 'In view of the pressing demands of the subjects I have ventured to experiment with the proposed constitution. The provision has been made to safeguard its failure. The council of ministers will take over the executive functions, the Durbar will necessarily be responsible to me only. Changes will have to be made in the rules for the administration of the State assembly.[34]

The Political Agent referred the proposed reforms to the Governor of Assam, who remarked that the Maharaja's proposed reforms would be '...so nebulous and questions such as the suitability to Manipur have been so insufficiently worked out that they are worth very little indeed.[35] It became apparent that the Maharaja's draft reforms meant almost nothing from a democratic point of view and in fact, if anything, tended to give more power to an autocratic ruler than what he actually possessed. The Governor considered that they were far less likely to satisfy and other element in the State. He assumed that the Maharaja's ruling passion was money. The Governor firmly believed that the reforms proposed by the Political Agent would be more suitable and practicable, and that they would really pacify the excited people. At the same time the Governor felt that if the British officers were to do their duty as trustees, in a sense, for Manipur, they were bound to try and force the Ruler to give his subjects a reasonably sound system of administration.[36]

The Assam Governor informed the Viceroy about his difficulties in convincing the Maharaja as he was unwilling to introduce the reforms in the British pattern. Moreover, the Maharaja was waiting for the introduction of the federation to take up the question of reforms. Keeping in view the critical situation of Manipur, the Governor-General agreed that the proposed reforms should be initiated without further delay. He observed that the question of further reductions in the Maharaja's privy purse that it might be left for later consideration. The Governor-General suggested that the Maharaja was generally inclined to adopt an obstructive attitude; therefore, '...the best course would, perhaps, be after an appropriately brief interval, for you (Assam Governor) to summon him and suggest to him that he should go on a pilgrimage or otherwise take a rest from his activities and leave the President under the instruction of the Political Agent and the Governor to proceed with putting matters straight.'[37]

The Maharaja was probably quite aware of the developments. He was sure that his proposed reforms were not going to be introduced in his State. Seeing no alternative, the Maharaja left Imphal for Calcutta for 'medical check-up'. At the same time, his intention was to delay the introduction of the reforms in his State. The Maharaja vaguely talked of announcing the British proposed reforms on the day of the golden jubilee of his reign. Sensing the obstructive attitude of the Maharaja, the Assam Governor immediately communicated with the Political Agent, expressing his views that '...it is no longer possible to postpone the introduction of reforms designed to bring the administration more into accord with accepted standards of good and efficient government.'[38] Later he felt that if the Government wanted to achieve success, it should go slowly.

Having reigned for fifty years, the Maharaja announced his intention to abdicate in favour of his eldest son. He died at Navadwip twenty-four days later on November 6, 1941.[39] The long drawn efforts of the British at constitutional reforms were of the demands of the Nikhil Manipuri Mahasabha. The British administrators suspected that the Maharaja aimed at concentrating all powers in his own hands. However, the colonial overlords themselves never intended to go beyond half-hearted constitutional reforms. To conclude, the women's agitation, which later turned into a mass movement, moved the British administration to plan and implement at least some reforms in the State essential to deal with its social and economic problems.

References

1. These women-workers purchased paddy from the whole-sellers and pounded and sold it in the form of rice at a very reasonable price. And what they got out of that was spent on their livelihood. As the price index moved up, the poor people were unable to purchase rice at the high rate for their daily consumption.
2. The *Khwairamband Keithel* or bazaar has been only a big market entirely run by the women. It was the main market in the British Reserve area. It opened at about four or five O'clock in the evening and closed at midnight.
3. E.F. Lyndall, *Administration Report, Manipur State, 1939-40* (Imphal: State Printing Press, 1943), p. 1.
4. Home Department, Political File No. 26 (23), 1940, NAI, New Delhi.
5. E.F. Lyndall, *Administration Report, Manipur State, 1939-40* (Imphal: State Printing Press, 1943), p. 1.

6. L. Ibungohal Singh, *Introduction to Manipur* (Imphal: Friends' Union Press, 1963), p. 49.
7. All India States Peoples' Conference File No. 18, 1939-1942, Nehru Memorial Museum and Library, New Delhi.
8. E.F. Lyndall, *Administration Report, Manipur State, 1939-40* (Imphal: State Printing Press, 1943), p. 1.
9. All India States Peoples' Conference File No. 12, 1940, NMML, New Delhi.
10. E.F. Lyndall, *Administration Report, Manipur State, 1939-40* (Imphal: State Printing Press, 1943), p. 1.
11. Defying the *hartal* some of the women leaders of small influence or reputation, about fifty in number, challenged to sit in the market, and they sat regularly. But the great majority werc intimidated. This time no attempt was made to interfere with the private business runners. A few of them conducted their business outside the British reserve. Here, the role of the new women leaders was not so successful, as they could not persuade the women-folk convincingly. They repeatedly failed in their attempts to stir up the sentiments of the women eventhough they held several meetings on several occasions.
12. *The Forward* (Calcutta), February 17, 1940, p. 11.
13. The Political Agent, acknowledging the service of the Assistant Sub-Inspector (including other constables) wrote to J.P. Mills, Secretary to Government of Assam, that '...I wish to place on record my appreciation of the persistence and tact with which the Assistant Sub-Inspector performed his duties and the willingness with which the constables supported him. They had very long hours of most anxious and unpleasant work and they were not found wanting. They kept their tempers even under the insults of women's tongues' *Ibid.* March 30, 1940, p. 14.
14. All India State Peoples' Conference File No. 18, 1939-42, NMML, New Delhi.
15. E.F. Lyndall, *Administration Report, Manipur State, 1939-40* (Imphal: State Printing Press, 1943), p. 1.
16. The Nikhil Manipuri Mahasabha, under the leadership of Hijam Irabot Singh, came into prominence early in 1939, when it submitted a memorial to the Governor-General requesting him to advise the Maharaja to establish a legislative council as a step towards the introduction of a responsible form of government in Manipur.
17. *The Amrita Bazar Patrika* (Calcutta), March 25, 1940, p. 4.
18. *Ibid*, April, 9, 1940, p. 10.
19. Particularly from this occurrence the movement had turned into a different shape as the men had started taking part actively in the women's agitation. Later, it converted into a constitutional movement.

20. Home Department, Political File No. 192, 1943, NAI, New Delhi.
21. E.F. Lyndall, *Administration Report, Manipur State, 1939-40* (Imphal: State Printing Press, 1943), p. 1.
22. Home Department, Political File No. 26(23), 1940, NAI, New Delhi.
23. *Ibid.*
24. *Ibid.*
25. *The Amrita Bazar Patrika* (Calcutta), April 21, 1940, p. 10.
26. The purpose of the establishment of this Agency was to function as a check-post. The Agent would have an opportunity of discussing matters with the State's people leaving the State and should soon get to know any outsiders who visit the State frequently.
27. Political Agent of Manipur to Secretary of Governor of Assam, 20 January 1940, Home Department File No. 11(7)/40-Poll 1940.
28. Maharaja of Manipur to Political Agent, 22 April 1940, Home Department File No. 26 (23), 1940, NAI, New Delhi.
29. E.F. Lyndall, *Administrative Report, Manipur State, 1940-41* (Imphal: State Printing Press, 1942), p. 1.
30. Political Agent of Manipur to Secretary of Governor of Assam, 20 May 1940, Home Department File No. 26(23)/40-Poll. 1940.
31. Maharaja of Manipur to Political Agent, 22 April 1940, *Ibid.*
32. *Ibid.*
33. Political Agent of Manipur to Secretary of Governor of Assam, 20 May 1940, *Ibid.*
34. Maharaja of Manipur to Political Agent, 8 May 1940, *Ibid.*
35. Governor of Assam to Governor-General, 4 June 1940, Home Department File No. 26(23)/40-Poll, 1940.

    Supporting the views of the Governor of Assam, the Governor-General was of the opinion that the scheme for constitutional reforms proposed by the Maharaja appeared to be impracticable and wholly unsuited to the needs of the State.
36. Secretary to the Governor-General, to Governor of Assam, 10 June 1940, *Ibid.*
37. Secretary to the Governor of Assam, to Secretary of Crown Representative, 7 June 1940, *Ibid.*
38. Secretary to the Governor of Assam, to Political Agent of Manipur, 6 September 1940, *Ibid.*
39. Home Department, Political File No. 160, NAI, New Delhi.

7
The Abortive Plan of a 'Purbachal Pradesh', 1948

Origin of the Movement

The idea of establishing an integrated eastern India frontier province consisting of parts of Assam and Manipur, was a brain-child of the frustrated Bengali elites, who were allegedly discriminated against and suppressed by the local Assamese majority in the heterogeneous province of Assam. The movement for the formation of Purbachal Pradesh on the eastern border of Assam, with a view to giving accommodation to the displaced Hindus of Sylhet and East Bengal (now in Bangladesh) soon began gaining popularity.

After Independence, the Bengalis of Assam were reduced to a tiny minority because the thickly populated district of Sylhet became a part of East Pakistan (now Bangladesh). As a result of the partition, the proportion of the Assamese people in the local population of Assam had risen from about a fifth to one-third. But the Bengalis, though much reduced in percentage, formed the largest single group in the province, particularly so because of the influx of the refugees after the partition.[1]

The Bengalis soon began to develop and suffer from a sense of minority complex. The Bengalis did not like the administrative and cultural domination of the Assamese. Above all the imagined superiority complex of the Assamese made the Bengali minority to think more about their community's integrity and safety. To save their identity they planned to arouse the sentiments of other minority groups who were inhabited in different parts of the Assam province.

Like the other minority groups in Assam, some of the political leaders of Manipur were also enthusiastically moved by the cause of the Bengalis, the largest minority in the province. The Manipuri political leaders came out in support of the demand for a united eastern frontier province. The proposed 'Purbachal Pradesh' was to comprise of some Hill districts, frontier areas or tracts, plain districts, and states of the Assam province.[2]

According to Professor J.K. Choudhary, the Purbachal Pradesh could have comprised of hill districts—the Khasi and Jaintia Hills, the districts including Shillong, the Garo Hills District, the Lushai Hills District, the Naga Hills District, the Mikir Hills, parts of Nowgong and the Sibsagar district except the *mouzas* of Barpathar and Sarupathar. In the frontier tracts, it could include the Sadiya and Balipara frontier tracts, the Tirap Frontier Tract with the Lakhimpur frontier and the Naga tribal areas. In the plain districts, the district of Cachar including Karimganj and the north Cachar sub-divisions. The district of Goalpara was also to be included. Further he felt that Purbachal could be formed with such states like Tripura, Manipur, Cooch-Behar and the Khasi states (including the above mentioned areas). But he did realize that it would finally depend on the will of the people of these states whether they would like to join Purbachal.[3] His argument was that 'Tripura, Manipur or Cooch-Behar are not such states according to the Government of India as can stand by themselves and bear the burden of a full-fledged modern-democratic administration; nor are they geographically contiguous to amalgamate with a view to forming one viable unit. The only alternative left to them is, therefore, a merger...'[4] But the formation of the proposed Pradesh would have resulted in the domination of the backward groups or tribes by the Bengalis and this would not have been palatable to the non-Bengali segments of the population.

Professor Choudhary's arguments were, however, neither cogent nor convincing. Tripura and Manipur have been constituted as different States. Not to talk of the small area which could not form a separate state, even today there are many small countries like Maldives, Sri Lanka, etc., who are even sovereign and independent. It is not the area but the capacity of the administrative efficiency which determines viability of a state. One cannot, however, fail to appreciate Professor Choudhury's plea that the people of every district and state should be allowed to have their own languages and script at the primary stage of education, with Hindustani as a compulsory language. The

Constitution has assured education and cultural rights to the linguistic minorities, and the national educational policy is also similarly oriented.

The formation of a new Purbachal might not be difficult, provided the people concerned willed it. The problem, however, was whether a strong and an efficient state could have been formed including all the components instead of dividing Assam into pieces. Perhaps a demand for more democratic decentralization in Assam might have been better. But Professor Choudhury seemed to believe that the Assamese and the Bengalis could never come to terms as if they had some deep-rooted animosities and irreconcilable aspirations. The Bengali elites, however, were not unnaturally apprehensive about their position and future under the new set-up as some of the Assamese leaders had given the impression as if they should like to liquidate Manipur culture, literature, script, language and customs. As a matter of fact, such leaders might not have had the slightest consideration for the minorities, whose demand then was to introduce Hindustani as state language. Referring to the vicious step taken by the Assam Government to introduce Assamese language in all the schools and the colleges of Manipur, Laishram Joychandra Singh of the Manipur State Congress sharply reacted: 'If the Assamese brush aside this logic facts and stick to the imposition of Assamese as State language, Manipur cannot come into Assam.'[5] It was, therefore, in the interest of both the Assamese and the Manipuris that there should be some safeguards for the proper development of the culture and language of the minorities.[6] The declaration that the Assam Government would have Assamese only as the provincial language made the Bengali people more excited.

The Bengali questioned the majority of the Assamese in Assam in view of the fact that they were only about two and half million, whereas the other different groups formed the six and half million of the whole Assamese population. All communities had the same rights in the state and could not accept domination by any one of them. But the fact that the Assamese enjoyed the monopoly in the government jobs was highlighted by Choudhury.[7]

There appeared to be some psychological misunderstanding between the two major groups and the Bengali elites openly criticized the anti-Bengali policy of the Assam Government. The Assam Government on the other hand did not relent and refused to provide settlement facilities to the Hindu Bengali refugees who had come from East Pakistan. B.C. Purkayastha however admitted that '...Assam with its heterogenous population and undeveloped regions need the Bengali talent for the development of the province. However, Bengali talent is temporarily reserved for Purbachal'.[8] The Assamese had burnt down and looted the houses of the Bengalis who had been the inhabitants from the time immemorial. Nalini Kanta Nag condemned the 'insular parochialism' of the Assamese to eliminate the non-Assamese, particularly the Bengalis from the province of Assam.[9] He vehemently criticized the Assamese for suppressing the Bengalis politically, economically, linguistically and culturally. The specific complaints, which he pointed out were the disallowance of suffrage to the Bengalis, no appointment of the qualified Bengalis to the vacant posts, no contract from the Assam Government, the ban on starting new industries and business, the forcible ejection of lands, the stoppage of the grants-in-aid to the Bengali institutions, etc.[10] Nalini Kanta Nag again condemned the Assam Government for 'a ruthless policy of extermination of Bengalis'.[11]

In view of the above facts the Bengalis were very much irritated. As a matter of fact, the idea for the formation of a new eastern Indian frontier province was the brain-child of the Bengalis. The Bengalis elite did not appreciate the pressure put by the Hindu Bengali refugees on the Assam Government to accept them as refugees. The main question was that how these landless refugees would be given settlement in the land of Assam, as Sylhet had already ceded to Pakistan. It gave birth to a movement which spread over the other eastern states of India. Some leaders from Cachar, Tripura, Manipur in cooperation with each other formed Purbachal Sangathan Committee and discussed the matter in order to find a solution to bring a peaceful atmosphere in the eastern region of India.

The Calcutta branch of the Purbachal Pradesh Sangathan Committee and the Cachar District Congress leaders also supported at a meeting held in Calcutta on October 25, 1948, the resolution adopted by the West Bengal Pradesh Congress Committee for the creation of a separate and a new Congress province with Manipur, Tripura, Cachar and Lushai Hills.[12]

On June 30, 1948, the demand for the creation of a separate Congress province having a separate administrative unit was put forward before the Congress Working Committee through a sub-committee. The deputation headed by Kalipada Mukherjee, Secretary of the Bengal Province Congress Committee, included Anil Chanda, the Principal, Paresh Choudhary and Dilip Chakravarty of the Cachar District Congress Committee.[13] It contended that 'this area have no cultural or linguistic link with the rest of Assam and even geographically is separated by a high range of hills.'[14]

The argument, however, did not carry much weight. From the foregoing statement we can draw a conclusion that the movement was sectarian in character. Assuming that there are no cultural and linguistic similarities among the Assamese and the tribal people it is worthwhile to examine to what extent this could be found in case of Purbachal Pradesh, with Manipuris, Cacharis, Bengalis, Tripuris and Lushais having so very distinct cultures and languages.

In a meeting held on August 22, 1948, the Cachar District Congress Committee demanded a separate administrative Committee demanded a separate administrative Congress Province with Manipur, Tripura and Lushai Hills. And a body named the Purbachal Province Organising Committee was also formed with Srijut Paresh Chandra Choudhury as the President and Nani Goswami and Rajendra Bhattacharya as the Joint Secretaries. The aim and object of the body was to ask for a separate Congress province. They insisted that the formation of a new province would be the only solution for the problem of upliftment of this backward area. It was further stated that 'the draft scheme...not only solves the vexed question of integrating the states but also assures complete autonomy for the districts and states in all internal matters to be administered through District or State Councils as envisaged in the sixth schedule of the draft constitution of India.'[15] It was pointed out that every component unit would not be able to maintain its own culture and language at the district level, until and unless it could arrange for a separate and an independent university and a High Court. The ultimate future was to be decided on the principle of self-determination.[16]

Professor Jogendra Kumar Choudhury repeatedly emphasized the hard need of an east India frontier province. He tried to convince the people through many lectures on the burning topic of Purbachal Pradesh. He emphasised the point that it would increase the spirit of the Indian nationalism and moreover, it would help in safe-guarding people's different cultures and languages.[17] He was of the opinion that the proposed Purbachal Pradesh should be centrally administered.[18] A resolution in appreciation and approval of the steps taken by the Cachar District Committee was unanimously adopted at a meeting presided over by Khan Saheb Rashid Ali Laskar, ex-Member of the Legislative Council.[19]

Causes of Failure

The Purbachal movement failed to arouse public opinion and was nipped in the bud mainly because it was undesirable cry for an unreasonable demand. The Congress Working Committee at its meeting held on November 18, 1948, turned down the request for a separate Purbachal Pradesh.

The Government considered the demand an outcome of the anti-Assamese feelings and never paid any serious attention to it. The demand was emotional and the justification given by N.K. Nag in his article was one-sided.[20] He got involved in petty politics and, it appears, was himself not very clear about it. He intentionally ignored the different components of the tribal groups of Manipur, who formed a considerable share of population. These tribals hardly knew Bengali language. As in the case of the Manipuris, it is a fact that they may be knowing Bengali script, but it is not necessary that they should understand Bengali language. It would be the same case with the Lushais. The Bengali language would be quite foreign to them. However, Nalinikanta Nag rightly pointed out the similarities of religion between the Hindu Manipuris and the Bengalis who followed Vaishnavism.[21] But he forgot to mention about the religion of the hill people of Manipur. Hence, his belief that religion would be able to bring unity also did not carry much weight. If we look back to the history we would be able to recall many incidents where religion had failed to play a unifying role. Therefore, Nag's force of argument does not appear to be fully logical.

To take up the case of Professor Debratta Datta's views supporting the proposal of forming a north-east India frontier province. He was in favour of immediate creation of a north-east India frontier province. He concluded that 'The Manipuris too, are afraid of the policy of Assamisation of the present Government of Assam, and hence they are reluctant to be tagged into Assam. If Manipur is put into Assam, it will be done defying the popular will and offering opportunities to our enemy. The more possibility of placing the state within the Assam has made the Manipur restless.'[22]

As the political propaganda was in high tone, a few of the leaders of Manipur were afraid of domination by the Assamese. Some of them openly supported the movement of Purbachal Pradesh. Laishram Joychandra Singh, one of the Congress leaders of Manipur, explained how the idea of a new state in north-east India came to be high-lighted. In his opinion it was purely a linguistic issue.[23] The Congress leaders of Manipur were tooth and nail against the imposition of Assamese language which was being introduced in all the schools and the colleges of Manipur. On the other hand, they were in favour of Hindustani as the State language of Assam. Only this could bring about a compromise on the language issue, the Manipur State appeared to be prepared to come out from the province of Assam and form a new administrative unit, i.e., the north-east India frontier province.[24]

The Assam Bengal Manipuri Society, Cachar District Congress Committee, Congress East Bengal Minority Rehabilitation and Citizenship Right Committee (Cachar), and Mar Mongolian Federation also criticized Gopinath Bordoloi, Premier of Assam, for his anti-Purbachal policies. They jointly condemned his statement on the need to maintain unity as itself disruptive and unwanted.[25]

It was decided to send a delegation to Delhi to emphasize upon the Congress High Command the indispensability of a separate congress administrative block. They proposed to submit a memorandum. The body passed a resolution in favour of Purbachal Pradesh consisting of Goalpara, Cooch-Behar, Garo Hills, Khasi Hills, Naga Hills, Lushai Hills, Cachar, Tripura State and State of Manipur. The meeting which was held at Gujrat Mansion in Bentick Street on November 6, 1948, appointed a Committee to mould public opinion in favour of this scheme.[26]

At the same time, a delegation of three men led by Gopinath Bordoloi with the intention to oppose the plan for Purbachal Province, left Gauhati for Delhi. It was to impress upon the Congress Working Committee for the inclusion of Cachar in the All India People's Conference Committee.[27] It was learnt that another deputation from Cachar had left for Delhi with a view to pressurize the Congress Working Committee on the point of a new province.[28]

But nothing happened to this effect as the Assam Government strongly opposed the Purbachal movement. The Premier of Assam rejected the theory on the geographical strategic grounds. He considered this as a very unwise and disruptive move. However, he conceded that such an important matter should be decided by democratic means in accordance with the wishes of the people.[29] An interesting aspect of the situation was that the Premier himself had been encouraging some organizations or persons to oppose the movement of Purbachal Pradesh. The body like 'Cachar Kalyan Samiti' became the forceful agent in propagating against the movement.[30] It got encouragement from the side of the Government of Assam.[31]

The Assam Governor was also reportedly interested in seeing the movement fizzle out. It was alleged that Sir Akbar Hydari, Governor of Assam, was also singing to the tune of Bordoloi.[32] He went out on tour with the purpose to dissuade the people from taking part in the movement of Purbachal Pradesh.[33] He went to Silchar and sought the views of pleaders, and also Muktear Bar on the Purbachal Pradesh movement; and was visibly annoyed when he came to know that they had enthusiastically supported the idea of Purbachal Pradesh. Both the Governor and Brigadier Habibur Rahman advised the people to abandon the idea on the plea that smaller provincial units would only weaken the defence of the country.[34]

The argument of strengthening the defence of the country, at the same time was used by Debratta Datta in favour of a separate province. The argument appeared to carry some weight when he remarked that the 'Discontent in those frontier districts is at such a high pitch at the present movement that our enemy will find a very fertile ground here for fomenting.'[35] He further alleged that there were some fascist in outlook among the Assamese who considered themselves having a close racial affinity with the Burmese, and looked upon them as their spiritual home.[36] He referred to the Communist movement which really threatened the internal peace and tranquility of the country, particularly, in the north-east India region. The neighbouring countries like Burma and Malaya had become victims of the Communist insurgency. The Government appeared to share some of his apprehensions and the closure of the Palel-Tummu road by an Ordinance of the Assam Government, was not without significance.

Datta recalled that the Burmese reign of Manipur as not an event of 'distant past' and felt stories of Burmese infiltration into Cachar and Upper Assam are yet fresh enough to be exploited by our enemy by raising the cry of the revival of old bonds.[37] Taking into consideration all these factors, Datta suggested that the only solution would be the formation of a new province directly to be administered by the Centre.

The Assam Government, however, never seriously took up the demand for Purbachal Pradesh and turned down it as impracticable. It appears that both the Assam Government as well as the Central Government had fully understood the game of the Bengali elites, who were guided more by their personal communal whims, than anything else. With the passage of time the problem got complicated. Then the matter was taken up by the Central Congress Committee. As earlier mentioned the congress Working committee had strongly criticized and outrightly rejected the proposal for the formation of Purbachal Pradesh in the north-eastern India. The Committee at the sametime promised to multi-culture character of the province of Assam.[38] Also the protection of diverse language was assured. Moreover the language of Manipuris and the Lushais were recognized by a resolution of the Congress Working Committee.[39] The people, it appeared, fully appreciated the line taken by the Congress Working Committee, which was under the circumstances the only reasonable course for maintaining solidarity in the north-eastern region without jeopardizing the culture and the linguistic interest of the heterogeneous community living there. And so in due course, the movement for the creation of a new province fizzled out.

References

1. J.K. Choudhary, 'A Case for Purbachal', *The Hindustan Standard*, November 14, 1948, p. 11.
2. *Ibid.*
3. *Ibid.*
4. *Ibid.*
5. *The Hindustan Standard* (Calcutta), November 3, 1949, p. 7.
6. *Ibid.*, November 3, 1948, p. 7.

   They further foresaw that if the Assamese brush aside this logic of facts and stick to the imposition of Assamese as the State language, Manipur could not come into Assam. Then in the interest of both Manipur and Assam a new administrative province should come into existence.

7. Birendra Chandra Purkayastha, 'Purbachala-A Home for Pakistan Refugees'. *The Hindustan Standard*, October 31, 1948, p. 11.
8. *Ibid.*, p. 5.
9. *Ibid.*
10. Choudhury felt that there were frantic efforts to exclude non-Assamese from the voter's list. This cultural, the economic and political conflict was likely to grow and lead to the disastrous consequences unless checked in time and it could be checked only by separating the non-Assamese areas from Assam. *Ibid.*, August 4, 1948, p. 8.
11. N.K. Nag, 'A Plea for Purbachal Province' *Ibid.*, October 31, 1948, p.11. Nag foresaw that there could never be a compromise on this score since a change of heart should precede any compromise, but the other side was lacking any desire for this.
12. *Ibid.*, October 27, 1948, p. 3.
13. *Ibid.*, July 3, 1948, p. 2.
14. *Ibid.*
15. *Ibid.*, p. 2.
16. *Ibid.* It was reported that there were indications that the authorities of Manipur (and Tripura) would support this move.
17. *Ibid.*, November 2, 1948, p. 3.
18. *Ibid.*, August 4, 1948, p. 8.
19. *Ibid.*
20. N.K. Nag, 'A Plea for Purbachal Province', *Ibid.*, October 31, 1948, p. 11.
21. *Ibid.*
22. Debratta Datta, 'Our North-Eastern Frontier-A Warning', *Ibid.*, September 12, 1948, p. 11.
23. *Ibid.*, November 3, 1948, p. 7.
24. *Ibid.*
25. They further said: 'Hon'ble Sri Bordoloi's undue stress on the indigenous' population and bespeaks of narrow parochialism that blatantly challenges all principles and policies pursued by the Indian National Congress and the ideals of Indian Nationalism. *Ibid.*, October 22, 1948, p. 5.
26. *Ibid.*, November 7, 1948, p. 3.
27. *Ibid.*, November 8, 1948, p. 3.
28. *Ibid.*
29. *The Amrita Bazar Patrika* (Calcutta), October 15, 1948, p. 7.
30. On the other hand, Bidyapati Singh, one of the members of the legislative assembly, supporting the move for Purbachal Pradesh warned the people to be on their guard against false, mischievous and reactionary

propaganda carried on by some organizations. *The Hindustan Standard* (Calcutta), November 2, 1948, p. 3.

31. D.C. Purkayasstha, 'Purbachal-A Home for Pakistan Refugees', *Ibid.*, October 10, 1948, p. 11.
32. Sir Akbar Hydari commented: 'I refer to the canker of provincialism now beginning to infect our body politic. Unless it is cut out and that soon, it will foul and whole of our national life. In the end this growth will strangle it; it will bring about the Balakinisation of India. The only, remedy is for us all to realize our mutual interdependence...' *Ibid.*, August 17, 1948, p. 9.
33. *Ibid.*
34. *Ibid.*, October 23, 1948, p. 2.
35. D. Datta, 'Our North Eastern Frontier-A Warning', *Ibid*, September 12, 1948, p. 11.
36. *Ibid.*
37. *Ibid.*
38. Beside that, even in the matter of election, sufficient safeguards had been provided so that any possible clique might not intervene or impose its will, which was another major reason which led a strong section to decide for the cessation from the Assam province Congress.
39. *The Amrita Bazar Patrika* (Calcutta), November 18, 1948, p. 1. The decision of the Working Committee had come as a devastating blow to the reactionary group of politicians, which was taking the advantage of this unfortunate controversy so long, trying to create chaos and confusion in the north-east region.

8
The Movement for Responsible Government 1946-49

Early Demands

By 1946, Manipur, like the rest of India, had reached the final stage of the nationalist struggle. Anticipating the withdrawal of the British from India, the Manipuri leaders came out with their own projections of the future political set up in Manipur. The Congress Party campaigned for the immediate establishment of the responsible government with an elected assembly to replace the monarchy; but the constitutional movement had only taken roots by the late 1930s, when the Women's Bazar Agitation led by Hijam Irabot Singh was launched for the ban on rice export and the establishment of the responsible government.

After the death of Sir Chura Chand Singh, his eldest son Bodha Chandra Singh took over the charge of the administration; for a pretty long year, the hereditary ruler supposed that he would be able to reign peacefully unhindered by any political trouble; but unfortunately he was seriously disturbed with the outbreak of the World War II. Manipur became in 1942 a target of the Japanese air raids and a battlefront. During the war the capital seemed to be completely deserted; the administration remained at a standstill for sometime then was taken over by the military.[1] With the end of the war in 1945 the Japanese retreated from Manipur. After the war the British Government had declared their intention to quit India forever. This news reached Manipur by passing through many tall mountains and valleys. This caused much political excitement and the demand for the responsible government was intensified.

A resolution passed by the All-Manipur Mahasabha Council's Working Committee on August 2, 1948, asked the Maharaja of Manipur to proclaim the establishment of the responsible government in the State within a year. It further requested him immediately to set up constitution-making machinery composed of the leaders of public opinion.[2]

The Nikhil Manipuri Mahasabha was the first political organization which took up the political issues of Manipur. Since then the party had been active in the State politics. It took the leading part in the compounder's strike and in the primary school teachers' demand for pay-hike. It also demanded the curtailment of the big salaries of the Durbar members and an increase in the pay of the low-paid public employees.

In one case it was decided in the Fifth Annual Session of the Manipur Students' Federation which was held at the Manipur Dramatic Union Hall under the Presidency of Dwijamani Dev Sharma, a leading political figure, that an immediate installation of a responsible government should be effected. The resolution also demanded the early introduction of the local self-government in the State.[3]

As the British Government made known its intention to transfer power to the Indian hands, a meeting of the Organizing Committee of the Socialist Party of Manipur was held at Imphal under the Presidentship of Bijoy Chandra Singh. It adopted a resolution for the early introduction of the popular government.[4]

Being apprehended the imminent political developments, the Maharaja instituted a constitution-making body for the future administration of the Manipur State. This was announced on December 12, 1946. The Manipur State Durbar after having a discourse with the Agent to the Governor-General had accepted to form an Interim Government, with some State officials of the present regime, for the time being before the making of a new constitution.[5] The Interim Council was inaugurated by the Maharaja on August 14, 1947. The Maharaj Kumar Priyabarta Singh, the younger brother of Maharaj Bodha Chandra Singh, became the first Chief Minister of the Manipur State. Four ministers from the plains and two from the hills were appointed.

The Era of Political Factionalism

With the creation of an Interim Council as the political executive, started the era of the factionalism in the Manipuri politics and the

State Congress Party split into two groups. The selection of the members of the Interim Council was left to the Maharaja's discretion. Those Congress leaders who had not been considered at all became angry with the Maharaja. They developed an inferiority complex. This dissatisfaction among a section of the Congressmen was responsible for the growth of the factionalism in the Party. As the chances of compromise narrowed down, a Congress group led by late Elangbam Tompok Singh separated from the united Congress Party. The remaining Congress group was headed by Tomal Singh. And both of them became the Presidents of their respective wings. It was a matter of question whether whose party would be the real and the genuine Congress. It was very difficult to answer because both of the Congresses claimed right. Both of the sections started condemning each other.

The Organising Committee of the Socialist Party of Manipur rejected the plea of the selection of the members of the Interim Council. It advocated only a popular Interim Government will be able to properly charge the responsibilities at the present juncture.'[6] The Committee was of the opinion that a constituent assembly elected on the adult franchise should immediately be established and recommended that the formation of an interim government should be left to the people and their organizations. The Committee did not favour the interference of the Maharaja with the affairs of the people.[7] Fairly speaking, the Maharaja should have approached in a democratic way, so that the people might have been satisfied. He could have arranged an election for the purpose. That would have credited more to him.

Laishram Achaw Singh, one of the members of the Congress Working Committee, issued a statement: 'There seems to be some confusions in the minds of the public about the reported move of the State Congress to come to some half-hearted arrangements with the State Authorities on the question of the Interim Ministry of Manipur State.'[8] Late Doctor (Physician) Leiren Singh, one of the supporters of the Congress led by Tompok, criticised the highhandedness from which it led to the splitting of the Congress.[9] This was reported to the President of the All India States People's Conference. The Congress led by Tompok charged against the Congress led by Tomal for violating the Congress discipline, as they joined the Interim Council.

The Congress problem started just after the so-called night 'secret negotiation', on the question of forming an Interim Government, between Pearson, Durbar President, and some Congress leaders namely, R.K. Bhubon Singh, the Congress President, Dwijamani Dev Sharma, Jogeshwar Singh and Khoimacha Singh, the Secretary of the Congress, on the other side. The content of the negotiation was unknown thoroughly. Naturally, this created more suspicions in the minds of the other Congress members.

Immediately after the incident took place a meeting of the Working Committee of the Congress was called in the night of July 16, 1947. But those suspected persons who took part in the secret negotiation did not turn up. The other members present in the meeting declined to disclose anything about the agreement. Achaw Singh tried in vain to let out something on the secret negotiation, and went on saying that if they could make a demand on the introduction of the Interim Government. But the matter was dropped for the following day the 17th instant at 9 a.m. This time the Working Committee discussed on the content of the letter given by Bhubon on the night of the 14th July. As Bhubon could not attend the meeting due to illness, Gouramani Sharma was appointed temporary President. In the meeting a charge-sheet was brought against Bhubon, Khoimacha Singh, Jogeshwar Singh that they were the gentlemen who recommended the names of two of them—Dwijamani Dev Sharma and Krishnamohan Singh—and two other State officials one of them a cousin of Bhubon for the ministership of the Council. The President in his letter specially mentioned the fact that the names of those two State officials could not be given out to the Committee even on that day. However, the discussion went on for about three hours. It was revealed in the meeting, that they went against the policy of the Committee itself as laid down in its resolutions, viz., the formation of an popular Interim Government in complete accord with the All India States Peoples' Conference resolutions, policies and decisions and also that they were, in so doing, acting against the discipline of the Congress organization.[10]

It was really a sinister game played by the unprincipled Congressmen to their colleagues. It was an act of crime to cheat the public by political manouvering with the help of Major Pearson. It was also a matter of shame on their part not to take the Working Committee into their confidence. It was not at all befitting on their part to finally submit the personnel of the ministry without prior consultation with the Committee. So the natural conclusion was that they had acted against the policy and discipline of the Manipur State Congress. The Committee, therefore, passed a censure motion on Bhubon and his associates by strong disapproving of their actions by nine votes to five.[11] The Committee further authorized Krishnamohan to call an urgent meeting of the Committee to take the requisite steps. The dissentients claimed that they should give minutes of dissent, quite contrary to the constitutional principles of any political organization. However, their motion was put down by a majority vote though the President of the day was a partisan on the side of the dissentients.[12]

In a special meeting of the Working Committee which was held on July 21, 1947, at Bhagyabati Press, the main topic of the discussion centred round the plan of the Interim Government. When the sitting commenced, a point of order was raised by one member stating that the appointment of the three additional Working Committee members was unconstitutional and arbitrary. But that was ruled out by the President. At that very moment, the same member demanded the resignation of the President as illogical conclusion of the censure motion passed on July 17, 1947. The President, however, refused to do so and urged the House to hear them again.[13]

The General Secretary began to move a counter resolution recommending the adoption of the secret plan to the Working Committee. Achaw raised a point of order on account of the fact that the plan was already considered and was disapproved and a censure motion passed on July 7, 1947. The dissentients confidently claimed that the matter should be reconsidered though they were in the minority. It was against the constitutional principle and the democratic practice of all political organisations in the world to manoeuver in this way so as to be able to impose their decision upon the Working Committee by a minority of official clique. The President showed his high-handedness and obstinacy by pressing the motion. The speaker once again demanded the resignation of the President. A point of information was also raised if the names of those two State officials who had been recommended to the Council could be divulged at that time. The President replied in the negative. It was a wonder that such a matter of public importance could not be given out in the Working Committee which was assumed to be the representative of the people. In spite of repeated demands of the resignation of the President and his bloc in the Working Committee. The President and his bloc in the Working Committee violated vagrantly the principle and the policy of the Congress and acted contrary to proper procedure. It was, therefore, vividly proved that they were the seceders who were somehow trying their utmost to maintain their position by political maneuvering and have refused to hand over office. They had set up an unconstitutional body and were creating an intricate sensation in the minds of the people.[14]

Soon after the incident, an emergency meeting of the Working Committee was held on the night of July 21, 1947, and Tompok was recommended as the President of the new Cabinet and Chandrahas Singh was authorized as the General Secretary to take up requisite steps for carrying on the activity of the Congress.

Tompok was duly elected as the President in the general meeting of the Congressmen convened for the purpose on July 24,1947, and a new Cabinet was formed and ratified by the meeting.[15]

When the matter came to a climax, the Chief Minister manoeuvred to pacify the rebellious Congress section by offering the post of Education Minister in the State Council to be formed, to their unquestioned leader Tompok, eventhough he did not recognize the new Cabinet. Tompok could not accept the position as the plan was quite defective and was not at all up to the expectations and in aspirations of the people. Because Krishnamohan and Tompok were only the peoples' representatives in the State Council of seven members. The Working Committee in the meantime rejected the proposal and demanded a truely popular Interim Government.

In the meanwhile, the Bhuban clique set up their own committee sponsored by the State Government and the Maharaja and they accepted the office in the name of the State Congress against the wishes of the vast majority of the public. Bhubon, himself belonged to the ruling family and Krishnamohan being brother-in-law of the Maharaja had allied themselves with the Maharaja to keep up the rule in power.[16]

Finally, the members of the Working Committee unitedly resolved to enquire into the matter and take proper steps to save from an impossible situation and to prevent from the imminent public disorder on sequent upon the secret alliance and the strengthening of the Maharaja's hands in taking repressive measures to put down the popular and the legitimate demand for a responsible form of a government. It would be illogical to form an Interim Government without prior consultation with the State Congress. The Working

Committee highly condemned the action of Major Pearson, the Chief Minister of the State Council, who in complete disregard of the people's wishes and demands entered into a secret negotiation with some politically self-motivated members of the Working Committee on the issue of the Interim Ministry.[17]

The Committee after analyzing the prevailing political situation considered the formation of a interim government highly essential, otherwise, the progress towards the responsible government might be hindered and arrested, and the disturbances and the troubles might break out in the State. The local authorities should in the case bear the responsibility. Besides, they out- rightly rejected the rules of the administration for the Manipur State, 1947, as introduced by the Maharaja could not be the basis of the Interim Government.[18]

To quote the words of Bipin Pal Dass, a Socialist leader of Assam, who happened to visit Manipur, addressing a public meeting held at the Manipur Dramatic Union Hall, that 'The Manipur State Rules for Administration, 1947 was a direct challenge to the people of Manipur and the State Congress. It was high time to reject the draft constitution of the constitution-making body which embodied provisions falling far short of full responsible government.'[19] Further, encouraging the people he drew the attention to Nehru's statement that the people's power would be supreme in all the Indian States. Sovereignty should go to the people and an intensified struggle for a responsible government should be advocated. Once again, Dass in a meeting of the Socialist workers held at Imphal, reminded, or rather excited the people that they should not stop their struggle for a responsible government, and be ready to face any source of trouble. Lastly, he further urged the people to endeavour to end the defective system of passport which prohibited free entry of the outsiders into Manipur without prior permission from the State Government. Really, many of the political leaders were disappointed, as they were not allowed to enter Manipur. Dass ironically commented that it was a great insult to the Manipuris.[20]

Coming back to the main theme of the problem of the formation of the State Council, the hill people and the Muslims protested on their exclusion in this respect. They alleged that the nomination of the present minister was illegal. In a meeting held on August 24, 1947, the attitude of the Maharaja was also condemned by the student's Congress wing, Krishak Sabha, etc. But the Maharaja seemed to be unheeded to such political development.[21]

If the Maharaja could have judged the political situation, he would have surely saved the Congress from the impending crisis. Neither his government nor he himself took the least interest in the welfare of the people and the State. He appointed in the constitutional making body only those persons who were his patrons. He appointed his younger brother as the first Chief Minister of Manpur; on the other hand, this would never serve the purpose of the proposal of compromise between the two Congress groups. The Maharaja should not have supported the Congress led by Tomal.

Negotiations for the Congress Unity

After the splitting of the Manipur State Congress into two rival groups, the efforts were continuously made for the reconciliation and the unity between the two while both continued to claim to be the genuine Congress Party. In Manipur, the united Congress Party was the only largest political organization before the split-up. Even before the satyagraha the matter was discussed to bring a compromise between the two groups; when the satyagraha was ended, the issue of the negotiation was a matter of daily question.

The only difference lied on the point: Tompok's Congress wanted the other Congress section headed by Tomal should follow them in spirit; only then they would be able to achieve their first and formost goal, i.e., the establishment of the full responsible government. If the Congress led by Tomal regretted the consequences of the split, and did not accept the constitution drafted by the constitution-making body, and demanded immediately the full resplonsible government, then there would be a definite chance of the normalization, as before, of the strained relationship between the two contending Congresses.[22] But, unfortunately this condition was not entertained by the Congress led by Tomal. In a meeting held on September 20, 1947, at Atom Babu Sharma's residence, the Tompok Congress came out with the following four points:

1. There should be re-election;
2. The President of the Congress should be elected by the primary members;

3. There should be a selection of fifteen members by the Working Committee according to the old constitution;
4. There should be a cancellation of three members from the category of the voter-candidate of the Congress, because they—Krishnamohan, Dwijamani Dev and Bhubon—illegally and secretly took part in the negotiation in connection with the formation of an interim government without prior consultation with the Congress Working Committee.[23]

With exception to the last point, Tomal's Congress accepted the remaining three conditions on the term of the compromise. It showed that the chance of the negotiation was broken down. Seeing the less chance of agreement between the two factions of the Congress, Sarangadhar, General Secretary of the All India States People's Conference, left Imphal on September 21, 1947, who came to solve the Manipur State Congress crisis.

On the eve of the satyagraha a Negotiating Committee was formed. On October 28, 1947, in a meeting, it was resolved that the two rival Congresses should unite together once again as before. Gourahari, the President of the Committee requested Tompok not to start any sort of agitation unless the two Congresses united.[24] The Committee asked the Congresses to send their suggestions on the term of compromise. Further the Committee informed them on November 2, that it might be handicapped in narrowing down the differences if there were no quick and definite replies from the Congresses. Despite, the Committee would be compelled to regret if any sort of agitation took place in the meanwhile. But all the attempts and the exertions of the Committee were in vain, as the Satyagraha movement had started already.

When the satyagraha was called off, the student Congress wing had taken the matter of the negotiation, and appealed to the leaders of both Congresses to work unitedly for the development and bring a socio-economic revolution in the State. Though the student wing referred to the successful satyagraha, they regretted the disunity among the Congressmen.[25]

Debeswar Sarma, the Indian Dominion Agent in Manipur, seemed to be interested in the Congress crisis of Manipur, as he invited four members from each Congress to the informal conference with a view to bring out a solution on the issue of replacing the present Council for a popular Interim Council and a Constituent Assembly in order to frame a constitution for the responsible government. But he failed consecutively to bring a common term of agreement.[26] On the first day of the meeting, the Congress led by Tompok raised certain points that the ministry should be distributed between the two Congresses in a proportionate ratio and an immediate dissolution of the present ministry. However, the other Congress led by Tomal accepted the dismissal of the present ministry and the substitution of the four Congress nominees if the dissentients were once again allowed to join the old Congress.[27] But such a condition was not acceptable to the Congress led by Tompok. As decided by the Working Committee (Resolution 1, 28.2.48), a sitting of the Manipur State Congress Parishad was arranged in Imphal at Manipur Dramatic Union Hall in connection with the settlement of the problem created by the split of the Congress. But the hope of bringing the two Congresses into one was never fulfilled.

Satyagraha against the Maharaja

As the Interim Council and the new rules for the administration of Manipur, 1947 did not meet the demand of the Tompok group, it eventually led to the launching of the first political satyagraha in Manipur. A dissident faction of the Tompok Congress did not think that a responsible government was going to be established very soon; so they decided to launch a satyagraha to press the demand for a responsible government in Manipur. It was massive satyagraha which spread to the far-flung villages of the capital. The satyagrahi's main aim was to bring an end of the autocratic rule, as 'For centuries together the Manipuris have been groaning under the yoke of the Rajas. Now with the course of events in the world at large and India in particular, the freedom-loving people of Manipur can no longer bear this medieval system in Manipur with the Raja as the sole dictator in the State'[28]

On August 15, 1947, a group of Congress led by Tompok using the Indian Congress caps and hoisting the National Flag tried to enter the palace with a view to worshipping the image of Govindji as a mark of the Independence Day celebration. They were not allowed to enter the palace by an order of the Maharaja because they came with the Indian National Flag and the Congress caps.[29] The Maharaja suspected the move was politically motivated; whatever the case might be, the Maharaja did commit a mistake in tackling the situation. In fact, he was deadly opposed to the Congress led by Tompok for their anti-feudal and anti-monarchical attitudes. Moreover, he should not have disrespected the National Flag. This irrational on his part had complicated the issue. This did not cause violence. However, many of them were arrested on the spot for breaking the laws of the State.[30] Subsequently, the arrest had incited the public sentiment from which it was likely to spread in the form of a large-scale agitation.

The General Secretary of the Manipur Socialist Party issued a press note declaring that 'They (Socialists) are now rising to end this feudalism once and for all and establish full responsible Government. They can no longer remain silent when the Tri-colour Flag, symbol of India's freedom, has been dishonoured by the Raja.'[31] The General Secretary further requested the people of Assam to help the Manipuris in their struggle for the achievement of the political and civil liberties.[32] This was responded by the Socialist Party of Assam. So far the Assam Socialist Party members and the workers were greatly excited by the satyagraha movement in Manipur and some of them came to Manipur to take part in the agitation. A few of them were arrested by the State police for not having obtained prior permission from the Government. Later, they were released at Mao, the border station in the north of Manipur.[33]

Sarangadhar, the General Secretary of the All India State Peoples' Conference and one of the members of the Constituent Assembly, issued a statement condemning the rude attitude of the local authorities of Manipur in holding up the members of the delegation of the Assam Socialist Party, namely, Hareswar Goswami, Principal Hem Barua, etc. He expressed with deep shock that 'we are free and the whole country is ours. You can go anywhere in your peaceful pursuits and no power on earth can stop you. Manipur claims to be independent but carries on this British system of permits imposed on non-Manipuris. This is absolutely no ground for it. There is no emergency nor any other condition. But feudalism still clutches at the British apron. I invite fighter all over to smash this citadel of old fashioned reaction'.[34]

When Dass was in Manipur, it was understood that he had conversation with Captain Priyabarta, Chief Minister of Manipur, regarding the 'pass system'. But his argument of hoisting up the National Flag in front of the Govindiji temple was unreasonable as it was not the general practice in all over India. It seemed to be politically motivated only to create a problem and tease the Maharaja. Anyway he admitted that the immediate cause of the satyagraha was the hoisting up of the National Flag in front of the temple and entering in the palace with the Gandhi caps.[35] He also talked to the Political Agent and Debeswar Sarma. He indicated that Manipur's case would be reviewed like the other states of India in the next session of the All India States Peoples' Conference.[36]

In September 1947, the Tompok Congress submitted an ultimatum to the State authorities in the following terms:

1. The interim government, which was recently introduced, should be reconstituted according to the popular demand, that is, all the members of the Government should be elected by the people and that no members should be nominated by the Maharaja as had been done.
2. A Constituent Assembly elected on the basis of the universal franchise should immediately be set up to draw up a constitution.
3. The 'pass system' whereby an outsider was to take a pass from the State authorities for the entry into Manipur should immediately be suspended.
4. The Indian Union Flag and the wearing of the Gandhi cap should be allowed in the temple of the palace, which had been disallowed even after the Manipur State had joined the Indian Union.
5. The land revenue, which was very high and the incidents of which were very high on the peasants, should be revised and redressed so as to give relief to the people.[37]

On November 6, 1947, a general strike was observed in the State. And all the Government offices like Police Station, Revenue Department, Registration Office, Chief Court, Palace, Chief Minister's residence, etc., were picketed.[38] But the Education Office was excluded as it was related to the sheet of learning. Subsequently, several public meetings were conducted, and long processions were taken out in Imphal. In defiance of the order of the Maharaja, the agitators started cutting bamboos and firewood's from the reserved forest of the Maharaja.[39] The satyagrahis' slogans like 'Bande Mataram' had thundered the air of Manipur. The reports of the clashes between the State police and the satyagrahis were coming in. In one of the happenings, on November 7th, the State police fired more than sixty rounds of blanks upon a large crowd of the satyagrahis gathering at police ground only to disperse them.[40] About twenty persons were reported injured and no death reported.[41] Some of the policemen were captured and detained by the satyagrahis but they were released stripped off their police uniforms.

On the tenth day of the non-cooperation movement in Manipur, an 'anti-repression day' was observed on November 14, under the leadership of Tompok, the Dictator of the Satyagraha Council of Action. The picketing was still continued. The majority of offices looked deserted. The State police was condemned for their rude and cruel handling of the satyagrahis. The satyagrahis vehemently denounced the police firing, the lathi-charge and the employment of the Assam Rifles to crush the demonstrators; they also de-cried the State's 'repressive policy'.[42] As a protest against the blatant use of the Assam Rifles in suppressing the peaceful satyagraha movement, the Manipur Satyagraha Aid Committee of the Assam Socialist Party sent telegrams to Sardar Patel, Jawaharlal Nehru and Sheikh Abdullah, the then President of the All India States Peoples' Conference.[43]

The satyagraha movement seemed to be not subsided before long. As the movement spread throughout Manipur, it also affected the student community. Now the State authorities instructed the school authorities to fine those students who took part in one incident of *hartal*. In a letter addressed to the President of the Manipur State Congress (the Tompok group), the students' General Secretary, on behalf of the Students' Strike Committee, expressed that the action of the Government was nothing except victimization of the girl and the boy students. The Committee further threatened that if the Government did not exempt the fine, it would turn into a serious consequence.[44]

A *Hindustan Standard* correspondent reported that the Maharaja's men were trying to sabotage the agitation by inciting people to violence.[45] The General Secretary of the Congress led by Tompok commented that the Maharaja and the Durbar could not fairly run the Government. Theirs became an administration of the police and the bullies. In a statement issued from the office of the Manipur Socialist Party, the people were warned to be vigilant against the activities of the anti-satyagraha movement, as they were trying to suppress the national movement by hook or by crook.[46]

By a resolution a conference of the Manipuris of the newly constituted district of Cachar held on October 28, 1947, at Masughat,

Silchar, congratulated the people of Manipur for their struggle for the full responsible government[47] The late Socialist leader Jaya Prakash Narayan sympathized with the cause. Wishing them all success in their struggle he said: '... I hope you too will soon be reaching your goal and that your progress would be rapid and sure...'[48]

The End of Satyagraha

After a long struggle between the State forces and the people's pressure, at last, the later had to win the ground. The Maharaja and his Government could not overlook all the time the rightful demand of the majority. The Government has been a machinery to look after the well-beings of the people; an autocratic ruler would never last long; it is only a question of time and tide; a change ought to take place sooner or later in due course. And, now people have been more and more politically conscious.

At the eleventh hour, the Maharaja's declaration came out that the draft constitution drawn up and submitted in the last July by the Constitution-Making Committee consisting of elected representatives from the plains and the hills would be introduced soon.[49] But the Chief Minister opined that 'there appears to be no reason why this constitution which, I am advised, ensures full responsible government, should not be given a trial. I am, however, prepared to invite and consider the opinion and advice of the Constitutional Advisor of the Constituent Assembly of the Indian Dominion on the draft constitution, as to whether any clause in its conflicts against the concept of responsible government.'[50] He further appealed to the people to work out the constitution. He also expressed his strong opinion to crush the anti-social elements for maintaining a strict law and order in the State.

The Dominion Agent in Manipur, speaking at a mammoth public meeting held at Imphal on April 23, assured the people that 'As the agent of the Dominion of India in Manipur, I have to say two things here. There are (1) Responsible Government is going to be introduced in Manipur State by April 1948. And (2) the Dominion of India cannot look upon chaos and disorder in this frontier State with equanimity. There should be peace, progress and rule of law here. The Dominion Government is interested in attainment of both objectives. I seek the whole-hearted cooperation of all peoples of Manipur State for this end.'[51]

The announcement of the Chief Minister affirmed the promise of the Maharaja for the establishment of the responsible government by April 1, 1948. This brought a change in the future political development in Manipur. Soon, the declaration of the Maharaja calmed down the satyagrahis. As a result of the recent change in the policy of the local government, the Manipur State Congress led by Tompok decided to call off the satyagraha on November 26, 1947.[52] The Dominion Agent said that it was a wise decision. On the other hand, the State Government accepted to fulfill their four demands, viz., the dissolution of the State Council, the introduction of the full responsible government, the institution of the constituent assembly and the grant of the people's civil liberties.[53]

As a celebration of the successful satyagraha movement, the Manipur State Congress led by Tompok made a programme for calling out a long procession on November 28, 1947; and in this way, the satyagraha in Manipur came to an end.

References

1. Home Department Political File No. 183, 1943, NAI, New Delhi.
2. The *Hindustan Standard* (Calcutta), September 2, 1946, p. 3.
3. *Ibid.*, June 21, 1946, p. 2. It also demanded the Calcutta University and the Manipur State Durbar for the recognition of the Manipuri vernacular in the Bachelor of Arts examination. It further emphasized the necessity of the establishment of a full-fledged college of Science and Arts, and a free and a compulsory primary education.
4. *Ibid.*, July 28, 1947, p. 5.
5. *Ibid.*
6. *Ibid.*, July 28, 1947, p. 5.
7. *Ibid.*
8. Elangbam Tompok to President of the All India States Peoples' Conference, 23 August 1947, Private Office Records, 19/MSC, 1947.
9. Telegram from Doctor Leiren Singh to President of the All India States Peoples' Conference, Manipur State Congress File No. 5, 1947-48 (Date is not mentioned).
10. General Secretary of the Manipur State Congress, to General Secretary of the All India States Peoples' Conference, 17 September 1947, Private Office Records, 1947, (File No. is not mentioned).
11. Proceedings of the Manipur State Congress, 17 July 1947, Manipur State Congress, 1947, *Ibid.*

12. It should be noted in their connection the fact that there was no higher authority of the Manipur State Congress other than the Working Committee. All the members of the Working Committee were accepted after the election of the President by a general meeting of the Congressmen. No representatives of the council of Congressmen existed on that day as of higher authority above the Working Committee.
13. Proceedings of the Manipur State Congress, 21 April, 1947, Private Office Records, 19/MSC., 1947.
14. Proceedings of the Manipur State Congress, 21 July 1947, Private Office Records, 19/MSC. 1947.
15. Elangbam Tompok to Chief Minister of Manipur, 25 July 1947, Private Office Records, 1947 (File No. is not mentioned).
16. Proceedings of the Manipur State Congress, 24 July 1947, Manipur State Congress, 1947, *Ibid.*
17. Proceedings of the Manipur State Congress, 31 July 1947, Manipur State Congress, 1947, *Ibid.*
18. *Ibid.*
19. *The Hindustan Standard* (Calcutta), July 28, 1947, p. 5.
20. The system of the 'inner line' permit had been adopted since the advent of the British rule in the State because the strategic considerations required it. Free entry might threaten the peace and tranquility of the border territory. Being conscious of this fact the British Government enforced the 'inner line' permit system. Even after the withdrawal of the British Government from India the same old system has been continued. Keeping in view of the advantage of the 'inner line' system the Maharaja and his Government intentionally did not abolish it. This would help to check the entry of the political mongers in Manipur. The Maharaja was really afraid of the outsiders who could instigate the people to revolt against his rule.
21. Manipur State Congress, Private Office Records, 1947 (File No. is not mentioned).
22. Manipur State Congress File No. 5, 1947, Congress Office, Imphal.
23. Manipur State Congress, Private Office Records, 1947 (File No. is not mentioned).
24. President of Negotiating Committee, to President of Manipur State Congress, 31 October 1947, *Ibid.*
25. Assistant Secretary of the Manipur State Students' Congress, to Manipur State Congress, 4 December 1947, Manipur State Congress File No. 5, 1948, Congress Office, Imphal.
26. Manipur State Congress, Publicity Department File No. 2, 1948, Congress Office, Imphal.
27. On the other hand, the Congress led by Tomal blamed the Congress group of Tompok that '... the seceder party went back upon their

words and demanded immediate unconditional dissolution of the present Ministry leaving the whole thing in chaos and thus giving them greater opportunity to aggravate the present disorder. They further wanted their party to continue as a separate Congress. The motive of the seceder party was evidently to leave every thing in melting pot for political adventurism.' *Ibid.*

28. *The Hindustan Standard* (Calcutta), September 30, 1947, p. 5.
29. Manipur State Congress, Publicity Department File No. 2, 1948, Congress Office, Imphal.
30. *The Hindustan Standard* (Calcutta), September 24, 1947, p. 7.
31. *Ibid.*, September 30, 1947, p. 5. A resolution was also passed in a public meeting held on August 24, 1947 that 'This meeting of the people of Manipur of all shades of opinion places on record its deep sense of grief at the dishonouring of the Indian Union Flag and the Gandhi cap and resolving that a Satyagraha movement will be launched to vindicate the honour of the flag and the cap.' Ibid, September 10, 1947, p. 8.
32. *Ibid.*
33. *Ibid.*, September 24, 1947, p. 7.
34. *Ibid.* Like Dass, Hareswar Goswami, one of the members of the National Executive of the Socialist Party of India, held the same views. He did not justify the arrest of the Socialist delegates on the ground of being they were foreigners. He added that "Nowhere in India this system (inner line permit) is in vogue. In Manipur too there can be no reason for its continuance after the withdrawal of the British from India. This only betrays a desire to remain independent and free from the Indian Union. Otherwise, how and why does Manipur restrict the freedom of movement of the people by such an obnoxious and medieval system, and that too, of an Indian. It does against the fundamenta rights of an Indian as enunciated by the Constituent Assembly. Every lover of freedom must fight this system. When too it is added the insult hurried by the Maharaja to the Union flag on August 15, the whole game becomes very clear. Manipur cannot at one and the same time join the Indian Union and disrespect its flag.' *Ibid.*
35. *Ibid.*, September 26, 1947, p. 4.
36. *Ibid.*, September 24, 1947, p. 7.
37. *Ibid.*
38. *The Daily Praja* (Imphal), November 12, 1947, p. 1.
39. Manipur State Congress, Publicity Department File No. 2, 1948, Congress Office, Imphal.
40. *The Hindustan Standard* (Calcutta), November 9, 1947, p. 1.
41. Later with the start of the satyagraha, i.e. between November 6 and November 19, about seventy people were reported injured. Manipur State Congress File No.5, 1947-48, Congress Office, Imphal.

42. *The Hindustan Standard* (Calcutta), November 14, 1947, p. 2.
43. Telegram from Elangbam Tompok to V.B. Patel, 8 November 1947, Manipur State Congress, 1947 (File No. is not mentioned).
44. Secretary of Students' Strike Committee, to President of Manipur State Congress, 11 October 1947, *Ibid.*
45. *The Hindustan Standard* (Calcutta), November 8, 1947, p. 5.
46. *Ibid.*, September 10, 1947, p. 8.
47. Proceedings of the Surma Valley Manipur Association, 28 October 1947, Manipur State Congress, 1947 (File No. is not mentioned).
48. Jaya Prakash Narayan to People of Manipur, 24 December 1947, Manipur State Congress, Publicity Department File No. 2, 1948, Congress Office, Imphal.
49. *The Hindustan Standard* (Calcutta), November 26, 1947, p. 3.
50. Manipur State Congress, Private Office Records, 1947 (File No. is not mentioned).
51. Elangbam Tompok to Dominion Agent in Manipur, 25 November 1947, Private Office Records, MSC/ 47, 1947.
52. Elangbam Tompok to Dominion Agent in Manipur, 26 November 1947, *Ibid.*
53. *The Hindustan Standard* (Calcutta), November 28, 1947, p. 1.

9

Manipur's Integration with the Indian Union : 1949

Prelude

When the British announced their intention to transfer power to the Indians some of the ambitious leaders saw an opportunity to reap a rich harvest by creating political upheaval in the State. They made out a case for the immediate installation of a full responsible government and a constituent assembly composed of elected members; subsequently, a satyagraha was launched in the State. An election to the Legislative Assembly thereafter was held in which no single party could secure an absolute majority to form a government.[1] It inevitably led to political instability in the State. In the meanwhile, the question of the merger of Manipur with the Indian Union became the principal political issue and the public opinion was sharply divided over it.

A section of people preferred rather the creation of a composite North-East India Frontier Province comprised of Cachar, Tripura, Manipur and Lushai hills; the another section desired to merge with Assam. Some leaders advocated the idea of an independent Manipur. The Congress group led by Tomal Singh was alone committed to Manipur's integration with the Indian Union; and some of this group even threatened to launch a satyagraha if the integration was not effected forthwith. The Government of India was anxious to complete the merger of the Princely states within the Indian Union to bring the political homogeneity and the democracy to all parts of India.[2] When the first phase of the mergers was over only eight states were left unmerged, namely, Kashmir, Hyderabad, Benares, Tripura, Cooch-Behar, Khasi Hills States (including sixteen small units), Mysore and Manipur.[3]

Impediments

However, Manipur underwent a great political turmoil before the merger was effected. *The Hindustan Standard* on May 28, 1947, reported that some leaders from the four adjoining states of Assam – Cooch-Behar, Tripura, Khasi Hills and Manipur – were to meet in a conference to be held in Shillong in June 1947, to discuss the problems arising out of the future constitutional changes.[4] It was also learnt that these states, excluding Cooch-Behar, had nominated some of their delegates to represent their case with the Constituent Assembly.[5] These small states were suspicious of whether their cultural identity would be preserved within the Indian Union.

The position of Manipur was rather delicate. According to an unconfirmed report, the Antifascist People's Federation League, the people of Manipur invited U Aung San, Deputy Chairman of the Burmese Interim Government, to visit their State. It was mentioned in the report that, the Manipuris wished to roll into one with the State of Burma in order to establish a permanent tie with the same. It was also reported that U Aung San was expected to be flown to Manipur in May 1947, to meet with the leaders of Manipur.[6] A news published in Rangoon on May 12, 1947, contained the clarification made by U Ba Choe, Information Minister of Burma, to the Associated Press of America, that '... his country would neither encourage the border State of Manipur to incorporate itself as a part of Burma, nor discourage the State from joining Burma'[7] U Ba Choe added, ' you may be certain the Burma Government will refrain from interfering'[8]with the decisions of the Manipuris. Further he firmly and confidently remarked that U. Aung San, Deputy Chairman of the Governor's Executive Council, would like to visit India for a discussion about the future of Manipur only if he were invited by Jawaharlal Nehru. But he was quite conscious of the desire of the Manipuris to mix with the Burmans; and he wished to go to Manipur for the purpose. At the same time U Ba Choe clarified that "Burma has no wish to encroach upon other's territories. When the Burmese Government has given to States within Burma the right of self determination for deciding whether they should amalgamate with Burma proper or not, it is unlikely that Burma would seek an outside state to merge irrespective of past associations between Burma and the State".[9]

Whatever the case might be the Burmese would have definitely liked the merger of Manipur with them. In a Rangoon information of

May 11, 1947, it was described clearly that Manipur was once a part of Burma some one hundred years ago. Later, it came out of Burma when the Britishers overran the country. Therefore, it would not be wrong to say, with no partiality, that the Burmese leaders wanted that Manipur should come and join Burma. In support of this view it would be appropriate to quote the words of U Ba Choe, which are as follows, 'The Manipuris being Hindus may not want association with Muslim Bengal, but that is a matter for the Indian Government to decide ...'[10]

In the meantime, the Communist Party of Manipur was carrying out subversive activities near the Burma-Manipur boundaries. The Communist infiltration in Manipur was repeatedly reported from time to time. It was reported from Shillong that a few Communist insurgents had entered into Ukhrul (in the north-east of Manipur) and lifted the rifles from the hill people.[11] It was also informed that considerable arms and ammunitions including the modern weapons had been smuggled by the underground Indian Communists into Assam through Manipur from the Red-held areas of Upper Chindwin and the Hukang Valleys in Burma. The Manipuri Communists were reported to have taken part in this activity. It was the time when the Communists movement in the north-east region of India was rapidly increasing.[12]

The report that there had been a move for the inclusion of Manipur in the Burmese territory was highly described as fabrication by two Congress leaders-cum-members of the executive of the Manipur State Congress Party. The two gentlemen–Krishna Mohan Singh and Jogeswar Singh–clarified their stand in a statement published in a local newspaper, that the 'Manipuris would resent this fantastic report.... The State Congress and the people could not even dream of it and were deadly against it'.[13] Further, it added, 'Not to speak of incorporation of Manipur into Burma, the State Government and the people now demanded for bringing under the direct control and administration of the Kabaw Valley, the area between the Ango hills in Burma and Moreh of Manipur for which the British Government have been passing an annual tribute to the State'.[14] These two leaders assured that Manipur being a Hindu State would not like to join Burma whose religion had been ethnically quite different from the Manipuris. Hence, Manipur would rather prefer to merge with the Indian Union.[15] The two Congresses posed that the Congress Party of Manipur as 'only a nationalist party' which represented the whole people of the State. The party had promised to resist any element which would come in the way of the merger of Manipur with the Indian Union, and to prevent the tendencies of the secessionists and the separatists from the same.[16]

A Delhi pressnote of July 22, 1949, commented on the Communist pressure in Manipur in this way: 'The autocratic and arbitrary ways of the Maharaja are denying the people democracy and have set at nought the state Constitutions. His pro-Communist attitude and his too weak and insufficient Government have combined to make a fertile soil for Communist'.[17] We could rightly remember the role of Hijam Irabot Singh during the constitutional movement in Manipur. He was the founder of the Communist Party in Manipur. He would be accountable for his role in the *nupi lan* or the women's agitation of 1939. He demanded the establishment of the State's assembly on the basis of the adult franchise and the abolition of the monarchial government. His views regarding the merger of Manipur with the Indian Union was equivocal. According to him Manipur being culturally different from other states would prefer to be independent.

As the Government was well informed of the Communist activities in Manipur, several efforts were made to arrest Irabot who had been underground for a long time; but the State Government could never catch hold of him alive. At last he died in Rangoon. The political situation in Manipur favoured the Communists to be dealt with firm hands. Analysing all the facts of the political development in Manipur, the Government of India decided to bring the State under the grip of the Centre. And it was the dream of Patel to see India consolidated.[18]

The problem of merger was to be solved urgently as Manipur has the international boundary with Burma. The Indian leaders were aware of the old feud between Burma and Manipur over the issue of the Kabaw Valley. The British Raj had ceded the Kabaw Valley to Burma under the treaty of Yandaboo signed in 1825. The Indian leaders foresaw that in the future the trouble might ensue on the issue of the Kabaw Valley. This would surely disturb the neighbourly relations of India with the independent Burma. In the meanwhile, the clashes on the Manipur Burma border had been reported from time to time.[19]

Besides, the Naga frontier problem was also there. Athiko Daiho, a Mao Naga leader openly and boldly demanded the separation of the Naga inhabited areas of Manipur and Assam with a view to form a separate Naga State. He wanted that the Nagas of Manipur should join their brethren Nagas of Assam. He further advocated for the establishment of an Eastern Frontier Hill Federation within or without an independent India so that the existence of their nationalities, rights and privileges would be recognised by Inda.[20] As to the reaction of the hill people's demand, Khoimacha Singh, a Congress leader, said that '... the Manipur State Congress stand for solidarity of His Highness's territories, the people of Manipur will resist any attempt as dismemberment of the State by any section.'[21] It was reported that Daiho's men were engaged in collecting taxes on potatoes. The cutting of the telephone-lines, the telegraph wires and the interference with the dispatch of the mails were also reported. For the security measures, the Assam Rifles were stationed at several disturbed areas.[22] The Mao Nagas demanded the Government for the immediate withdrawal of the imposition of rice duty on them. They thought that it was a repressive measure on the part of the State Council in the Mao Nagas who were fighting and leading the other Naga tribes of the State to amalgamate themselves with the Nagas of the Naga Hills on the basis of their closer affinity with them.[23] Later, the Naga National League was formed in the early part of 1948 under the Presidentship of Pukeni and Athikho Daiho as its Secretary.[24] The political aim of the League was to represent the cause of the Nagas. On January 24, 1949, the Mao Nagas submitted a memorandum to the Deputy Prime Minister of Indian Dominion, demanding the consolidation of the Naga inhabited areas under one administrative unit. They further suggested that a referendum might be called to ascertain the wishes of the Nagas of Manipur.[25]

In the Naga Hills (now Nagaland), Imti Aliba Ao, the first President of the 'Naga National Council', said that he would be giving an ultimatum to the Prime Minister of India and the Assam Governor.[26] He threatened: If the authorities failed to look into the matter, the Naga Hills would automatically discontinue to be a part of the Indian Union from December 6, 1947.[27] A delegation of the Naga leaders had flown to New Delhi to discuss with the appropriate authorities and the leaders what they described as 'their claim for independence' after the British withdrawal from India on August 15, 1947.[28] It was understood that the delegation already met Gandhi and Jinnah and placed before them their view points.[29] It was presumed that the movement was instigated by the Communist elements in Assam.[30]

Angami Zapu Phizo, who became the President of the Naga National Council on December 11, 1950, was the person who dreamt of a larger Nagaland comprising of the whole Naga inhabited areas in the northeast frontier of India and the northwest frontier of Burma.

But the movement of Naga self-determination was as old as 1929; the issue had well-gripped the Naga minds and public opinion had already been moulded against the continual dominance of the Britishers over the Nagas. It was in the same year the Nagas had requested His Majesty's Government of Great Britain in vain 'to leave us alone to determine for ourselves as in ancient times'.[31] The Naga problem was discussed in the British parliament; the Government, however, was reluctant to endorse the Nagas' claim to self-determination.

Sir Reginald Coupland, a British constitutional expert, drew up a plan for the creation of a crown colony comprising of all the Naga contiguous areas of India and Burma; at the same time, the territorial integrity of it should be guaranteed by the Governments of India and Burma.[32] But the Coupland plan was strongly criticised by Sir Andrew Clow, Governor of Assam, as impracticable, eventhough it received appreciations and supports from several British politicians and officials. Sir Charles Pawsey, the last British Deputy Commissioner in the Naga Hills, made his own effort to revive the Coupland plan as an alternative to the Naga demand for complete independence, just before the termination of the British rule in India; but the Government of India was openly against his proposal and rejected the Coupland plan. Phizo outrightly branded it as a policy of British imperialism and colonialism.

On February 20, 1947, the Naga National Council submitted a memorandum to His Majesty's Government and the Government of India, demanding the setting up of an interim government of the people with financial provisions for a period of ten years at the end of which the Nagas should be left to choose an appropriate government under which they themselves choose to live. But unfortunately, on the issues of Naga self-determination and interim government, no agreement could be arrived at between the Naga National Council and the Government of India, despite many efforts on both sides.

On June 26, 1947, the then Assam Governor Sir Akbar Hydari held a three-day negotiation with the members of the Naga National Council. Engulfed in a controversy on the interpretation of Clause 9 of the Hydari Agreement, 1947, the negotiation ended in a fiasco; otherwise Phizo asserted that the agreement envisaged that the Nagas would be independent after the expiry of the ten-year period.[33]

A seven-member delegation of the Naga National Council consisting of Phizo, Khrisanisa, Kughato, Kezehol, John Angami, Theyiechuthie Sakhrie and Lhousituo met Gandhi on July 19, 1947, at Bhangi Colony, New Delhi. The delegation told Gandhi that the Nagas were never Indians and the Naga Hills had never been a part of the Indian territory; independence was certainly an inalienable right of the Naga people. Further, the delegates well apprised the Father of Nation that the Nagas would be celebrating August 15 as their Independence Day. They also complained of the intimidation of Hydari to use force if the Nagas declared independence, informing their apprehension to Gandhi. Gandhi replied that if the Nagas were not really willing to join the Indian Union, nobody would force them to do that. He further rapped out: Hydari was wrong, and I would ask militarymen to shoot me first before one Naga was shot.[34]

Discarding the Hydari Agreement on August 14, 1947, the Naga National Council sent a telegram to the Government of India, intimating that the Nagas would be free to decide their own future at the end of the ten-year period. It so happened, Gandhi was assassinated by Nathuram Godse, a religious fanatic, on January 30, 1948, before he could come to Kohima, Nagaland, and settle the Naga case as he had promised. Then, Hydari came to an untimely end, on December 28, 1948, of a heart stroke at Thumbuthong in Manipur, leaving the Nagas in the lurch. After this tragedy, the Nagas thought that the then Chief Minister Gopinath Bordoloi could be something for them; but he had frustrated the Naga delegates whom he met on November 9, 1949, informing that the Government of India had no longer considered the Hydari Agreement to be existing. Destroyed the hopes of further negotiation, the Nagas now decided to change their future course of politics, as they had developed in their minds some sort of doubts and misgivings on the good faith of the Indian government.

On July 9, 1948, Phizo was arrested on the ground of possessing certain documents prejudicial to India's security. On the compassionate ground, he was released from the Presidency Jail of Calcutta on parole on December 18, 1948; then the Government of India extended the period of parole for a special medical treatment at the Welsh Mission

Hospital, Shillong, as his wife and baby had met a vehicle accident on December 4, 1948, between the village of Khonoma and Jotsoma in Nagaland. Believing that Phizo had given up the anti-Indian political activities, Nari Rustomji, the then Political Advisor to the Assam Government, unconditionally set him free from the jal. But Phizo never changed his old path of the political propagation of the Naga independence and the anti-national activities.[35] Later, the Phizoites resorted to violence as a means of achieving Nagas' freedom; but even today, this had not brought a permanent solution in spite of relentless efforts by the Government to bring peace in Nagaland.

At the same time, the Mizo problems could not be overlooked; in other incident, the Mizo Union demanded Mizos' independence. A conference of the Mizo Union consisting of representatives from Manipur,Lushai Hills and Cachar was held at Lakhipur (in Cachar district), on November 21, 1946, with Bawichhuaka as the President. It resolved that all the Mizo areas in Manipur, Lushai Hills, Cachar district, Chittagong Hills tract and other adjacent places should be amalgamated into one administrative unit and designated as the Mizoram District because all these people have a common culture, language, religion, geographical contiguity and the most important of all is that the area occupies a strategic position from the point of defence.[36] It demanded that the widest autonomy should be given to the Mizo District along with the right of representing in the Constituent Assembly; Not even before completing two months, it wrote to the President of the Constituent Assembly that its representative should be given membership in the Advisory Committee for the Tribal areas of Assam. If it was excluded from the Constituent Assembly, the Mizo Union threatened that they would form a separate constitution exclusively for the Mizos. Then, they would decide whether they would seek the British protection for the time being, or join the Chin Hills in Burma and form a separate province within Burma, or declare an independent sovereign country.

The intricate politics among the members of the Mizo Union undermined the cause of independence: The leftists submitted a memorandum to the Bordoloi Committee when it visited Aizawl, present capital of Mizoram, on April 17, 1947, stating that the Mizoland should be a part of India for a period of at least ten years after which they would decide what they would do with themselves. During this period they would govern themselves through a district council. The Rightists stood for complete independence; on the other hand, the two co-opted members of the Bordoloi Committee, Khawtinkhuma and Saprawnga, on behalf of the Mizo people agreed to be a part of the Indian Union. Lalmawia, the founder of the United Mizo Freedom Organization, made up his mind to form an independent Chin state; later on, he opted to merge the Mizo Hills with Burma. But his proposal did not get much support from U Nu, Prime Minister of Burma.[37]

In late 1948, the civil disobedience started in the Mizo Hills; it took mainly in the form of riotous assaults on the chiefs whom the commoners branded as exploiters. The Unionists reiterated their demand for the abolition of the oppressive systems of the village chiefs and the installation of the district council. The Government of Assam hesitated to launch upon a drastic legislation as demanded by the Mizo Union. The Unionists, however, were pacified by Nari Rustomji, Political Advisor to the Governor on tribal affairs, when he visited the district in January 1949 with a promise to implement the Sixth Schedule; as a result, prior to the formation of the district council, the Lushai Hills District along got an Advisory Council.[38] But the solution of the Mizo problem remained unfulfilled; in fact, the Mizos resorted to political violence as an immediate means of achieving independence. Nevertheless, the Government of India was not at all prepared to accept an independent Mizo-homeland.[39]

Manipur's Accession Achieved

Being aware of the political problems of the north-eastern region the Indian leaders were afraid that Assam might possibly developed fissiparous tendencies. The eastern region important as it was the geographically and strategically needed the fullest integration with the Indian Union to forestall all the possible dangers. The Union Government took the matter very seriously. It was understood that the discussion was started among the high political circles of Assam regarding the merger of the small states like Manipur, Cooch Behar and Tripura in the Assam Province like that of eight states of Orissa, eight states of Deccan, etc. The matter was put up before Patel when he came to Assam.[40]

With due reference to the question of the merger of Manipur with the Indian Union, a team of Sri Prakasa, Governor of Assam, A.B.

Chatterjee, Joint Secretary, States Ministry of the Government of India and Rustomji, arrived at Imphal on March 22, 1949. This was followed up after the declaration of the States Ministry of the Government of India to corporate some of the states namely, Benaras, Rampur, Tehri Garewal states, Khasi Hills states, Cooch-Behar, Tripura and Manipur with the Indian Union as these with due regard to their geographical positions and other consideration.[41]

The need for an immediate Central take-over of Manipur's administration was emphasized by Gopinath Bordoloi, Primier of Assam, in a letter which he sent to Patel on May 4, 1949, in which he informed that '... the central C.I.D. sometimes suspected the Communist leaders, Irabot Singh of Manipur as having received shelter in the place itself. It is now suspected that Irabot Singh is somewhere in Burma, acting in league with the Communists of Manipur. You have already seen what the R.C.P. is doing in Dum Dum. I have not the slightest doubt that the Manipur Government will not be able to do anything substantial to help the Assam Rifles or our Forces, if a serious situation arises'.[42] further, he cautioned Patel that it would be '... dangerous to maintain a weak and vacillating State near our borders and also to give them independence to act as they liked'.[43] Patel himself confirmed that 'From a careful study of international affairs, it appears almost certain that the danger, if it comes to India, is likely to come from this Burma borders'.[44]

During this time the Manipur State Congress led by Tomal Singh was uproarious in demanding the abolition of the Maharaja's *gaddi* and the immediate take-over of the Manipur administration by the Centre. They had been agitating for a long time. Such an action of Tomal was never sympathized by the other Congress group led by Elangbam Tompok Singh. They were in the advocacy of the formation of 'Purbachal Pradesh' comprised of Tripura, Cachar, Lushai Hills and Manipur. This demand was even prevalent when the two rival Congresses were one; but the difference of opinion developed after the Congress split.

Criticising the resolution of Tomal's Congress, Laishram Achaw Singh, Secretary of the Manipur Socialist Party and one of the members of the Manipur State Assembly commented, ' The Manipur State Congress in its annual sitting on the 30th April last has committed another great blunder by asking the Government of India to take over the administration of Manipur State as a centrally administered area.

The Congress while advocating the necessity of a strong government in this frontier State of Manipur has sought the direct intervention of the Centre, in spite of the fact that a more or less democratic form of Government has been set up in Manipur since the introduction of the Manipur State Constitution Act, 1947'.[45] But the Socialist Party of Manipur rejected the idea of a separate province. And 'It should be the duty of the Indian Government to consult the leaders of public opinion before they take any step on this matter. The Socialist Party of Assam has given the right lead by adopting the principle of a Federated Province of Assam where in the different cultural and linguistic groups in Assam should enjoy full cultural autonomy. The principle has never been questioned for the solution nor has any alternative been suggested for the solution of this complicated problem. The Socialist Party would rather welcome a referendum in deciding the future relation of Manipur State with the Indian Union'.[46]

Not long ago, the Congress led by Tomal decided to launch a satyagraha in the whole State in order to abolish the autocracy of the Maharaja. It was known that a delegation of three men—Krishnamohan Singh, a member of the Congress Working Committee, a Shaugaizam Somorendra Singh and Dwijamani Dev Sharma—had left Imphal for Delhi in connection with the recent political development. The programmes of the political mission was to meet some Congress high commands like, Pattabi Sitaramayya, President of the Indian National Congress, Patel, Deputy Prime Minister of India, etc. They discussed the matter of the merger of Manipur with the Indian Union; and they gave word that if the Centre delayed and failed to work out the integration, they would immediately launch a satyagraha movement. It was expected that the three delegates would be laying down their demands before the Congress Working Committee's meeting to be held shortly in New Delhi on July 16, 1949.[47] The delegation would also put up an issue on the merger of Manipur with the Assam Province as totally unacceptable on the cultural and the economic grounds.[48]

Not later than a few days ago, Prakasa, Governor of Assam accompanied by Rustomji, left Gauhati for Benaras en route to Delhi by air on September 4, 1949. The Primier of Assam was already in Delhi in connection with the future administration of Manipur (and other states).[49] In Delhi they had an hours-long discussion with the

States Ministry on September 6, 1949. After the talk was over the Governor had left for Bombay. On September 8, 1949 the Governor accompanied by Rustomji met Sardar Patel, who was ailing at that time, at Birla House in Bombay. They apprised him of the political situation in Manipur. Patel reportedly asked him:'... is there no our Indian Brigadier?'[50] It meant that force should be used if Manipur opposed the merger with the Indian Union. Now, the Governor fully understood what to do next; immediately he left Bombay for Shillong.

As soon as Prakasa reached Shillong, he invited Maharaja Bodha Chandra Singh, as advised by the Central leaders, to meet him at Shillong at an early date. It was clearly understood that the Maharaja had to be pressurized to sign the Instrument of Accession.[51] As directed by the Governor of Assam, the Maharaja came to Shillong to discuss the future of his State. The policy and programme of the Government of India was placed before the Maharaja. After going through the typed documents prepared by the Assam Government according to the advice of the Central Government, the Maharaja did not wish to sign them as some of their provisions were unsavoury to him; in the meantime, the Assam Governor informed Sardar Patel about his reluctance.[52] The telegram of September 18, 1949, reads: 'Begins had discussions with H.H. (High Highness) of Manipur this morning H.H. threatens returning to Manipur without holding any discussion or signing agreement. H.H. must not under any circumstances be allowed to return to Manipur with his advisors and I have accordingly instructed police to be detained here his party if they attempt to return before signing of agreement. Please telegraph immediately repeat immediately authority for detention of H.H. and Advisors under Regulation Ill or by whatever other means you consider might be appropriate. Have already warned sub-area to be prepared for any eventuality in Manipur. Grateful for further instructions. Ends. Will keep you closely informed of further development (if) here addressed'[53]

It was very clear that the Maharaja was not agreeable to certain conditions of the document of the merger agreement. He also knew that force would be used against him if he did not sign the agreement. He was in a confused state of mind. To avoid technical complications, the Maharaja requested the Governor to allow him to go back home as he would not be able to sign the agreement unless he consulted with the State Assembly. But that was political gimmick only to escape from the critical situation. This intention of the Maharaja was already sensed by the Governor and his Advisor; so they were very eager to finalize the agreement as soon as possible before he left Shillong for Manipur. On the other hand, the Central leaders would have probably been apprehensive of a possible rebellion like that of 1891 to break out if the Maharaja was allowed to return to his State. The security arrangements, therefore, were tightened along the borders of Manipur. The Maharaja had to be detained in Shillong unless he signed the documents of the agreement. The Governor pressurized the Maharaja at his best to do it; and he tempted the Maharaja that he would get a privy purse of a few lakhs for the whole of his life if he signed the agreement.[54] At this moment, the Maharaja was conveyed a rumour that his younger brother Maharajkumar Priyabrata was to be installed as the Maharaja of Manipur. For him (Maharaja) this was just like a thunder in his brain. At last, the Maharaja afraid of the use of force on the part of the Government, jealous of his younger brother and lusty of the privy purse reconciled with his fate and agreed to sign the agreement. The final arrangements were made for the ceremony in the Government House in Shillong. Maharaj Bodha Chandra Singh executed the documents of the agreement of the merger of Manipur with the Indian Union on September 21, 1949.[55]

The culmination of Sardar Patel's 'Bloodless Revolution' was gradually completed.[56] The Union Government took over the administration of Manipur on October 15, 1949, and a Chief Commissioner was appointed.[57] The State Assembly was dissolved. Rawal Amar Singh, the erstwhile Dewan of Manipur, designated as the first Chief Commissioner took charge on the morning of October 15.[58]

References

1. In the election that was held in June 1948, the State Congress Party secured nineteen seats in a House of fifty-three. The ministry was formed by the Praja Santi Party in coalition with other parties. But the fall of the ministry was brought because of the lack of the cohesion among the members.
2. *The Amrita Bazar Patrika* (Calcutta), August 15, 1949, p.2.
3. *Ibid.*
4. *The Hindustan Standard* (Calcutta), May 11, 1947, p. 3.
5. *Ibid.*, April 28, 1947, p. 1.
6. *Ibid.*, May 12, 1947, p. 2.

7. *Ibid.*, May 12, 1947, p. 2.
8. *Ibid.*
9. *Ibid.*, May 14, 1949, p. 5.
10. *Ibid.*
11. *The Amrita Bazar Patrika* (Calcutta), March 5, 1949, p. 5.
12. *Ibid.*, July 23, 1949, p. 5.
13. *The Hindustan Standard* (Calcutta), May 21, 1947, p. 5.
14. *Ibid.*
15. *Ibid.*
16. *Ibid.*
17. *The Amrita Bazar Patrika* (Calcutta), July 24, p. 5.
18. *The Hindustan Standard* (Calcutta), July 6, 1947, p. 5.
19. *Ibid.*, September 12, 1949, p. 3.
20. Home Department, Political File No. 333, 1946, NAI, New Delhi.
21. *Ibid.*
22. *The Hindustan Standard* (Calcutta), September 1, 1948, p. 3.
23. The Mao Nagas in Manipur consumed a fair amount of rice from the Manipur valley. No duty was ever known to be imposed on rice movement within Manipur when the white-folk (Britishers) were in power. Immediately after the resumption of power by the locals the imposition of duty on rice commenced at the rate of four *annas* per mound in December (1947) last. Since then the duty had been enhanced up to two rupees per mound and was actually realised.
24. The Naga National League was the only political organization set up in order to work and consolidate the Nagas of Manipur. It pledged itself to stand together with other hill tribes in the State as well as outside it in order to demand self-determination of the hill people in general without in any way injuring the general interest of Assam and India.
25. Memorandum submitted by Naga Leaders to Deputy Prime Minister, 24 January 1948, Manipur State Congress File No. 5, 1948.
26. The Naga Hills District Tribal Council which was established under the Chairmanship of Charles Pawsey in 1945 with an object to train the Nagas in the art of self-administration, had changed its name and the whole set-up to the Naga National Council in 1946. It stands in 1946: The solidarity of the Naga tribes, including those in the unadministered areas, which scattered all over the north-east hilly region of India and the north-west frontier of Burma. Its aim was to bring about amity and understanding among the different tribes. It strongly protested against the grouping of Assam with Bengal. It demanded the Naga Hills should be continuously included in an autonomous Assam in a free India, with

local autonomy and due safeguards for the interests of the Nagas; and the Nagas should have a separate electorate.

27. *The Hindustan Standard* (Calcutta), November 26, 1947, p. 3.
28. *Ibid.*, July 22, p. 2.
29. *Ibid.*
30. *Ibid.*, November 26, 1947, p. 3.
31. *Memorandum on Naga-Self-determination* submitted to the Simon Commission on January 10, 1929.
32. R. Reid, *Years of Change in Bengal and Assam* (London: 1966), p. 110.
33. P.D. Stracey, *Nagaland Nightmare* (Bombay: Allied Publishers Private Limited, 1968), p. 69.
34. V. Venkata Rao, *A Century of Tribal Politics in North East India*, 1874-1974 (New Delhi: S. Chand & Company Ltd., 1976), pp. 314-315.
35. Phizo quietly slipped out of India in 1957 and took political asylum in England. The seventy-four year old Phizo has been the President of the Naga National Council in absentia ever since his self-exile in London. He never came back to India. Still he claimed that the Nagas were never Indian citizens and Nagaland was never an integral part of India. This was proved by his first ever dialogue, that hardly lasted some twenty minutes, with the Prime Minister Morarji Desai in India House, London, on June 14, 1977.

    Even today, Phizo has been the source of political inspiration to the Naga people who have been demanding Naga independence for the last thirty-three years. The Nagas firmly believe that their problem cannot be solved without Phizo. Even after his death, the underground movement for a sovereign state of Nagaland is still in continuance.
36. V. Venkata Rao, *A Century of Tribal Politics in North East India, 1874-1974* (New Delhi: S. Chand & Company Ltd., 1976), p. 497.
37. *Ibid.*, p. 515.
38. Shibanikinokar Chaube, *Hill Politics in North-East India* (Calcutta: Orient Langman, 1973), p. 164.
39. Ever since the birth of the Mizo National Front, Laldenga as its President was preaching openly complete independence. Laldenga who had been living in Delhi since July 1976 as a guest of the Government of India was arrested on July 6, 1979 from his residence on the ground of sedition, conspiracy and waging war against the State. On October 30, 1965, the Mizo National Front submitted a memorandum to the late Prime Minister Pandit Jawaharlal Nehru, stating that the Mizos, from the time immemorial lived in complete independence. The Mizo Hills had never been an integral part of India.

    It was thirteen years ago that the Mizo movement suddenly erupted into large-scale violence; the revolt came in the wake of a devastating famine in 1959. By March 1966, the Mizo National Front declared independence. The outlawed Mizo National Front launched the quit Mizoram movement on the plea that the non-Mizos were agents of the Centre; and in occupation of the Mizoram, they were spoiling Mizo nationalism. They were given ultimatum for leaving Mizoram for all by July 1, 1979. This had created a panic among the non-Mizos. However, the timely action of the police brought the tense situation under control. Subsequently, the Government has suppressed the Mizo insurgency with the help of a strong military operation. But force could not be an only means for the permanent solution of the Mizo problem. The repressive measures would make the local people more hostile to the Government. It would be better if the Centre could understand the real happenings in Mizoram; and this would mean initiating a dialogue with the Mizo leaders on sorting out things and evolving a satisfactory and a lasting solution to the problem plaguing that area.

Movement for sovereignty is a thing of past. Today. Mizoram has become one of the Indian states on February 23, 1987 after the signing of an accord between the Union Government and the leader of the Mizo National Front (MNP).

40. *The Hindustan Standard* (Calcutta), January 12, 1948, p. 5.
41. *The Amrita Bazar Patrika* (Calcutta), March 23, 1949, p. 5.
42. Durga Das (Ed.), *Sardar Patel's Correspondence*, VIII (Ahmedabad: 1974), p. 527.
43. *Ibid.*
44. *Ibid.*, pp. 517-18.
45. *The Hindustan Standard* (Calcutta), April 16, 1949, p. 3. He further said: 'Any change of Government can only be brought about by peaceful and democratic means. We wonder how a political party wedded to non-violence and Khadi can adopt extra-constitutional methods for their own political end by calling their rivals bad names. Moreover, a centrally administered automous unit of Manipur would become just a military outpost with little political and civic freedom, for which the Manipur people have fought since 1939. Their decision is premature and inopportune as they lack the necessary backing of the masses of Manipur'. *Ibid.*
46. *Ibid.*
47. *Ibid.*, July 10, 1949, p. 3.
48. *The Amrita Bazar Patrika* (Calcutta), July 13, 1949, p. 8.
49. *The Hindustan Standard* (Calcutta), September 6, 1949, p. 1.
50. *The Amrita Bazar Patrika* (Calcutta), September 9, 1949, p. 10.
51. Sudhkar Bhat, *The Challenge of the North-East* (Bombay: Popular Prakashani, 1975), p. 47.

52. On the other hand, it was learnt that the Maharaja had informed the Chamber of Princes that he wanted Manipur to be grouped with Sikkim and the Khasi states and not with Tripura. Home Department, Political File No. 5(9), 1947, NAI, New Delhi.
53. Durga Das (Ed.), *Sardar Patel's Correspondence*, VIII (Ahmedabad: Navajivara Publishing House, 1973), p. 528.
54. After the merger of Manipur with the Indian Union, the Maharaja received a payment of Rs.300,000/- annually free of all taxes to cover all expenses of the Ruler and his family including expenses on account of his personal staff, maintenance of his residence, marriages and other ceremonies. *The Amrita Bazar Patrika* (Calcutta), December 27, 1949, p. 4.
55. *White Paper on Indian States* (Delhi, Government of India Press, 1950), pp. 232-234.
56. *The Amrita Bazar Patrika* (Calcutta), October 13, 1949, p. 1.
57. *Ibid.*, October 16, 1949, p. 1.
58. *Ibid.*, October 17, 1949, p. 7.

10
Conclusion

The present study aims at a historical survey of political development in Manipur since the revolt of 1890-91. Nine distinct periods of this process have been singled out for the detailed treatment in the preceding chapters.

The important events of these periods which have had any significant impact on the course of the State's political development have been thoroughly researched. To mention only few of them in December 1917, the Thado Kukis who had responded poorly to the calls for the Labour Corps sent to France early in the year, broke into open armed rebellion. In 1930-32, Jadonang and Gaidinliu revolted against the British power in Manipur with a view to establishing a 'Naga Raj'. The question of Manipur's accession to the proposed Indian federation was greatly controversial during 1936-38. The Women's Bazar Agitation that took place in 1939 was a product of the economic and the political pressures in the State. From 1946 onwards Manipur saw a movement of political and constitutional reforms. Immediately after the independence a movement was started by the intelligentia to form a North-East India Frontier Province along with Manipur, Cachar, Tripura and Lushai Hills. But due to the lack of the popular support the political movement soon fizzled out.

Manipur in its present territorial limits has existed as an independent political unit for about 2,000 years. Ruled by a succession of dynasties, the State has in the past undergone many periods of civil strife, mutual killings, bloodshed and turmoil; the absolute rule of the rajahs came to an end with the dawn of the Indian independence in 1947.

Manipur differs from other states in history and culture due to its peculiar geographic location. It is situated in the most isolated and neglected eastern part of the Indian Union. It was a British protected

State, under the superintendence and the control of the Assam administration. Though of small size, Manipur is rich in history. The State which came under the British control as a princely State in 1891, as merged in the Indian Union on October 15, 1949, and made the administrative charge of a Chief Commissioner.

The origins of political development of Manipur may be traced to the period of the Kuki Insurgency (1917-1919) which had a direct bearing on the policy of the British Indian Government towards this princely State. It was a first major revolt by the tribals after the Manipur uprising of 1891. For a long period, it could not be subdued by the authorities, the normalcy was restored only when the British took a strong military 'punitive measure' against the rebels. Some of the British Officers even thought of using hand-grenades and powerful guns and planes to crush the rebellion but that idea was dropped immediately because of the non-availability of ammunition.

The British policy of 'forced recruitment' from the hill tribes, especially the Kukis, for the establishment of a Labour Corps which was supposed to serve in the British Army in Mesopotamia (Iraq) during the World War I, was the immediate cause of the Kuki Rebellion. At the beginning of 1917, the Assam Government was assigned a quota for supply of the labourers for the deployment in Mesopotamia; the matter was referred to the Maharaja of the Manipur State. Immediately, the Maharaja started recruiting labourers or *coolies* from the hill tribes, two thousands in number. But a further requirement of two thousand labourers, for the establishment of a Second Labour Company, could not be raised up because of the size and frequency of the drafts demanded for the first corps of the hillmen; therefore, he offered a Second Corps (Labour), to be recruited, when required, from his Valley. Lord Chelmsford, Viceroy and Governor-General in India, wrote to Maharaja informing a further Second Labour Corps was not required for the purpose at present. After some time, the Government of India felt the need of a second Labour Company; the matter was discussed in a political conference held in Shillong. The British Political Agent in Manipur, Higgins, was confident at this time that he would be able to raise up a Second Labour Corps of the hillmen. A dialogue was arranged between the Political Agent and the Kuki village heads. But the Kuki Chiefs declined to supply the labourers. The Political Agent, with an escort of fifty rifles, left Imphal with a view to having another conversation; as the Kuki chiefs did not turn up, he burnt the Mombi village which he found deserted. The burning of a Kuki village was a blunderous offence ever committed by a Political Agent which provoked the restless tribals to rioting and violence. The recalcitrant Kuki chiefs (*Luchingba*) now flatly refused to carry out the orders of the Government of India, and an open armed rebellion broke out.

The rebellion in most of the hill areas of Manipur soon spread to the bordering territory. The Kukis of the unadministered area of Somra Tract and some adjacent area within the neighbouring Burma had been affected seriously. The revolt was politically embarrassing to the governments of Manipur and Burma. To cope with the situation, some seasoned British Officers proposed to construct a new road at Mawleik (Burma) running to Manipur State, but dropped the idea due to an inevitable economic pressure on the State exchequer.

An Armistice was signed in May 1919 and many British military officers were rewarded with higher ranks in appreciation, of their services during the Kuki outbreak. The military campaign nevertheless ended up with a huge loss of human lives and the destruction of a large number of cattle and several tribal villages. It cost a few laks of rupees. However, the villages affected by the punitive expedition were compensated to some extent for their sufferings.

As the uprising came to a close, a number of riotous and unruly Kuki chiefs were convicted and executed; and the other prisoners were lodged in the Sadiya Jail.

The main causes of the rebellion may be ascribed to the apathy on the part of the State administration and misunderstanding of the critical situation and of the Kuki psychology; but the immediate provocation was provided by the burning of the Mombi village. The role of the corrupt *lambus* (interpreters) was also responsible for the outbreak. A lack of direct link between the hill tribes and the State Government and want of mutual understanding between them created a cleavage between them. Moreover, the Kukis were afraid of going to a foreign land which was quite unknown to them; adding to this, they were unwilling to leave their villages at a critical juncture, as the rival Nagas might take an advantage of attacking their families. It seemed that both the Political Agent and the Maharaja were oblivious to the traditional feud between the Nagas and the Kukis; above all, it very well be suspected that the information regarding the ill-treatment of the Indians in Mesopotamia had been leaked out to the Kukis; they were, therefore, ready to pay money rather than serve as labourers.

The significance of the Kuki uprising lay in its political repercussions; the political bearing of the rebellion, however, whatever the case might be, aimed at the overthrow of the British Government and the suppression of the Nagas whom the Kukis had been grudging for the last many years. A no-tax campaign was also launched during the Kuki rebellion. It was the only local armed political uprising against the British India Government and the State administration in Manipur.

When the rebellion subsided, the British Government fully realized the strong feelings of the rebels and thereafter took steps for the reform of the tribal administration and for the mutual understanding and benefit. Finally, the rules for the administration of the Manipur State, originally framed in 1916, were revised keeping in view the need for the better administration among the hill tribes.

The Naga unrest spans the two phases marked by the rise, growth and suppression of the rebellious cults of Jadonang and Gaidinliu respectively.

The political aim of Jadonang's movement was to establish a Kabui Naga Raj by overthrowing the domination of the British, of the Kukis and valley population.

Jadonang was the chief leader of this unique movement; he who professed to be starting a new cult. He was regarded as god or messiah of the Kabui Naga group. Originally as a 'maiba' or medicine-man he played on the minds of the Kabuis to such an extent that they began to look upon him as a god who would overthrow the existing British administration. Jadonang sent words to all the Kabuis: 'There is a word (prophecy) that Milong (Nagas) will become great; let us try and kill the *Sarkar* (British administration-mine)'. He just came to the notice of the British authority in 1927 when he caused unrest amongst the Kabuis. In 1928, he was put into jail telling the people the British Raj was coming to an end and that a Kabui Naga Raj was to be established in its place. Jadonang told all the Kabui Nagas not to pay any more revenue to the British Government from 1931-32 and that all revenue was to be paid to him. There was suspicion that he had got Congress infection from Lakhipur (Assam).

Jadonang was wanted not only as the leader of the new movement but also as a murderer. After his arrest the criminal investigations were started against him and others of his village for the brutal murder, in 1929, of four unarmed Hindu Manipuris who were journeying towards Cachar. It appeared likely that the victims were put to death at the instance of Jadonang probably as sacrifices to his gods as well as to show his followers his power and defiance of the existing laws of the State. He was convicted with six other Kabui Nagas of the village of Kambiron and was sentenced to be hanged. The human sacrifice brought him to the gallows in August 1931. The other convicts were sentenced to imprisonment.

Gaidinliu, the torch-bearer of Jadonang, took up the mission of her master after his execution. She preached the same political religion of her leader. In season and out season it was preached that when Gaidinliu's day would come those who had supported her would be blessed in every way, and those who had opposed her would certainly meet with disaster. Jadonang who was believed then to be present in spirit was held to be that 'Naga King', who would reign jointly with Gaidinliu. 'The day of Nagas is coming' was the slogan. This really involved the dis-appearance of the British rule in India. As long as Gaidinliu was at large her influence would diminish little.

When the civil disobedience movement was in full swing in the plains in 1930, Gaidinliu launched a no-tax campaign in the hills. To get rid of the British control meant to them the establishment of a 'Naga Raj', evidently because these illiterate highlanders had little knowledge of the world outside their hill abodes in the frontiers of Assam. The British authorities tried to nip the movement in the bud by capturing the Naga leaders though it was not an easy task for them. Even after the execution of Jadonang, Gaidinliu wielded tremendous influence over the hill tribes. Her movement became the cause of the serious alarm to the governments of Assam and Manipur. The local British authorities had to take recourse to repressive measures including the burning of the villages and the mass arrests. The repression was intensified with the failure of the government to trace the whereabouts of Gaidinliu.

With the arrest of Gaidinliu her movement disintegrated gradually. She was sentenced to transportation for life on a charge of murder by the Political Agent in Manipur. She was praised by Jawaharlal Nehru as a powerful freedom fighter. She was released from the jail at his instance when India became free.

The Government of India Act, 1935, posed a serious problem to Manipur with regard to its federal scheme. The Government of India was anxious to bring in it all the states still in relations with the local governments of India. But in the case of Manipur so many difficult problems were found to stand in the way that it was decided that when the new Act came into force relations with the State should be conducted by the Governor of Assam province in his personal capacity as the Agent of the Crown Representative. He was authorized under Section 287 of the Government of India Act, 1935, to discharge such functions of the Crown in its relations with the Manipur State as had hitherto been performed by the Governor-in-Council in Assam. This in fact led no practical change in the erstwhile political set-up.

One of the principal subjects of the controversy was, of course, the administration of the hill areas. Though they covered some 7,000 square miles out of the State's total area of 8,000 square miles and contained a population of about 150,000, it had never, and with good reason, been adjudged safe to leave their administration in the hands of the ruler. The opinion of the Governor of Assam as regards the administration of the hill portions was that they could not possibly be handed over to the ruler of Manipur; the Government of India accepted the views of the Government of Assam.

Some two years later, i.e., in 1930, the Maharaja of Manipur again raised the question of the hills during the course of the discussion on the details of the federation, but he agreed this time to federate on terms which covered the exclusion of the hill areas from his direct control. Previously he was unwilling to join the proposed federation due to his vanity. He wanted a free hand in the administration of the plains and the hills of Manipur without any interference from the British authorities. But the hopes that the federation would be established by 1936, i.e., a year after the inauguration of the provincial autonomy were never fulfilled. Further talks on the question of the federation were brought to an abrupt end by the outbreak of the Second World War in September 1939. A Government of India letter informed that it was not expected that in view of the war pre-occupation, Her Majesty's Government would be able to give active attention to the federal problem.

This massively organized women's agitation was the first of its kind in Manipur. The agitation took place because of the scarcity of rice; in its later phase, the agitation acquired the political overtones as well. The slogans like 'Britishers go back' became popular during the movement; however, the agitation never got out of control.

It was from Nepal to Travancore and Cochin: All the states of the British Indian Empire were witnessing the beginnings of the political awakening. Manipur, though far away in the north-eastern corner of India, could not lag behind the others. The women's agitation was a sort of reaction against the administration of the Manipur State where the autocratic powers were exercised by the Durbar members and the Maharaja.

The agitation had its origin in the acute scarcity of rice in Manipur owing to the floods. A ban was imposed on the export of rice. In November, however, when the harvest season was on, the ban was suddenly lifted and the price of rice shot up causing acute hardship to the people of the State.

The sheer economic necessity had disturbed the placid life of the people of Manipur, so to say, the womenfolk had been forced to agitate due to the ruthless economic dispensation under the rule of the Maharaja. This resulted in political confusion in the State. Having no other alternative, the Government had to ban the export of rice again and fulfilled some of the demands of the women agitators. Gradually the movement subsided.

The demand for the formation of a new Eastern India Frontier Province came in the wake of the partition of Bengal. The movement was mainly guided by the Bengali elites who needed a safeguard against the majority rule of the Assamese in Assam.

It is worthwhile to ponder why on earth there had been such a sudden demand at all. According to the views of the Bengali elites it had been evident that the Assamese people have been suffering from the narrow 'Valley Jealousy'. Even the body politic of Assam was no exception. The inhabitants of Assam thought that since the province bore the name 'Assam' which they interpreted, was a corruption of the term 'Ahom' the whole of the province was their own homeland and all others were but outsiders. The insular parochialism of the Assamese had prompted them to seek an opportunity just to eliminate the non-Assamese, especially the Bengalis who happened to be a part and parcel of the province.

A consequence of a short-sighted policy on the part of the Assamese people was Bengali-baiting in political, economic, linguistic and cultural spheres. The Bengalis were being manhandled, their hearth and home being burnt down and looted, their means of living being snatched away, even those domiciles who had been living in the province for generations together. Further, the elites complained that the Assamese had been following a ruthless policy of the extermination of the Bengalis.

The Bengalis declared that there could never be a compromise on this score since a change of hearts should precede any compromise, but that was not to be on the other side. Therefore, to rehabilitate the immirgrants of Assam and thousands of the unfortunate refugees from Bengal there was no other way out but the immediate formation of the proposed 'Purbachal Province'.

The proposed North-East India Frontier Province might comprise of Manipur, Cachar, Tripura, Lushai Hills, Naga Hills and Khasi and Jaintia Hills; geographically these states represent a compact area. The elites justified the joining of Manipur to the proposed new province for the reason that the Manipuris well understood Bengali and spoke it too; besides, the Hindu Bengalis and the Hindu Manipuris had a common religious tie, both being the followers of Vaishnavism. Some of the political leaders of Manipur advocated the formation of a new province in the north-east of India. But this idea was not incorporated with that of the Central leaders of India. The Government of India was tooth and nail against the formation of a North-East India Frontier Province. By a resolution, the Congress Working Committee rejected the idea of the formation of a separate North-East India Frontier Province. As the movement was one-sided it could not endure.

The years 1946-49 saw the assimilation of the democratic ideas by the Manipuris; they consequently started agitating for the establishment of a responsible government. A draft constitution was passed by the Manipur State Durbar on July 26, 1941. On September 26, 1947, the Maharaja promised an announcement on the constitution within eight months from that date. In the meantime, to replace the State Durbar presided over by Pearson, an interim state council was set up consisting of two ministers from the Manipur State Congress, two ministers representing the hills and two ministers nominated by the Manipur State Congress from amongst the State officials and the chief minister nominated by the Maharaja. The new cabinet of the ministers was thus set up and began to function from August 14, 1947. Some members of the Manipur State Congress disapproved of the method and personel taken into the newly formed State Council seceded and formed themselves into a group of Congress. Now two separate Congress parties appeared on the political scene of Manipur both of them demanding the immediate establishment of responsible government.

The splinter Congress group suggested that the Maharaja should establish a popular interim council by dissolving the present Interim Council. Further, they appealed to the State Government that a new constitution providing full responsible government should be framed through a constituent assembly elected on the adult franchise.

The new Congress started satyagraha and civil resistance on November 6, 1947. Seeing this state of affairs the old Congress adopted a resolution on November 11, 1947, reiterating its demand for a full responsible government in Manipur with a view to removing discontent in the State. The Maharaja introduced in 1948 a responsible government in Manipur. The first Manipur State Assembly, elected on the universal adult franchise, was inaugurated by him on October 18, 1948.

At the end of the World War II, the British were planning to quit India and transfer power to the native hands.

While the whole of India was amidst political excitement, in Manipur too, some leaders started agitation against the Maharaja demanding a responsible government. The Congress agitated and urged the Government of India to merge Manipur with the Indian Union as Manpur in their view could not become a viable State. No doubt, some political leaders who were not in favour of the merger with the Indian Union, had also been agitating throughout the year. Besides, one of the political parties was very much interested in unison with Burma (Myanmar); the ill-design, however, was nipped in the bud.

The Maharaja was strongly opposed to the integration with the Indian Union on terms offered by the British. But the Prime Minister, Jawaharlal Nehru, assured that the State of Manipur would retain its separate identity. Mahatma Gandhi also made it public that no state would be merged without the consent of its people. The Maharaja, however, remained complacent in this regard. But the political parties restlessly worked and got the sympathy of the Central Congress leaders of India. At last, on September 21, 1949, the Maharaja of Manipur signed the merger agreement in Shillong.

With the integration of Manipur into the Indian Union as the last State, Sardar Patel's dream of unification of India by abolishing the native state was practically realized. The State Assembly and the Council of Manipur State stood abolished in consequence of the merger agreement and Manipur then became a Chief Commissioner's Province exercising the powers of the Maharaja-in-Council. A new chapter in the political history of Manipur was thus opened ending up the age long political hierarchy in Manipur. Today Manipur has become one of the full-fledged states of the Indian Union, and stand equal in status with the other states.

Appendix–I

Rules for the Management of the State of Manipur, 1916*

General Administration

1. **Administration:** His Highness the Raja will be responsible for the administration of the State. He will be assisted by a Darbar, which will consist of an officer specially selected by the Government of Assam who will be styled the President, and of at least three Manipuri Members who may hold charge of departments and shall be called ordinary members. Three additional members may be appointed, who while not holding charge of any deparment, will attend all meetings of the Darbar and speak and vote equally with the other members.

2. **Appointment of Members:** His Highness, in consultation with the Political Agent, will appoint the ordinary and additional members of the Darbar. No member shall be removed without the express consent of the Political Agent in writing.

3. **Meeting of the Darbar:** The Darbar will meet for the transaction of business under the presidency of the President, whose presence is obligatory, unless dispensed with by the Political Agent. Four shall form a quorum and, in cases of equality of voters, the presiding officer shall have a casting vote.

4. **Distribution of works:** The President wll be responsible to His Highness for the proper administration of the finance and Revenue Departments and will on behalf of His Highness, exercise general supervision over the working of all other departments. His Highness in consultation with the Political Agent will arrange for the distribution of work between himself and the ordinary members.

---

* Extracts from the *Rules for the Management of the State of Manipur* 1916 (Imphal).

5. **Responsibility of Members:** Each ordinary member will be responsible to His Highness for the proper administration of the department committed to his charge. He will dispose of all ordinary business, but must bring questions of importance to His Highness's notice, through the Darbar, which in forwarding matter to His Highness may make any representation it sees of it. His Highness's orders will be notified to the Darbar in writing. His Highness may call on any member to submit to him any matter connected with his department and pass orders thereon such orders shall be notified to the Darbar in writing.

6. **His Highness's Powers as Regards Resolutions Passed by the Darbar:** The Darbar will submit copies of its proceedings to His Highness, who may (1) approve thereof, (2) refer any matter back to the Darbar for further discussion, (3) veto any resolution and issue what orders he sees fit, stating his reasons in writing. After His Highness has passed his orders, copies of the proceedings and the orders passed thereon will be submitted to the Political Agent in English.

7. **Darbar's Position:** The Darbar has the right to be consulted in all matters of importance affecting the State and with reference to any proposed alteration in established procedure or custom. The Darbar may communicate with the Political Agent, through His Highness regarding any matters of importance.

8. **Appointments of Officials:** His Highness will appoint all title-holders and officials drawing pay of more than Rs. 15 a month and the members of the Cherap and all Panchayat Courts. Other officials will be appointed by the Members in charge of the department. Members in charge of departments will submit to His Highness the names of suitable persons to fill vacancies which may occur in posts which are in His Highness's gift.

9. **President's Powers of Reference:** The President may, after consultation with His Highness refer any matter affecting any State department to the Political Agent. The Political Agent may refer any matter which has been submitted to him under this rule or under the provisions of rule 6 for the orders of the government of Assam but before doing so he shall consult His Highness. The Political Agent may, if he considers it necessary, direct that any order to which he takes exception and which he is referring

under this rule shall be held in suspense until the orders of the Government of Assam have been received.

10. **The Budget:** The annual budget will consist of two parts, one part relating to the hills tribes and other part of the State generally the budget in both parts will be drafted by the President, and will be laid by him before the Darbar for examination. After the Darbar has recorded its suggestions if any, for modifications in the President's draft budget, His Highness will record his own opinion. If His Highness desires any modification in the budget proposed by the Darbar, His Highness will communicate his opinion to the Darbar in order to give them an opportunity of reconsidering their views and submitting a further minute to His Highness. His Highness will then record his own final opinion indicating clearly the forum in which he desires that the budget shall be accepted by the Government of Assam and will forward all the papers to the Political Agent for submission to the Governor of Assam. The Government of Assam after giving due consideration to the wishes of His Highness and the Darbar, will finally approve the budget with such modifications as it sees fit. When once approved by the Government of Assam the budget must be adhered to subject to such modifications as are allowed by the rules sanctioned by the Government of Assam for the keeping of the State Accounts.

11. **Hill Administration:** The hill tribes are administered by the President assisted by one or more Officers on His Highness's behalf in accordance with rules approved by the Government of Assam but His Highness shall be consulted in all matters of importance and the Political Agent, in consultation with the President shall give effect to His Highness's wishes so far as is consistent with the orders of the Government of Assam. If the Political Agent is unable to agree to His Highness's proposals, the matter shall, if His Highness so wishes, be referred to the Government of Assam.

Appendix–II

[The] Government of India Act, 1935*

Be it enacted by the King's most Excellent Majesty, by and with the advice and consent of the Lords Spiritual and Temporal, and Commons, in this present Parliament assembled, and by the authority of the same, as follows: -

1. This Act may be cited as the Government of India Act, 1935.

2. (1) All rights, authority and jurisdiction heretofore belonging to his Majesty the King, Emperor of India, which appertain or are incidental to the Government of the territories in India for the time being vested in him, and all rights, authority and jurisdiction exercisable by him in or in relation to any other territories in India, are exercisable by His Majesty, except in so far as may be otherwise provided by or under this Act, or as may be otherwise directed by His Majesty:

   Provided that any powers connected with the exercise of the functions of the Crown in its relations with Indian States shall in India, if not exercised by His Majesty, be exercised only by, or by persons acting under the authority of, His Majesty's Representative for the exercise of those functions of the Crown.

   (2) The said rights, authority and jurisdiction shall include any rights, authority or jurisdiction heretofore exercisable in or in relation to any territories in India by the Secretary of State, the Secretary of State in Council, the Governor-General, the Governor-General in Council, any Governor or any Local Government, whether by delegation from his Majesty or otherwise.

* Extract from the *Government of India Act, 1935.*

3. (1) The Governor-General of India is appointed by His Majesty by a Commission under the Royal Sign Manual

   (a) All such powers and duties as are conferred or imposed on him by or under this Act; and

   (b) Such other powers of His Majesty, not being powers connected with the exercise of the functions of the Crown in its relations with Indian States, as His Majesty may be pleased to assign to him.

(2) [His Majesty's Representative for the exercise of the functions of the Crown in its relations with Indian States] is appointed by His Majesty in like manner and has such powers and duties in connection with the exercise of those functions (not being powers or duties conferred or imposed by or under this Act on the Governor-General) as His Majesty may be pleased to assign to him.

(3) It shall be lawful for His Majesty to appoint one person to fill both the said offices].

(4) There shall be a Commander-in-Chief of His Majesty's Forces in India appointed by Warrant under the Royal Sign Manual.

PART II
THE FEDERAL EXECUTIVE

CHAPTER 1.
ESTABLISHMENT OF FEDERATION AND ACCESSION OF INDIAN STATES

5. (1) It shall be lawful for His Majesty, if an address in that behalf has been Proclamation of presented to him by each House of Parliament and if the condition hereinafter mentioned is satisfied, to declare by Proclamation that as from the day therein appointed there shall be united in Federation under the Crown, by the name of the Federation of India,—

   (a) the Provinces hereinafter called Governors' Provinces; and

   (b) the Indian States which have acceded or may thereafter accede to the Federation;

and in the Federation so established there shall be included the Provinces hereinafter called Chief Commissioners' Provinces.

(2) The condition referred to is that States —

(a) the Rulers whereof will, in accordance with the provision contained in Part II of the First Schedule to this Act be entitled to choose not less than fifty-two members of the Council of State; and

(b) the aggregate population whereof, as ascertained in accordance with the said provisions, amounts to at least one-half of the total population of the States as so ascertained, have acceded to the Federation.

(1) A State shall be deemed to have acceded to the Federation if His Majesty has signified his acceptance of an Instrument of Accession executed by the Ruler thereof, whereby by the Ruler for himself, his heirs and successors —

(a) declares that he accedes to the Federation as established under this Act, with the intent that His Majesty the King, the Governor-General of India, the Federal Legislature, the Federal Court and any other Federal authority established for the purpose of the Federation shall by virtue of his Instrument of Accession, but subject always to the terms thereof, and for the purposes only of the Federation, exercise in relation to his State such functions as may be vested in them by on under this Act; and

(b) assumes the obligation of ensuring that due effect is given within his State to provisions of this Act so far as they are applicable therein by virtue of his Instrument of Accession:

Provided that an Instrument of Accession may executed conditionally on the establishment of the Federation on or before a specified date, and in that case the State shall not be deemed to have acceded to the Federation is not established until after that date.

(2) An Instrument of Accession shall specify the matters which the Ruler accepts as matters with respect to which the

Federal Legislature make laws for his State, and the limitations, if any, to which the power of the Federal Legislature to make laws for his State, and the exercise of the executive authority of the Federation in his State, are respectively to be subject.

(3) A Ruler may, by a supplementary Instrument executed by him and accepted by His Majesty, vary the Instrument of Accession of his State by extending the functions which by virtue of that Instrument are exercisable by His Majesty or any Federal Authority in relation to his State.

(4) Nothing in this section shall be construed as requiring His Majesty to accept any Instrument of Accession or supplementary Instrument unless he considers it proper so to do, or as empowering His Majesty to accept any such Instrument if it appears to him that the terms thereof are inconsistent with the scheme of Federation embodied in this Act;

Provided that after the establishment of the Federation, if any Instrument has in fact been accepted by His Majesty, the validity of that Instrument or of any of its provisions shall not be called in question and the provisions of this Act shall, in relation to the State, have effect subject to the provisions of this Act shall, in relation to the State, have effect subject to the provisions of the Instrument.

(5) It shall be a term of every Instrument of Accession that the provisions of this Act mentioned in the Second Schedule thereto, may, without affecting the accession of the State, be amended by or by authority of Parliament, but not such amendment shall, unless it is accepted by the Ruler in a supplementary Instrument, be construed as extending the functions which by virtue of the Instrument are exercisable by His Majesty or any Federal Authority in relation to the State.

(6) An Instrument of Accession or supplementary Instrument shall not be valid unless it is executed by the Ruler himself, but, subject as aforesaid, references in this Act to the Ruler of a State include references to any persons for the time being exercising the powers of the Ruler of the State,

whether by reason of the Ruler's minority or for any other reason.

(7) After the establishment of the Federation the request of a Ruler that his State may be admitted to the Federation shall be transmitted to His Majesty through the Governor-General, and after the expiration of twenty years from the establishment of the Federation the Governor-General shall not transmit to His Majesty any such request until there has been presented to him by each Chamber of the Federal Legislature, for submission to His Majesty, an address praying that His Majesty may be pleased to admit the State into the Federation.

(8) In this Act a State which has acceded to the Federation is referred to as a Federal State, and the Instrument by virtue of which a State has so acceded, construed together with any supplementary Instrument executed under this section, is referred to as the Instrument of Accession of that State.

(9) As soon as may be after any Instrument of Accession or supplementary Instrument has been accepted by His Majesty under this section, copies of the Instrument, and of His Majesty's Acceptances thereof shall be laid before Parliament, and all courts shall take judicial notice of every such Instrument and Acceptance.

CHAPTER II
THE FEDERAL, EXECUTIVE

The Governor General

7. (1) Subject to the provisions of this Act, the executive authority of the Federation shall be exercised on behalf of His Majesty by the Governor-General either directly or through officers subordinate to him, but nothing in this section shall prevent the Federal Legislature from conferring function, upon subordinate authorities, or be deemed to transfer to the Governor-General any functions conferred by any existing Indian law on any court judge or officer, or on any local or other authority.

(2) References in this Act to the functions of the Governor-General shall be construed as references to his powers and

duties in the exercise of the executive authority of the Federation and to any other powers and duties conferred or imposed on him as Governor-General by or under this Act, [other than powers exercisable by him reason that they have been assigned to him by His Majesty under Part 1 of this Act].

(3) The provisions of the Third Schedule to this Act shall have effect with respect to the salary and allowances of the Governor-General and the provision to be made for enabling him to discharge conveniently and with dignity the duties of his office.

(1) Subject to the provisions of this Act, the executive authority of the Federation extends

(a) to the matters with respect ιo which the Federal Legislature has power to make laws;

(b) to the raising in British India on behalf of His Majesty of naval, military and air forces and to the governance of His Majesty's forces borne on the Indian establishment;

(c) to the exercise of such rights, authority and jurisdiction as are exercisable by His Majesty by treaty, grant, usage, sufferance, or otherwise in and in relation the tribal areas:

Provided that —

(i) the said authority does not, save as expressly provided in this Act, extend in any Province to matters with respect to which the Provincial Legislature has power to make laws;

(ii) the said authority does not, save as expressly provided in this Act, extend in any [Federal] State save to matters with respect to which the [Federal] Legislature has power to make laws for that State, and the exercise thereof in each State shall be subject to such limitations, if any, as may be specified in the Instrument of Accession of the State;

(iii) the said authority does not extend to the enlistment of enrolment in any forces raised in India of any person unless he is either a subject of His Majesty or a native of India or of territories adjacent to India; and

(iv) commissions in any such force shall be granted by His Majesty save in so far as he may be pleased to delegate the power by virtue of the provisions of Part I of this Act or otherwise.

(2) This executive authority of the Ruler of [a Federal] State shall notwithstanding anything in this section, continue to be exercisable in that State with respect to matters with respect to which the [Federal] Legislature has power to make laws for that State except in so far as the executive authority of the [Federation] becomes exercisable in the State to the exclusion of the executive authority of the Ruler by virtue of a [Federal] law.

Administration of Federal Affairs

9. (1) There shall be a council of ministers, not exceeding ten in number, to aid and advise the Governor-General in the exercise of his functions, [except in so far as he is by or under this Act required to exercise his functions or any of them in his discretion:

Provided that nothing in this sub-section shall be construed as preventing the Governor-General from exercising his individual judgment in any case where by or under this Act he is required so to do.

(2) The Governor-General in his direction may preside at meetings of the council of ministers.

(3) If any question arises whether any matter is or is not a matter as respects which the Governor-General is by or under this Act required to act in his direction or to exercise his individual judgment, the decision of the Governor-General in his discretion shall be final, and the validity of anything done by the Governor-General shall not be called in question on the ground that he ought or ought not to have acted in his discretion, or ought or ought not to have exercised his individual judgment].

10. (1) The Governor-General's ministers shall be chosen and summoned by him, shall be sworn as members of the council, and shall hold office during his pleasure.

(2) A minister who for any period of six consecutive months is not a member of [either Chamber of] the Federal Legislature shall at the expiration of that period cease to be a minister.

(3) The salaries of ministers shall be such as the Federal Legislature may from time to time by Act determine and, until the Federal Legislature so determine, shall be determined, by the Governor-General:

Provided that the salary of a minister shall not be varied during his term of office.

(4) The question whether any and, if so, what advice was tendered by ministers to the Governor-General shall not be inquired into in any Court.

(5) The functions of the Governor-General, with respect to the choosing and summoning and the dismissal of ministers, and with respect to the determination of their salaries, shall be exercised by him in his discretion].

11. (1) The functions of the Govenior-General with respect to defence and ecclesiastical and with respect to external affairs, except the relation between the Federation and any part His Majesty's dominions, shall be exercised by him in his discretion, and his functions in or in relations to the tribal areas shall he similarly exercised.

(2) To assist him in the exercise of those functions the Govemor-General may appoint counsellors, not exceeding three in number, whose salaries and conditions of service shall be such as may be prescribed by His Majesty in Council.

12. (I) In the exercise of his functions the Governor-General shall have the following special responsibilities, thai is to say,—

(a) the prevention of any grave menace to die peace or tranquility of India or any part thereof;

(b) the safeguarding of the financial stability and credit of the Federal Government;

(c) the safeguarding of the legitimate interests of minorities;

(d) the securing to, and to the dependants of, persons who are or have been members of the public services of any rights provided or preserved for them by or under this Act and the safeguarding of their legitimate interests;

(e) the securing in the sphere of executive action of the purposes which the provisions of Chapter III of Part V of this Act are designed to secure in relation to legislation;

(f) the prevention of action which would subject goods of United Kingdom or Burmese origin imported into India to discriminatory or penal treatment;

(g) the protection of the rights of any Indian State and the rights and dignity of the ruler thereof; and

(h) the securing that the due discharge of his functions with respect to matter with respect to which he is by or under this Act required to act in his discretion, or to exercise his individual judgment, is not prejudiced or impeded by any course of action taken with respect to any other matter.

(2) If and in so far as any special responsibility of the Governor-General is involved, he shall in the exercise of his functions exercise his individual judgment as to the action to be taken.

13. (1) The Secretary of State shall by before Parliament the draft of any Instrument of Instructions (including any Instrument amending or revoking an Instrument previously issued) which it is proposed to recommend His Majesty to issue to the Governor-General, and no further proceedings shall be taken in relation thereto except in pursuance of an address presented to His Majesty in both Houses of Parliament praying that the Instrument may be issued.

(2) The validity of anything done by the Governor-General shall not be called in question on the ground that it was done otherwise than in accordance with any Instrument of Instructions issued to him.

14. (1) In so far as the Governor-General is by or under this Act required to act in his discretion or to exercise his individual judgment; he shall be under the genera!

Control of, and comply with such particular directions, if any, as may from time to time be given to him by, the

Secretary of State, but the validity of anything done by the Governor -General shall not be called in question on the ground that it was done otherwise than in accordance with the provisions of this section.

(2) Before giving any directions under this section the Secretary of State shall satisfy himself that nothing in the directions requires the Governor-General to act in any manner inconsistent with any Instrument of Instructions issued to him by His Majesty.

15. (1) The Governor-General may appoint a person to be his financial adviser.

(2) It shall be the duty of the Governor- General's financial adviser to assist by his advice the Governor-General in the discharge of his special responsibility for safeguarding the financial stability and credit of the Federal Government, and also to give advice to the Federal Government upon any matter relating to finance with respect to which he may be consulted.

(3) The Governor-General's financial adviser shall hold office during the pleasure of the Governor-General, and the salary and allowances of the financial adviser and the numbers of his staff and their conditions of service shall be such as the Governor-General may determine.

(4) The powers of the Governor-General with respect to the appointment and dismissal of a financial advisor, and with respect to the determination of his salary and allowances and the numbers of his staff and their conditions of service shall be exercised by him in his discretion:

Provided that, if the Governor-General has determined to appoint a financial adviser he shall, before making any appointment other than the first appointment, consult his ministers as to the person to be selected.

16. (1) The Governor-General shall appoint a person, being a person qualified to be appointed a judge of the Federal Court, to be Advocate-General for the [Federation].

(2) It shall be the duty of the Advocate-General to give advice to the [Federal] Government upon such legal matters, and

to perform such other duties of a legal character, as may be referred to assigned to him by the Governor-General, and in the performance of his duties he shall have right of audience in all courts in British India and, in a case in which [federal] interests are concerned, in all courts in any [Federated] State.

(3) The Advocate- General shall hold office during the pleasure of the Governor-General, and shall receive such remuneration as the Governor-General may determine.

(4) In exercising his powers with respect to the appointment and dismissal of the Advocate-General and with respect lo the determination of his remuneration, the Governor-General shall exercise his individual judgment.

7. (1) All executive action of the [Federal] Government Shall be expressed to be taken in the name of the Governor-General.

(2) Orders and other instruments made and executed in the name of the Governor-General shall be authenticated in such manner as may be specified in rules to be made by the Governor-General, and the validity of an order or instrument which is so authenticated shall not be called in question on the ground that it is not an order or instrument made or executed by the Governor-General.

(3) The Governor-General shall make rules for the more convenient transaction of the business of the [Federal] Government, and for the allocation among ministers of the said business [in so far as it is not business with respect to which the Governor-General is by or under this Act required to act in his discretion].

(4) The roles shall include provisions requiring ministers and Secretaries to Government to transmit to the Governor-General all such information with respect to the business of the Federal Government as may he specified in the rules, or as the Governor-General may otherwise require to be so transmitted, and in particular requiring a minister to bring to the notice of the Governor-General and the appropriate secretary to bring to the notice of the minister concerned and of the Governor-General, any matter under consideration by him which involves, or appears to him likely to involve, any Special responsibility of the Governor-General.

(5) In the discharge of his functions under sub-sections (2), (3) and (4) of this section the Governor-General shall act in his discretion after consultation with his ministers.

CHAPTER III
THE FEDERAL LEGISLATURE

General.

(1) There shall be a Federal Legislature which shall consist of His Majesty, represented *by* the Govern or-General, and two chambers, to be known respectively as the Council of State and the House of Assembly (in this Act referred to as "the Federal Assembly").

(2) The Council of State shall consist of one hundred and fifty-six representatives of British India and not more than one hundred and four representatives of the Indian States, and the Federal Assembly shall consist of two hundred and fifty representatives of British India and not more than one hundred and twenty-five representatives of the Indian States.

(3) The said representatives shall be chosen in accordance with the provisions in that behalf contained in the First Schedule to this Act.

(4) The Council of State shall be a permanent body not subject to dissolution, but as near as may be one-third of the members thereof shall retire in every third year in accordance with the provisions in that behalf contained in the said First Schedule.

(5) Every Federal Assembly, unless sooner dissolved, shall continue for five years from the date appointed for their first meeting and no longer, and the expiration of the said period of five years shall operate as a dissolution of the Assembly.

19. (1) The [Chambers of the Federal] Legislature shall be summoned to meet once at least in every year, and twelve months shall not intervene between their last sitting in one session and the date appointed for their first sitting in the next session.

(2) Subject to the provisions of this section, the Governor-General may in his discretion from time to time —

(a) summon the [Chambers or either Chamber] to meet at such time and place as he thinks fit;

(b) prorogue the Chambers;

(c) dissolve the Federal Assembly.

(3) The Chambers shall be summoned to meet for their first session on a day not later than such day as may be specified in that behalf in His Majesty's Proclamation establishing the Federation,

20. (1) The Governor-General may in his discretion address [either Chamber of] the Federal Legislature [or both Chambers assembled together], and for that propose require attendance of members.

(2) The Governor-General may [in his discretion] and messages to [either Chamber of] the Federal Legislature, whether with respect to a Bill then pending in the Legislature or otherwise, and [a Chamber to whom any message is so sent] shall with all convenient dispatch consider any matter which they are required by the message to take into consideration.

21. Every minister [every counsellor] and the Advocate-General shall have the Rights to speak in, and otherwise to take part in the proceedings of, [either Chamber, any joint sitting of the Chambers, and any committee of the Legislature] of which he may be named a member, but shall not by virtue of this section be entitled to vote.

22. (1) The Council of State shall, as soon as may be, choose two members of the Council to be respectively President and Deputy President thereof and, so often as the office of President or Deputy President becomes vacant, the Council shall choose another member to be President or Deputy President as the case may be.

(2) A member holding office as President or Deputy President of the Council of State shall vacate his office if he ceases to be a member of the Council, may at any time resign his office by writing under his hand addressed to the Governor-General, and may be removed from his office by a resolution of the Council passed by a majority of all the then members of the Council; but no resolution for the purpose of this

sub-section shall be moved unless at least fourteen days' notice has been given of the intention to move the resolution.

(3) While the office of President is vacant, the duties of the office shall be performed by the Deputy President or, if the Office of Deputy President is also vacant, by such member of the Council as the Governor-General may in his discretion appoint for the purpose, and during any absence of the President from any sitting of the Council the Deputy President or, if he is also absent,, such person as may be determined by the rules of procedure of the Council, or, if no such person is present, such other person as may be determined by the Council, shall act as President.

(4) There shall be paid to the President [and the Deputy President o* the Council of State] such ''[salaries] as may be "[respectively] fixed by Act of the Federal Legislature, and, until provision in that behalf is so made such salaries as the Governor-General may determine.'

(5) The foregoing provisions of this section shall apply in relation to the Federal Assembly as they apply in relation to the Council of State with the substitution of the titles "Speaker" and ''Deputy Speaker" for the titles "President" and "Deputy President" respectively, and with the substitution of references to the Assembly for references to the Council:

Provided that, without prejudice to the provisions of sub-section (2) this section as applied by this sub-section, whenever the Assembly is dissolved, the Speaker shall not vacate his office until immediately before the first meeting of the Assembly after the dissolution.

23. (1) Save as provided in the last preceding section, all questions at any sitting "for joint sitting of the Chambers] shall be determined by a majority of votes of the members present and voting, other than the President "[or Speaker] or person acting as such.

The President "[or Speaker] or person acting as such shall not vote in the first instance, but shall have and exercise a casting vote in the case of an equality of votes.

(2) [A Chamber of] the [Federal] Legislature shall have power to act not with standing any vacancy in the membership thereof and any proceedings in the Legislature shall be valid notwithstanding that it is discovered sub-sequent that some person who was not entitled so to do so at or voted or otherwise look part in the proceedings.

(3) If at any time during a meeting of [a Chamber] less than one-sixth of the total number of members of [the Chamber] are present, it shall be the duty of the President [or Speaker] or person acting as such either to adjourn the Chamber, or to suspend the meeting until at least one-sixth of the members are present.

Provisions as to Members of Legislature

24. Every member of either Chamber shall, before taking his seat, make and subscribe before the Governor-General, or some person appointed by him, an oath according to that one of the forms set out in the Fourth Schedule to this Act which the member accepts as appropriate in his case,

25. (1) No person shall be a member of both Chambers, and rules made by the Governor-General exercising his individual judgment shall provide for the vacation by a person who is chosen a member of both Chambers of his seat in one Chamber or the other.

(2) If a member of either Chamber—

(a) becomes, subject to any of the disqualifications mentioned in sub-section (1) of the next succeeding section; or

(b) by writing under his hand addressed to the Governor-General resigns his seat, his seat shall thereupon become vacant.

(3) If for sixty days a member of either Chamber is without permission of the Chamber absent from all meetings thereof, the Chamber may declare his seat vacant:

Provided that in computing the said period of sixty days no account shall be taken of any period during which the Chamber is prorogued, or is adjourned for more than four consecutive days.

26. (1) A person shall be disqualified for being chosen as, and for being, a member of either Chamber—

(a) if he holds any office of profit under the Crown in India, other than an office declared by Act of the Federal Legislature not to disqualify its holder;

(b) if he is of unsound mind and stands so declared by a competent Court;

(c) if he is an undischarged insolvent;

(d) If, whether before or after (he establishment of the Federation, he has been convicted, or has, in proceedings for questioning the validity or regularity of an election, been found to have been guilty, of any offence or corrupt or illegal practice relating to elections which has been declared by Order in Council or by an Act of the Federal Legislature to be an offence or practice entailing disqualification for membership of the Legislature, unless such period has elapsed as may be specified in that behalf by the provisions of that Order or Act;

(e) if, whether before or after the establishment of the Federation, he has been convicted of any other offence by a Court in British India or in a State which is a Federated State and sentenced to transportation or to imprison men I for not less than two years, unless a period of five years, or such less period as the Governor-General, acting in his discretion, may allow in any particular case, has elapsed since his release;

(f) if, having been nominated as a candidate for the Federal or any Provincial Legislature or having acted as an election agent of any person so nominated, he has failed to lodge a return of election expenses within the time and in the manner required by any Order in Council made under this Act or by any Act of the Federal or the Provincial Legislature, unless five years have elapsed from the date by which the return ought to have been lodged or the Governor-General, acting in his discretion, has removed the disqualification:

Provided that a disqualification under paragraph (f) of this sub-section shall not take effect until the expiration of one month from the date by which the return ought to have been lodged or of such longer period as the Governor-General, acting in his discretion, may in any particular case allow.

(2) A person shall not be capable of being chosen a member of either Chamber while he is serving a sentence of transportation or of imprisonment for a criminal offence.

(3) Where a person who, by virtue of a conviction or a conviction and a sentence, becomes disqualified by virtue of paragraph (d) or paragraph (e) of sub-section (1) of this section is at the date of the disqualification a member of the Legislature, his seat shall, notwithstanding anything in this or the last preceding section, not become vacant by reason of the disqualification until three months have elapsed from the date thereof or, if within those three months an appeal or petition for revision, is brought in respect of the conviction or the sentence, until that appeal or petition is disposed of, but during any period during which his membership is preserved by this sub-section he shall not sit or vote.

(4) For the purposes of this section a person shall not be deemed to hold an office of profit under the Crown in India by reason only that—

(a) he is a minister either for the Federation or for a Province: or

(b) while serving a State, he remains a member of one of the services of the Crown in India and retains all or any of his rights as such.

27. If a person sits or votes as a member of .cither Chamber when he is not qualified or is disqualified for membership or thereof when he is prohibited from so doing by the provisions of sub-section (3) of the last preceding section, he shall be liable in respect of each day on which he so sits or votes to a penalty of five hundred rupees lo be recovered as a debt due to the [Federation].

(1) Subject to the provisions of this Act and lo the rules and standing orders regulating the procedure of the [Federal]" Legislature, there shall be freedom of speech in the Legislature, and no member of the Legislature shall be liable to any proceedings in any Court in respect of anything said or any vote given by him in the Legislature or any committee thereof, and no person shall be so liable in respect of the publication by or under the authority of "(cither Chamber of] the Legislature of any report, paper, votes or proceedings.

(2) In other respects, (no privileges of members of the [Chambers] shall be such as may from time to time be defined by Act of the Federal Legislature and, until so defined, shall be such were immediately before the establishment of the Federation enjoyed by members of the Indian Legislature.

(3) Nothing in any existing Indian Act, and, notwithstanding anything in the foregoing provisions of this section, nothing in this Act, shall be construed as conferring, or empowering the [Federal] Legislature to confer, on either Chamber or on both Chambers sitting together, or on any committee or officer of the Legislature, the status of the Court, or any punitive or disciplinary powers other than a power lo remove or exclude persons infringing the rules or standing orders, or otherwise behaving in a disorderly manner.

(4) Provision may be made by an Act of the [Federal]— "Legislature for the punishment, on conviction before a Court, of persons who refuse to give evidence or produce documents before a committee of a Chamber when duly required by the chairman of the committee so to do:

Provided that any such Act shall have effect subject to such rules for regulating the attendance before such committees of persons who are, or have been, in the service of the Crown in India, and safeguarding confidential matter from disclosure, as may be made by the Governor-General exercising his individual judgment.

(5) The provisions of sub-sections (1) and (2) of this section shall apply in relation to persons who by virtue of this Act

have the right to speak in, and otherwise take part in the proceedings of, [a Chamber] as they apply in relation to members of the Legislature.

29. Members of [either Chamber] shall be entitled to receive such salaries and allowances as may from time to time be determined by Act of the [Federal Legislature] and, until provision in that respect is so made allowances at such rates and upon such conditions as were immediately before the date of the establishment of the [Federation] applicable in the case of members of the Legislative Assembly of the Indian Legislature.

Legislative Procedure

30. (1) Subject to the special provisions of this Act with respect to financial Bills, a Bill may originate in cither Chamber.

(2) Subject lo the provisions of the next succeeding section, a Bill shall not be deemed to have been passed by the Chambers of the Legislature unless it has been agreed to by both Chambers, either without amendment or with such amendments only as are agreed to by both Chambers.

(3) A Bill pending in the Legislature shall not lapse by reason of the prorogation of the Chambers.

(4) A Bill pending in the Council of Stale which has not been passed by the Federal Assembly shall not lapse on dissolution of the Assembly.

(5) A Bill which is pending in the Federal Assembly or which having been passed by the Federal Assembly is pending in tht: Council of State shall, subject to the provisions of the next succeeding section, lapse on dissolution of the Assembly.

31. (1) If after a Bill has been passed by one Chamber and transmitted to the other Chamber—

(a) the Bill is rejected by the other Chamber; or

(b) the Chambers have family disagreed as to the amendments to be made in the Bill; or

(c) more than six months elapse from the dale of the reception of the Bill by the other Chamber without the Bill being presented to the Governor-General to his assent, the Governor-General may, unless the Bill has lapsed by reason of a dissolution of the Assembly, notify to the Chambers, by message if they are sitting or by public notification if they are not sitting, his intention to summon "them to meet in a joint sitting for the purpose of deliberating and voting on the Bill.

Provided that, if it appears to the Governor-General that the Bill relates to finance or to any matter which affects die discharge of his functions in so far as he is by or under this Act required to act in his discretion or to exercise his individual judgment, he may so notify the Chambers notwithstanding that there has been no rejection of or final disagreement as to the Bill notwithstanding that the said period of six months has not elapsed, if he is satisfied that there is no reasonable prospect of the Bill being presented to him for his assent without undue delay.

In reckoning any such period of six months as is referred to in this sub-section, no account shall be taken of any time during which the Legislature is prorogued or during which both Chambers are adjourned for more than four days.

(2) Where the Governor-General has notified his intention of summoning the Chambers to meet in a joint sitting, neither Chamber shall proceed further with the Bill but the Governor-General may at any time in the next section after the expiration of six months from the date of his notification summon the Chamber to meet in a joint sitting for the purpose specified in his notification and, if he does so, the Chambers shall meet accordingly:

Provided that, if it appears lo the Governor-General that the Bill is such a Bill as is mentioned in the proviso to sub-section (1) of this section, he may summon the Chambers to meet in a joint sitting for the purpose aforesaid at any date, whether in the same session or in the next session.

(3) The functions of the Governor-General under the provisos to the two last preceding sub-sections shall be exercised by him in his discretion.

(4) If at the joint sitting of the two Chambers the Bill, with such amendments, if any, as are agreed to in joint sitting,

is passed by a majority of the total number of members of both Chambers present and voting, it shall be deemed for the purposes of this Act to have been passed by both Chambers:

Provided that at a joint sitting—

(a) if the Bill, having been passed by one Chamber, has not been passed by the other Chamber with amendments and returned to the Chamber in which it originated, no amendment shall be proposed to the Bill other than such amendments (if any) .is are made necessary by the delay in the passage of the Bill; (b) if the Bill has been so passed and returned, only such amendments ns aforesaid shall be proposed to the iiill and such other amendments as are relevant to the matters with respect to which the Chambers have not agreed, and the decision of the person presiding as to the amendments which are admissible under this sub-section shall be final.

(5) A joint sitting may be held under this section and a bill passed thereat notwithstanding that dissolution of the Assembly has intervened since the Governor-General notified his intention to summon the Chambers to meet therein.

32. (1) When a Bill has been passed by the [Chambers,] it shall be presented to the Governor-General, and the Governor-General shall in his discretion declare either that he assents in His Majesty s name to the Bill, or that he withholds assent there from, [or that lie reserves the Bill for the signification of His Majesty's pleasure.]

Provided that the Governor-General may in his discretion return the Bill to the Chambers with a message requesting that they will reconsider the Bill or any specified precisions (hereof and, in particular, will consider tie desirability of introducing any such amendments as he may recommend in his message, and the Chambers shall reconsider the Bill accordingly.

(2) A Bill reserved for the signification of His Majesty's pleasure shall not become an Act of the Federal Legislature unless and until, within twelve months from the day on which it

was presented to the Governor-General, the Governor-General makes known by public notification that His Majesty has assented thereto.

(3) Any Act assented to by the Governor-General may be disallowed by His Majesty within twelve months from the day of the Governor-General's assent, and where any Act is so disallowed the Governor-General shall forthwith make the disallowance known by public notification, and as from the date of the notification the Act shall become void.

Procceder in Financial Matters.

33. (1) The Governor-General shall in respect of every financial year cause to be laid before [both Chambers] of the Federal Legislature, a statement of the estimated receipts and expenditure of the Federation for that year, in this Part of tliis Act referred to as the "annual financial statement".

(2) The estimates of expenditure embodied in the annual financial statement shall show separately-

(a) The sums required to meet expenditure described by this Act as expenditure charged upon. The revenues of the Federation; and

(b) the sums required to meet expenditure proposed lo be made from the revenues of the Federation, and shall distinguish expenditure on revenue account from other expenditure, [and indicate the sums, if any, which are included solely because the Governor-General has directed their inclusion as being necessary for the due discharge of any of his special responsibilities.]

(3) The following expenditure shall be expenditure charged on the revenues of the Federation:-

(a) the salary and allowances of the Governor-General and other expenditure relating to his office for which provision is required lo be made by Order in Council];

(b) debt charges for which the Federation is liable, including interest, sinking fund charges and redemption charges, and other expenditure relating to the raising of loans and the service and redemplion of debt:

(c) the salaries, and allowances of ministers, [of counsellors, of the financial adviser], of the advocate-general, of chief commissioners, [and of the staff of the financial adviser];

(d) the salaries, allowances and pensions payable to or in respect of judges of the Federal Court, and the pensions payable to or in respect of judges of any High Court;

(e) expenditure for the purpose of the discharge by the Governor-General of his functions with respect to defence and ecclesiastical affairs, his functions with respect to external affairs in so far as he is by or under this Act required in the exercise thereof to act in his discretion, his functions in or in relation to tribal areas, and his functions in relation to the administration of any territory in the direction and control of which he is under this Act required to act in his discretion: provided that the sum so charged in any year in respect of expenditure on ecclesiastical affairs shall not exceed forty-two lakhs of rupees, exclusive of pension charges;

(f) the sums payable to His Majesty under this Act out of the revenues of the Federation in respect of the expenses incurred in discharging the functions of the Crown in its relations with Indian Slates;

(g) any grants for purpose connected with the administration of any areas in a Province which are for the time being excluded areas;

(h) any sums required to satisfy any judgment, decree or award of any Court or arbitral tribunal;

(i) any other expenditure declared by this Act or any Act of the Federal Legislature to be so charged.

(4) Any question whether any proposed expenditure falls within a class of expenditure charged on the revenues of the. Federation shall be decided by the Governor-General in his discretion.

34. (1) So much of the estimate of expenditure as relates to expenditure charged upon the revenues of the Federation

shall not be submitted to the vote of the legislature, but nothing in this sub-section shall be construed as preventing the discussion in either Chamber of] the Legislature of any of those estimates other than estimates relating to Expenditure referred to in paragraph (a) [or paragraph (f)] of sub-section (3) of the preceding section.

(2) So much of the said estimates as relates to other expenditure shall he submitted in the form of demands for grants to the [Federal Assembly and thereafter to the Council of State, and either Chamber] shall have power to assent or to refuse to assent to any demand, or to assent to any demand subject to a reduction of the amount specified therein:

Provided that, where the Assembly have refused to assent to any demand, that demand shall not be submitted to the Council of State, unless the Governor-General so directs and, where the Assembly have assented to a demand subject to a reduction of the amount specified therein, a demand (or the reduced amount only shall be submitted to the Council of State, unless the Governor-General otherwise directs; and where, in either of the said cases, such a direction is given, the demand submitted to (he Council of State shall be for such amount, not being a greater amount than that originally demanded, as may be specified in the direction.

(3) If the Chambers differ with respect to any demand the Governor-General shall summon the two Chambers to meet; in a joint silting for the purpose of deliberating and voting on the demand as to which they disagree, and the decision of the majority of the member of both Chambers present and voting shall be deemed to be the decision of the two Chambers.

(4) No demand for a grant shall be made except on the recommendation of the Governor-General.

35. (1) The Governor-General shall authenticate by his signature a schedule specifying—

(a) the grants made by the [Chambers] under the last preceding section;

(b) the several sums required to meet the expenditure charged on the revenues of the Federation but not exceeding, in the case if any sum, the sum shown in the statement previously laid before the Legislature:

Provided that, if the Chambers have not assented to any demand for a giant or have assented subject to a reduction of the amount specified therein, the Governor-General may, if in his opinion the refusal or reduction would affect the due discharge of any of his special responsibilities, include in the schedule such additional amount, if any, not exceeding the amount of the rejected demand or the reduction, as the case may be, as appears to him necessary in order to enable him to discharge that responsibility.

(2) The schedule so authenticated shall be laid before [both Chambers] but shall not be open to discussion or vote therein.

(3) Subject to the provisions of the next succeeding section, no expenditure from the revenues of the [Federation] shall be deemed to be duly authorised unless it is specified in the schedule so authenticated.

36. If in respect of any financial year further expenditure from the revenues of the Federation becomes necessary over and above the expenditure herefore authorised for that year, the Governor-General shall cause to be laid before [both Chambers of] the [Federal] Legislature a supplementary statement showing the estimated amount of that expenditure, and the provisions of the preceding sections shall have effect in relation to that statement and that expenditure as they lave effect in relation to the annual financial statement and expenditure mentioned therein.

37. (1) A Bill or amendment making provision—

(a) for imposing or increasing any tax; or

(b) for regulating the borrowing of money or the giving of any guarantee by the Federal Government, or for amending the law with respect to any financial obligations undertaken or to be undertaken by the Federal Government; or

(c) for declaring any expenditure to be expenditure charged on the revenues of the Federation, or for increasing the amount of any such expenditure, shall not be introduced or moved except on the recommendation of the Governor-General, [and a Bill making such provision shall not be introduced in the Council of State.]

(2) A Bill or amendment shall not be deemed to make provision for any of the purposes aforesaid by reason only that it provides for the imposition of fines or other pecuniary penalties, or for the demand or payment of fees for licences or fees for services rendered.

(3) A Bill which, if enacted and brought into operation, would involve expenditure from the revenues of the [Federation] shall not be passed by [either Chamber] unless the Governor-General has recommended to [that Chamber the consideration of the Bill.]

Procedure generally

38. (1) [Each Chamber of the [Federal] Legislature may make rules for regulating, subject to the provisions of this Act, their procedure and the conduct of their business:

[Provided that as regards each Chamber the Governor-General shall in his direction, after consultation with the President or the Speaker, as the case may be, make rules.

(a) for regulating the procedure of, and the conduct of business in the Chamber in relation to any matter which affects the discharge of his functions in so far as he is by or under this Act required to act in his discretion or to exercise his individual judgment;

(b) for securing the timely completion of financial business;

(c) for prohibiting the discussion of, or the asking of question on, any matter connected with any Indian State, other than a matter with respect to which the Federal Legislature has power to make laws for that State, unless the Governor- General in his discretion is satisfied that the matter affects Federal interests or affects a British subject, and has given his consent to the matter being discussed or the question being asked;

(d) for prohibiting, save with the consent of the Governor-General in his discretion,—

(i) the discussion of, or the asking of questions on, any matter connected with relations between His Majesty or the Governor-General and any foreign State or Prince; or

(ii) the discussion, except in relation to estimates of expenditure, of, or the asking of questions on, any matter connected with the tribal areas or the administration of any excluded area; or

(iii) the discussion of, or the asking of questions on, any action taken in his discretion by the Governor-General in relation to the affairs of a Province; or

(iv) the discussion of, or the asking of questions on, the personal conduct of tbe Ruler of any Indian State, or of a member of the ruling family thereof; and, if and in so far as any rule so made by the Governor-General is inconsistent with any rule made by a Chamber, the rule made by the Governor-General shall prevail.

(2) The Governor-General, after consultation with the President of the Council of State and the Speaker of the Legislative Assembly, may make rules as to the procedure with respect to joint sittings of, and communications between, the two Chambers.

The said rules shall make such provision for the purposes specified in the proviso to the preceding sub-section as the Governor-General in his discretion may think fit.

(3) Until rules are made under this section, the rules of procedure and standing orders in force immediately before the establishment of the Federation with respect to the Indian Legislature shall have effect in relation to the Federal Legislature subject to such modifications and adaptations as may be made therein by the [Governor-General in his discretion].

(4) At a joint sitting of the two Chambers the President of the Council of State, or in his absence such person as may be determined by rules of procedure made under this section, shall preside.

39. All proceedings in the Federal Legislature shall be conducted in the English language:

Provided that the rules of procedure of each Chamber and the rules with respect to joint sittings shall provide for enabling persons unacquainted, or not sufficiently acquainted, wilh the English language to use another language.

40. (1) No discussion shall take place in the Federal Legislature with respect to the conduct of any judge of the Federal Court or a High Court in the discharge of his duties.

In this sub-section the reference to a High Court shall be construed as including a reference to any court in a Federated State which is a High Court for any of the purposes of Part IX of this Act.

(2) If the Governor-General in his discretion certifies that the discussion of a Bill Introduced or proposed to be introduced in the Federal. Legislature, or of any specified clause of a Bill, or of any amendment moved or proposed to be moved to a Bill, would affect the discharge of his special responsibility for the prevention of any grave menace to the peace or tranquillity of India or any part thereof, he may in his discretion direct that no proceedings, or no further proceedings, shall be taken in relation to the Bill, clause or amendment, and effect shall be given to the direction,

41. (1) The validity of any proceedings in the Federal Legislature shall not be called in question on the ground of any alleged irregularity of procedure.

(2) No officer or other member of the Legislature in whom powers are vested by or under this Act for regulating procedure or the conduct of business, or for maintaining order, in the Legislature shall be subject to the jurisdiction of any Court in respect of the exercise by him of those powers.

CHAPTER IV
LEGISLATIVE POWERS OF GOVERNOR-GENERAL

42. (1) If at any time: when the Federal Legislature is not in session the Governor-General is satisfied that circumstances exist which render it neessary for him to take immediate action, he may promulgate such ordinances as the circumstances appear to him to require:

Provided that the Governor-General —

(a) shall exercise his individual judgment as respects the promulgation of any ordinance under this section if a Bill containing the same provisions would under this Act have required his previous sanction to the introduction thereof into the Legislature; and

(b) shall not, without instructions from His Majesty, promulgate any such ordinance if he would have deemed it necessary to reserve a Bill containing the same provisions for the signification of His Majesty's pleasure thereon.

(2) An ordinance promulgated under this section shall have the same force and effect as an Act of the Federal Legislature assented to by the Governor-General, but every such ordinance —

(a) shall be laid before the Federal Legislature and shall cease to operate at the expiration of six weeks from the reassembly of the Legislature or, if before the expiration of that period resolulions disapproving it are passed by both Chambers, upon the passing of the second of those resolutions:

(b) shall be subject to the provisions of this Act relating to the power of His Majesty to disallow Acts as if it were an Act of the Federal Legislature assented to by the Governor-General ; and

(c) may be withdrawn at any time by the Governor-General.

(3) If and so far as an ordinance under this section makes any provision which the Federal Legislature would not under this Act be competent to enact, it shall be void.

43. (1) If at any time the Govenor-General is satisfied that circumstances exist which render it necessary for him to take immediate action for the purpose of enabling him satisfactorily to discharge his functions in so far as he is by or under this Act required in the exercise thereof to act in his discretion or ,to exercise his individual judgment, he may promulgate such ordinance as in his opinion the circumstances of the case require.

(2) An ordinance promulgated under this section shall continue in operation for such period not exceeding six months as may be specified therein, but may be a subsequent ordinance be extended for a further period not exceeding six months.

(3) An ordinance promulgated under this section shall have the same force and effect as an Act of the Federal legislature assented to by the Governor-General, but every such ordinance—

(a) shall be subject to the provisions of this Act relating to the power of His Majesty to disallow Acts as if it were an Act of the Federal Legislature assented to by the Governor-General;

(b) may be withdrawn at any time by ihe Governor-General; and

(c) if it is an ordinance extending previous ordinance for a further period, shall be communicated forthwith to the Secretary of State and shall be laid by him before each House of Parliament

(4) If and so far as an ordinance under this section makes any provision which the Federal Legislature would not under this Act be competent to enact, it shall be void.

(5) The functions of the Governor-General under this section shall be exercised by him in his discretion.

44. (1) If at any time it appears to the Governor-General that, for the purpose of enabling him satisfactorily to discharge his functions in so far as he is by or under this Act required in the exercise thereof to act in his discretion or to exercise his individual judgment, it is essential that provision should be made by legislation, he may by message to both of the

Legislature explain the circumstances which in his opinion render legislation essential, and either—

(a) enact forthwith, as a Govern or-General's Act, a Bill containing such provisions as he considers necessary; or

(b) attach to his message a draft of the Bill which he considers necessary.

(2) Where the Governor-General takes such action as is mentioned in paragraph (b) of the preceding sub-section, he may at any time after the expiration of one month enact, as a Governor-General's Act, the Bill proposed by him to the Chambers either in Ihe form of the draft communicated to them or owith such amendments as he deems necessary, but before so doing he shall consider any address which may have been presented to him within the said period by either Chamber with reference to the Bill or to amendments suggested to be made therein.

(3) A Governor-General's Act shall have the same force and effect, and shall be subject to disallowance in the same manner, as an Acf of the Federal Legislature assented to by the Governor-General and, if and in so far as a Governor-General's Act makes any provision which the Federal Legislature would not under this Act be competent to enact, it shall be void.

(4) Every Governor-General's Act shall be communicated forthwith to the Secretary of State and shall be laid by him before each House of Parliament.

(5) The functions of the Governor-General under this section shall be exercised by him in his discretion.

CHAPTER V
PROVISIONS IN CASE OF FAILURE OF CONSTITUTIONAL MACHINERY

45. If at any time the Governor-General is satisfied that a situation has arisen in which the governmnt of the Federation cannot be carried on in accordance with the provisions of this Act, he may by proclamation—

(a) declare that his functions shall be such extent as may be specified in the Proclamation be exercised by him in his discretion;

(b) assume to himself all or any of the powers vested in or exercisable by any Federal body or authority, and any such Proclamation may contain such incidental and consequential provisions as may appear to him to be necessary or desirable for giving effect to the objects of the Proclamation, including provisions for suspending in whole or in part the operation of any provisions of this Act relating to any Federal body or authority:

Provided that nothing in this sub-section shall authorise the Govenor-Gencral to assume to himself any of the powers vested in or exercisable by the Federal Court or to suspend, either in whole or in part, the operation pf any provision of this Act relating to the Federal Court.

(2) Any such Proclamation may be revoked or varied by a subsequent Proclamation.

(3) A Proclamation issued under this section—

(a) shall be communicated forthwith to the Secretary of State and shall be laid by him before each House of Parliament;

(b) unless it is a Proclamation revoking a previous Proclamation, shall cease to operate at the expiration of six months:

Provided that, if and so often as a resolution approving the continuance in force of such a Proclamation is passed by both Houses of Parliament, the Proclamation shall, unless revoked, continue in force for a further period of twelve months from the date on which under this sub-section it would otherwise have ceased to operate.

(4) If at any time the government of the Federation has for a continuous period of three years been carried on under and by virtue of a Proclamation issued under this section, then, at the expiration of that period, the Proclamation shall cease to have effect and the government of the Federation shall be carried on in accordance with the other provisions of this Act, subject to any amendment thereof winch

Parliament may deem it necessary to make, but nothing in this sub-section shall be construed as extending the power of Parliament to make amendments in this Act without affecting the accession of a State.

(5) If the Governor-General, by a Proclamation under this section, assumes to himself any power of the Federal Legislature to make laws, made by him in the exercise of that power shall, subject to the terms thereof, continue to have effect until two years have elapsed from the date on which the Proclamation ceases to have effect, unless sooner repealed or re-enacted by Act of the appropriate Legislature, and any reference in this Act to Federal Acts, Federal laws, or Acts or laws of the Federal Legislature shall be construed as including a reference to such a law.

(6) The functions of the Governor-General under this section shall be exercised by him in his discretion.

PART III
THE GOVERNORS' PROVINCES

CHAPTER I
THE PROVINCES

46. (1) Subject to the provisions of the next succeeding section with respect to Berar, the following shall be Governors' Provinces, that is to say, Madras, Bombay,[Bengal, the United Provinces, the Punjab, Bihar, the Central Provinces and Berar, Assam, the North-West Frontier Province, Orissa, Sind], and such other Governors' Provinces as may be created under this Act.

(2) Burma shall cease to be part of India.

(3) In this Act the expression "Province" means, unless the context otherwise requires, a Governor's Province, and "Provincial" shall be constructed accordingly.

47. Whereas certain territory (in the Act referred to as "Bearar") is under the sovereignty of His Exalted Highness the Nizam of Hyderabad, but is at the date of the passing of this Act, by virtue of certain agreements subsisting between His Majesty and His Exalted Highness, administered together wiih the Central Provinces.

And whereas it is in contemplation that an agreement shall be concluded between His Majesty and His Exalted Highness whereby, notwithstanding the continuance of the sovereignty of His Exalted Highness over Berar, the Central Province's and Berar may be governed together as one Governor's Province under this Act by the name of the Central Provinces and Berar:

Now, therefore—

(1) While any such agreement is in force—

(a) Berar and the Central Provinces shall, notwithstanding the continuance of the sovereignty of His Exalted Highness, be deemed to be one Governor's Province by the name of the Central Provinces and Berar;

(b) any reference in this Act or in any other Act to British India shall be construed as a reference to British India and Berar, and any reference in this Act to subjects of His Majesty shall, except for the purposes of any oath of allegiance, be deemed to include a reference to Berari subjects of His Exalted Highness :

(c) any provision made under this Act with respect to the qualifications of the voters for the Provincial Legislature of the Central Provinces and Berar, or the voters for the Council of State, shall be such as to give effect to any provisions with respect to those matters contained in the agreement.

(2) If no such agreement is concluded, or if such an agreement is concluded but subsequently ceases to have effect, references in this Act to the Central Provinces and Berar shall be construed as references to the Central Provinces, and His Majesty in Council may make such consequential modifications in the provisions of this Act relating to the Central Provinces as he thinks proper.

CHAPTER II
THE PROVINCIAL EXECUTIVE

The Governor

(1) The Governor of a Province is appointed by His Majesty by a Commission under the Royal Sign Manual.

(2) The provisions of the Third Schedule to this Act shall have effect with respect to the salary and allowances of the Governor and the provision to be made for enabling him to discharge conveniently and with dignity the duties of his office.

49. (1) The executive authority of a Province shall be exercised on behalf of His Majesty by the Governor, either directly or through officers subordinate to him, but nothing in this section shall prevent the Federal or the Provincial Legislature from conferring functions upon subordinate authorities, or be deemed to transfer to the Governor any functions conferred by any existing Indian law on any court, judge or officer or any local or other authority.

(2) Subject to the provisions of this Act, the executive authority of each Province extends to the matters with respect to which the Legislature of the Province has power to make laws.

Administration of Provincial Affair

50. (1) There shall he a'council of ministers to aid and advice the Governor in the exercise of his functions except in so far as he is by or under this Act required to exercise his functions or any of them in his discretion:

Provided that nothing in this sub-section shall be construed as preventing the Governor from exercising his individual judgment in any case where by or under this Act he is requited so to do.

(2) The Governor in his discretion may preside at meetings of the council of ministers.

(3) If any Question arises whether any matter is or is not a matter as respects which, the -Governor is by or under this Act required to act in his discretion or to exercise his individual judgment, the decision of the Governor in his discretion shall be final, and the validity of anything done by the Governor shall not be called in question on the ground that he ought or ought not to have acted in his discretion, or ought or ought not to have exercised his individual judgment.]

51. (1) The Governor's ministers shall be chosen and summoned by him, shall be sworn as members of the council, and shall hold office during his pleasure.

(2) A minister who for any period of six consecutive months is not a member of the Provincial Legislature shall at the expiration of that pericd cease to be a minister.

(3) The salaries of ministers shall be such as the Provincial Legislature may from time to time by Act determine, and, until the Provincial Legislature so determine, shall he determined by the Governor:

Provided that the salary of a minister shall not be varied during his term of office.

(4) The question whether any, and, if so what, advice was tendered by ministers to the Governor shall not be inquired into in any Court.

(5) The functions of the Governor under this section with respect to the choosing and summoning and the dismissal of ministers, and with respect to the determination of their salaries, shall be exercised by him in his discretion.

52. (1) In the exercise of his functions the Governor shall have the following special responsibilities, that is to say:—

(a) the prevention of any grave menace to the peace or tranquility of the Province or any part thereof;

(b) the safeguarding of the legitimate interests of minorities:

(c) the securing to, and to the dependants of, persons who are or have been members of the public services of any rights, provided or preserved for them by or under this Act and the safeguarding of their legitimate interests;

(d) the securing in the sphere of executive action of the purposes which the provisions of chapter III of Part V of this Act are designed to secure in relation to legislation;

(e) the securing of the peace and good government of areas which by or under the provisions of this Part of this Act are declared to be partially excluded areas;

(f) the protection of the rights of any Indian State and the rights and dignity of the Ruler thereof; and

(g) the securing of the execution of orders or directions lawfully issued io him under Part VI of this Act by the Governor-General in his discretion.

(2) The Governor of the Central Provinces and Berar shall also have die special responsibility of securing that a reasonable share of the revenues of any Province is expended in or for the benefit of Berar; the Governor of any Province which includes an excluded area shall also have the special responsibility of securing that the due discharge of his functions in respect of excluded areas is not prejudiced or impeded by any course of action taken with respect to any other matter; any Governor who is discharging any functions are agent for the Governor-General shall also have the special responsibility of securing that the due discharge of those functions is not prejudiced or impeded by any course of action taken with respect to any other matter, and the Governor of Sind shall also have the special responsibility of securing the proper administration of the Lloyd Barrage and Canals Scheme.

(3) If and in so far as any special responsibility of the Governor is involved, he shall in the exercise of his functions, exercise his individual judgment as to the action to be taken.

53. (1) The Secretary of State shall lay before Parliament the draft of any Instructions (including any Instructions amending or revoking Instructions previously issued) which it is proposed to recommend His Majesty issue to the Governor of a Province, and no further proceedings shall be taken in relation thereto except in pursuance of an address presented to His Majesty by both Houses of Parliament praying that the Instructions may be issued.

(2) The validity of anything done by the Governor of a Province shall not be called in question on the ground that it was done otherwise than in accordance with any Instrument of Instructions issued to him.

54. (1) In so far as the Governor of a Province is by or under this Act required to act in his discretion or to exercise his

individual judgment, he shall be under the general control of, and comply with such particular directions, if any, as may from time to time be given to him by the Governor-General in his discretion, but the validity of anything done by a Governor shall not be called in question on the ground that it was done otherwise than in accordance with the provisions of this section.

(2) Before giving any directions under this section, the Governor-General shall satisfy himself that nothing in the directions requires the Governor to act in any manner inconsistent with any Instrument of Instructions issued to the Governor by His Majesty.

55 (1) The Governor of each Province shall appoint a person, being a person qualified to be appointed a judge of a High Court, to be Advocate-General for the Province.

(2) It shall be the duty of the Advocate-General to give advice to the Provincial Government upon such legal matters, and to perform such other duties of a legal character, as may from time to time be referred or assigned him by the Governor.

(3) The Advocate-General shall hold office during the pleasure of the Governor, and shall receive such remuneration as the Governor may determine.

(4) In exercising his powers with respect to the appointment and dismissal of the Advocate-General and with respect to the detenuination of his remuneration, the Governor shall exercise his individual judgment.

56. Where it is proposed that the Governor of a Province should be virtue of any powers vested in him make or amend, or approve the making or amendment of any rules, regulations or orders relating to any police force whether civil or military, be shall exercise his individual judgment with respect to the proposal, unless it appears to him that the proposal does not relate to or affect the organisation or discipline of that force,

57. (1) If it appears to the Governor of a Province that the peace or tranquillity of the Province is endangered by the operations of any persons committing, or conspiring, preparing or attempting to commit, crimes of violence which, in the opinion of the Governor, are intended to overthrow

the government as by law established the Governor may, if he thinks, that the circumstances of the case require him so to do for the purpose of combating those operations, direct that his functions shall, to such extent as may be specified in the direction, be exercised by him in his discretion and, until otherwise provided by a subsequent direction of the Governor, those functions shall to that extent be exercised by him accordingly.

(2) While any such direction is in force, the Governor may authorise an official to speak in and otherwise take part in the proceedings of the Legislature, and any official so authorised may speak and take part accordingly in the proceedings of the Chamber of the Legislature any joint sitting of ihe Chambers, and any committee of the Legislature of which he may be named a member by the Governor, but shall not be entitled to vote.

(3) The functions of the Governor under this section shall be exercised by him in his discretion.

(4) Nothing in this section affects the special responsibility of the Governor for the prevention of any grave menace to the peace or tranquillity of the Province or any part thereof.

58. The Governor in his discretion shall make rules for securing that no records or information relating to the sources from which information has been or may be obtained with respect to the operations of persons committing, or conspiring, preparing, or attempting to commit, such crimes as are mentioned in the last preceding section, shall be disclosed or given —

(a) by any member of any police force in the Province to another member of that force except in accordance with directions of the Inspector General of Police or Commissioner of Police, as the case may be, or to any other person except in accordance with directions of the Governor in his discretion; or

(b) by any other person in the service of the Crown in the Province to any person except in accordance with directions of the Governor in his discretion.

59. (1) All executive action of the Government of a Province shall be expressed to be taken in the name of the Governor.

(2) Orders and other instruments made and executed in the name of the Governor shall be authenticated in such manner as may be specified in rules to be made by the Governor, and the validity of an order or instrument which is so authenticated still not be called in question on the ground that it is not an order or instrument made or executed by the Governor.\

(3) The Governor shall make rules for the more convenient transaction of the business of the Provincial Government, and for the allocation among ministers of the said business [in so far as it is not business with respect to which the Governor is by or under this Act required to act in his discretion].

(4) The rules shall include provisions requiring ministers and secretaries to Government to transmit to the Governor all such information with respect to the business of the Provincial Government as may be specified in the rules, or as the Governor may otherwise require to be so transmitted, and in particular requiring a minister to bring to the notice of the Governor, and the appropriate secretary to bring to the notice of the minister concerned and of the Governor, any matter under consideration by him which involves, or appears to him likely to involve, any special responsibility of the Governor.

(5) In the discharge of his functions under sub-section (2), (3) and (4) of this section the Governor shall act in his discretion after consultation with his ministers.

CHAPTER III
THE PROVINCIAL LEGISLATURE

General

60 (1) There shall for every Province be a Legislature which shall consist of His Majesty, represented by the Governor, and

(a) in the Provinces of Madras; Bombay, [Bengal] the United Provinces, Bihar [and Assam], two Chambers;

(b) in other Provinces, one Chamber.

(2) Where there are two Chambers of a Provincial Legislature, they shall be known respectively as the Legislative Council

and the Legislative Assembly, and where there is only one Chamber, the Chamber shall be known as the Legislative Assembly.

61. (1) The Composition of the Chamber of Chambers of the Legislature of a Province shall be such as is specified in relation to that Province in the Fifth Schedule to this Act.

(2) Every Legislative Assembly of every Province, unless sooner dissolved, shall continue for five years from the date appointed for their first meeting and no longer, and the expiration of the said period of five years shall operate as dissolution of the Assembly.

(3) Every Legislative Council shall be a permanent body not subject to dissolution but as near as may be one-third of the members thereof shall retire in every third year in accordance with the provision in that behalf made in relation to the Province under the said Fifth Schedule. .

62. (1) The Chamber or Chambers of each Provincial Legislature shall be summoned to meet once at least in every year, and twelve months shall not intervene between their last sitting in one session and the date appointed for their first sitting in the next session.

(2) Subject to the provisions of this section, the Governor may in his discretion from time to time—

(a) summon the Chambers or either Chamber to meet at such time and place as he thinks fit;

(b) prorogue the Chamber or Chambers;

(c) dissolve the Legislative Assembly.

[(3) The Chamber or Chambers shall be summoned to meet for the first session of the Legislature on a day not later than six months after the commencement of this Part of this Act.]

63. (1) The Governor may in his discretion address the Legislative Assembly or in the case of a Province having a Legislative Council, either Chamber of the Provincial or both Chambers assembled together, and may for that purpose require the attendance of members.

(2) The Governor may in his discretion send messages to the Chamber or Chambers of the Provincial Legislature, whether with respect to a Bill then pending in the Legislature or otherwise, and a Chamber to whom any message is so sent shall with all convenient dispatch consider any matter which they are required by the message to take into consideration.

64. Every minister and the Advocate-General shall have the right to speak in, and otherwise take part in the proceeding of, the Legislative Assembly of the Province or, in the case of a Province having a Legislative Council, both Chambers and any joint sitting of the Chambers, and to speak in, and otherwise take part in the proceedings of, any committee of the Legislature of which he may be named a member, but shall not, by virtue of the section, be entitled to vote.

65. (1) Every Provincial Legislative Assembly shall as soon as may be, choose two members of the Assembly to be respeciively Speaker and Deputy Speaker thereof and, so often as the office of Speaker or Deputy Speaker becomes vacant, the Assembly shall choose another member to be Speaker or Deputy Speaker, PS the case may be.

(2) A member holding office as Speaker or Deputy Speaker of an Assembly shall vacate his office if he ceases to be member of the Assembly, may at any time resign his office by writing under his hand addressed to the Governor, and may be removed from his office by a resolution of the Assembly passed by a majority of all the then members of the Assembly; but no resolution for the purpose of this sub-section shall be moved unless at least fourteen days notice has been given of the intention to move the resolution:

Provided that, whenever the Assembly is dissolved, the Speaker shall not vacate his office until immediately before the first meeting of the Assembly after the dissolution.

(3) While the office of Speaker is vacant, the duties of the office shall be performed by the Deputy Speaker or, if the office of Deputy Speaker is also vacant, by such member of the Assembly as the Governor may in his discretion appoint for the purpose, and during any absence of the Speaker from any sitting of the Assembly the Deputy

Speaker or, if he is also absent, such person as may be determined by the rules of procedure of the Assembly, or, if no such person is present, such other person as may be determined by the Assembly, shall act as Speaker.

(4) There shall be paid to the Speaker and the Deputy Speaker of the Legislative Assembly such salaries as may be respectively fixed by Act of the Provincial Legislature and, until provision in that behalf is so made, such salaries as the Governor may determine.

(5) In the case of a Province having a Legislative Council, the foregoing provisions of this section [other than the provision to sub-section (2) thereof] shall apply in relation to the Legislative Council as they apply in relation to the Legislative Assembly, with the substitution of the titles "President" and "Deputy President" for the titles "Speaker" and "Deputy Speaker" respectively, and with the substitution of references to the council for references to the Assembly.

66. (1) Save as in this Act otherwise expressly provided, all questions in a Chamber, or a joint sitting of two Chambers, of a provincial Legislature shall be determined by a majority of votes of the members present and voting other than the Speaker or President, or person acting as such.

The Speaker or President, or person acting as such shall not vote in the first instance, but shall have and exercise a casting vote in the case of an equality of votes.

(2) A Chamber of a Provincial Legislature shall have power to act notwithstanding any vacancy in the membership thereof, and any proceedings in a Provincial Legislature shall be valid notwithstanding that it is discovered, subsequently that some person who was not entitled so to do, sat or voted or otherwise look part in the proceedings.

(3) If at any time during a meeting of a Provincial Legislative Assembly less than one-sixth of the total number of members of the Chamber are present, or if at any time during a meeting of a Provincial Legislative Council less than ten members are present, it shall be the duty of the Speaker or President or person acting as such either to adjourn the Chamber, or to suspend the meeting until at least one-sixth

of the members, or, as the case may be, at least ten members, are present. Provisions as to Members of Legislatures.

67. Every member of a Provincial Legislative Assembly or Legislative Council shall, before taking his seat, make and subscribe before the Governor, or some person appointed by him, on oath according to that one of the forms set out in the Fourth Schedule to this Act which the member accepts as appropriate in his case.

68. (1) No person shall be a member of both chambers of a Provincial Legislature and rules made by the Governor exercising his individual judgment shall provide for the vacation by a person who is chosen a member of both Chambers of his seat in one Chamber or the other.

[(2) No person shall be a member both of the Federal Legislature and of a Provincial Legislature and if a person is chosen a member both of the Federal Legislature and of a Provincial Legislature, then, at the expiration of such period as may be specified in rules made by the Governor of the Province exercising his individual judgment, that person's seat in the Provincial Legislature shall become vacant, unless he has previously resigned his seat in the Federal Legislature.]

(3) If a member of a Chamber—

(a) becomes subject to any of the disqualifications mentioned in sub-section (1) of the next succeeding section; or

(b) by writing under his hand addressed to the Governor resigns his seat, his seat shall thereupon become vacant.

(4) If for sixty days a member of a Chamber is without permission of the Chamber absent from all meetings thereof the Chamber may declare his seat vacant:

Provided that in competing the said period of sixty days no account shall be taken of any period during which the Chamber is prorogued, or is adjourned for more than four consecutive days.

69. (1) A person shall be disqualified for being chosen as, and for being, a member of a Provincial Legislative Assembly or Legislative Council—

(a) if he holds any office of profit under the Crown in India, other than an office declared by Act of the Provincial Legislature not to disqualify its holder;

(b) if he is an unsound mind and stands so declared by a competent court

(c) if he is an undischarged insolvent;

(d) if, whether before or after the commencement of this Part of this Act, he has been convicted or has, in proceedings for questioning the validity or regularity of election, been found to have been guilty, of any offence or corrupt or illegal practice relating to elections which has been declared by Order in Council or by an Act of the Provincial Legislature, to be an offence or practice entailing disqualification fcr membership of the Legislature, unless such period has elapsed as may be specified in that behalf if the provisions of that Order or Act;

(e) if, [whether before or after the commencement of this Part of this Act], he has been convicted of any other offence [by a Court in British India or in a State which is a Federated State] and sentenced to transportation or to imprisonment for not less than two years, unless a period of five years, or such less period as the Governor, acting in his discretion may allow in any particular case, has elapsed since his release;

(f) if, having been nominated as a candidate for the Federal or any Provincial Legislature or having acted as an election agent of any person so nominated he has failed to lodge a return of election expenses within the time and in the manner required by any Order in Council made under this Act or by any Act of the [Federal] or the Provincial Legislature, unless five years have elapsed from the date by which the return ought to have been lodged or the Governor, acting in his discretion, has removed the disqualification;

Provided that a disqualification under paragraph (f) of this sub-section shall not take effect until the expiration of one month from the date by which the return ought to have been lodged or of such longer period as the Governor, acting in his discretion, may in any particular case allow.

(2) A person shall not be capable of being chosen a member of a Chamber of a Provincial Legislature while he is serving a sentence of transporation or of imprisonment for a criminal offence.

(3) Where a person who, by virtue of a conviction or a conviction and a sentence, becomes disqualified by virtue of paragraph (d) or paragraph (e) of sub-section (1) of this section is at the date of the disqualification a member of a Chamber, his seat shall, notwithstanding anything in this or the last preceding section, not become vacant by reason of the disqualification until three months have elapsed from the date thereof or, if within those three months an appeal or petition for revision is brought in respect of the conviction or the sentence, until that appeal or petition is disposed of, but during any period which his membership is preserved by this sub-ection, he shall not sit or vote.

(4) For the purpose of this section a person shall not be deemed to hold an office of profit under the Crown in India by reason only that he is a minister either for the Federation or for a Province.

70. If a person sits or votes as a member of a Provincial Legislative Assembly or Legislative Council when he is not qualified or is disqualified for membership thereof, or when he is prohibited from so doing by the provisions of sub-section (3) of the last preceding section, he shall be liable in respect of each day an which he so sits or votes to a penalty of five hundred rupees to be recovered as a debt due to the Province.

71. (1) Subject to the provisions of this Act and to rules and standing orders regulating the procedure of the Legislature there shall be freedom of speech in every Provincial Legislature, and no member of the legislature shall be liable to any proceeding in any Court in respect of anything said

or any vote given by him in the Legislature or any committee thereof, and no person shall be so liable in respect of the publication by or under the authority of a Chamber of such a Legislature of any report, paper, votes or proceedings.

(2) In other respects the privileges of members of a Chamber of a Provincial Legislature shall be such as may from time to time be defined by Act of the Provincial Legislature, and. until so defined, shall be such as were immediately before the commencement of this Part of this Act enjoyed by members of the Legislative Council of the Province.]

(3) Nothing in any existing Indian law, and, notwithstanding anything in the foregoing provisions of this section, nothing in this Act, shall be construed as conferring, or empowering any Legislature to confer on a Chamber thereof or on both Chambers sitting together or any committee or officer of the Legislature, the status of a court, or any punitive or disciplinary powers other than the power to remove or exclude persons infringing, the rules or standing orders, or otherwise behaving in a disorderly manner.

(4) Provision may be made by an Act of the Provincial Legislature for the punishment, on conviction before a Court, of persons who refuse to give evidence or produce documents before a committee of a Chamber when duly required by the chairman of a committee so to do:

Provided that any such Act shall have effect subject to such rules for regulating the attendance before such committees of persons who are, or have been, in the service of the Crown in India, and safeguarding confidential matter from disclosure, as may be made by the Governor exercising his individual judgment,

(5) The provisions of sub-sections (1) and (2) of this section shall apply in relation to persons who by virtue of this Act have the righs to speak in and otherwise take part in the proceedings of a Chamber as they apply in relation to members of the Legislature.

72. Members of Provincial Legislative Assemblies and Legislative Councils shall be entitled to receive such salaries and allowances as may from time to time be determined by Act of the Provincial

Legislature [and until provision in that respect is so made, allowances at such rates and upon such conditions as were immediately before the commencement of this Part of this Act applicable in the case of members of the Legislative Council of the Province.]

Legislative Procedure.

73. (1) Subject to the special provisions of this Part of this Act with respect to financial Bills, a Bill may originate in either Chamber of the legislature of a Province which has a Legislative Council.

(2) A Bill pending in the Legislature of a Province shall not lapse by reason of the prorogation of the Chamber or Chambers thereof.

(3) A Bill pending in the Legislative Council of a Province which has not been passed by the Legislative Assembly shall not lapse on dissolution of the Assembly.

(4) A Bill which is pending in the Legislative Assembly of a Province, or which having been passed by the legislative Assembly is pending in the Legislative Council, shall lapse on dissolution of the Assembly.

74. (1) Subject to the provisions of this section, a Bill shall not be deemed to have been passed by the Chambers of the Legislature of a Province having a Legislative Council unless it has been agreed to by both Chambers, either without amendments or with such amendments only as are agreed to by both Chambers.

(2) If a Bill which has been passed by the Legislative Assembly and transmitted to the Legislative Council is not, before the expiration of twelve months from its reception by the Council, presented to the Governor for his assent, the Governor may summon the Chambers to meet in a joint sitting for the purpose of deliberating and voting on the Bill:

Provided that, if it appears to the Governor that the Bill relates to finance [or affects the discharge of any of his special responsibilities], he may summon the Chambers to meet in a joint sitting for the purpose aforesaid notwithstanding that the said period of twelve months has not elapsed.

[The functions of the Governor under the proviso to this sub-section shall be exercised by him in his discretion.]

(3) If at a joint sitting of the two Chambers summoned in accordance with ihe provisions of this section the Bill, with such amendments if any, as are agreed to in joint sitting, is passed by a majority of the total number of members of both Chambers present and voting it shall be deemed for the purposes of this Act to have been passed by both Chambers:

Provided that at a joint sitting —

(a) unless the Bill has been passed by the Legislative Council with amendments and returned to the Legislative Assembly, no amendment shall be proposed to the Bill other than such amendments, if any, as are made necessary by the delay in the passage of the Bill;

(b) if the Bill has been so passed and returned by the Legislative Council, only such amendments as aforesaid shall be proposed to the Bill and such other amendments as are relevant to the matters with respect to which the Chambers have not agreed, and the decision of the person presiding as to, the amendments which are admissible under this sub-section shall be final.

75. A Bill which has been passed by the Provincial Legislative Assembly or, in the case of a Province having a Legislative Council, has been passed by both Chambers of the Provincial Legislature, shall be presented to the Governor, and the Governor in his discretion shall declare either that he assents in His Majesty's name to the Bill, or that he withhold assent therefrom, or that he reserves the Bill for the consideration of the Governor-General:

Provided that the Governor may in his discretion return the Bill together with a message requesting that the Chamber or Chambers will consider the Bill or any specified provisions thereof and, in particular, will consider the diserability of introducing any such amendments as he may recommend in his message and, when a Bill is so returned, the Chamber or Chambers shall reconsider it accordingly.

76. (1) When a Bill is reserved by a Governor for the consideration of the Governor-General, the Governor-General shall in his discretion declare, either that he assents in His Majesty's name to the Bill, or that he withholds assents therefrom, [or that he reserves the Bill for the signification of his Majesty's pleasure thereon]

Provided that the Governor-General may, if be in his discretion thinks fit, direct the Governor to return the Bill to the Chamber, or, as the case may be, the Chambers, of the Provincial Legislature together with such a message as in mentioned in the proviso to the last preceding section and, when a Bill is so returned, the Chamber or Chambers shall reconsider it accordingly and, if it is again passed by them with or without amendment, it shall be presented again to the Governor-General for his consideration.

[(2) A Bill reserved for the signification of His Majesty's pleasure shall not become an Act of the Provincial Legislature unless and until, within twelve months from the day on which it was presented to the Governor, the Governor makes know by public notification that His Majesty has assented thereto].

[77. Any Act assented to by the Governor or the Governor-General may be disallowed by His Majesty within twelvefrom the date of the assent, and where any Act is so disallowed the Governor shall forthwith make the disallowance known by public notification and as from the date of the notification the Act shall become void.]

Procedure in Financial matters.

78. (1) The Governor shall in respect of every financial year cause to be laid before the Chamber or Chambers of the Legislature of statement of the estimated receipts and expenditure of the Province for that year, in this Part of this Act referred to as the "annual financial statement".

(2) The estimates of expenditure embodied in the annual financial statement shall show separately—

(a) The sums required to meet expenditure described by this Act as expenditure charged upon the revenues of the Province; and

(b) the sums required to meet other expenditure proposed to be made from the revenues of the Province, and shall distinguish expenditure on revenue account [from other expenditure, and indicate the sums, if any, which are included solely because ihe Governor has directed their inclusion as being necessary for the due discharge of any of his special responsibilities.]

(3) The following expenditure shall be expenditure charged on sthe ri-venues of each Province—

(a) the salary and allowances of the Governor and other expenditure relating to his office for which provision is [required to be made by Order in Council]

(b) debt charges for which the Province is liable, including interest, sinking fund charges and redemption charges, and Other expenditure relating to the raising of loans and the service and redemption of debt;

(c) the salaries and allowances of ministers, and of the Advocate-General:

(d) expenditure in respect of the salaries and allowances of judges of any High Court;

(e) any sums required to satisfy any judgment, decree or award of any court or arbitral tribunal;

(f) any other expenditure declarcd by this Act or any Act of the Provincial Legislature to be so charged.

[(4) Any question whether any proposed expenditure falls within a class of expenditure charged on the revenues of the Province shall be decided by the Governor in his discretion.]

79. (1) So much of the estimates of expenditure as relates to expenditure charged upon the revenues of Provincial not be submitted to the vote of the Legislative Assembly, but nothing in this sub-section shall be construed as preventing the discussion in the Legislature of those estimates, other than estimates relating to expenditure referred to in paragraph (a) of sub-section (3) of the last preceding section.

(2) So much of the said estimates as relates to other expenditure shall be submitted, in the form of demands for grants, to

the Legislative Assembly, and the Legislative Assembly shall have power to assent, or to refuse to assent, to any demand, or to assent to a demand subject to a reduction of the amount specified therein.

(3) No demand for a grant shall be made except on the recommendation of the Governor.

80. (1) The Governor shall authenticate by his signature as schedule specifying—

(a) The grants made by the Assembly under the last proceeding section;

(b) the several sums required to meet the expenditure charged or the revenues of the Province but not exceeding, in the case of any sum, the sum shown in the statement previously laid before the Chamber or Chambers:

[Provided that, if the Assembly have refused to assent to any demand for grant or have assented to such a demand subject to a reduction of the Amount specified therein, the Governor may, if in his opinion the refusal or reduction would affect the due discharge of any of his special responsibilities, include in ihe schedule such additional amount, if any, not exceeding the amount of the rejected demand or the reduction, as the case may be, as appears to him necessary in order to enable him to discharge that responsibility].

(2) The schedule so authenticated shall be laid before the Assembly but shall not be open to discussion or vote in the Legislature.

(3) Subject to the provisions of the next succeeding section, no expenditure from the revenue of the province shall be deemed to be duly authorised unless it is specified in the schedule so authenticated.

81. If in respect of any financial year further expenditure from the revenues of the Province becomes necessary over and over the expenditure authorized for that year, the Governor shall cause to be laid before the Chambers a supplementary statement showing the estimated amount of the expenditure, and the provisions of

the preceding sections shall have effect in relation to that statement and that expenditure as they have effect in relation to the annual financial statement and the expenditure mentioned therein.

82. (1) A Bill or amendment making provision.

(a) for imposing or increasing any tax; or

(b) for regulating the borrowing of money or the giving of any guarantee by the Province, or for amending the law with respect to any financial obligations undertaken or to be undertaken by the Province; or

(c) for declaring any expenditure to be expenditure charged on the revenues of the Province, or for increasing the amount of any such expenditure, shall not be introduced or moved except the recommendation of the Governor and a bill making such provision shall not be introduced in a Legislative Council.

(2) A Bill or amendment shall not be deemed to make provision for any of the purposes aforesaid by reason only that it provides for the imposition of fines or other pecuniary penalties or for the demand and payment of fees for licences or fees for services rendered.

(3) *A* Bill which, if enacted and brought into operation, would involve expenditure from the revenues of a Province shall not be passed by a Chamber of the Legislatures unless the Governor has recommended to that Chamber the consideration of the Bill.

[83. (1) If in the last complete financial year for the commencement of this Part of this Act a grant for the benefit of the Anglo-Indian and European communities or either of them was included in the grants made in any Province for education, then in each subsequent financial year, not being a year in which the Provincial Legislative Assembly otherwise resolve by a majority which includes at least three-fourths of the members of the Assembly, a giant shall be made for the benefit of the said community or communities not less in amount than the average of the grants made for its or their benefit in the ten financial years ending on the thirty first day of March, nineteen hundred and thirty-three:

Provided that, if in any financial year the total grant for education in the Province is less than the average of the total grams for education in the Province in the said ten financial years, then, whatever fraction the former may be of the latter, any grant made under this sub-section in that financial year for the benefit of the said community or communities need not exceed that fraction of the average of the grants made for its or their benefit in.the said ten financial years.

In computing for the purposes of this sub-section the amount of any grants, grants for capital purposes shall be included.

(2) The provisions of this section shall cease to have effect in a Province if at any time the Provincial Legislative Assembly resolve by a majority which includes at least three-fourths of the members of the Assembly that those provisions shall cease to have effect.

(3) Nothing in this section affects the special responsibility of the Governor of a Province for the safeguarding of the legitimate interests of minorities].

Procedure generally.

84. (1) A Chamber of a Provincial legislature may make rules for regulating, subject to the provisions of this Act, their procedure and the conduct of their business:

[Provided that, as regards either a Legislative Assembly or a Legislative Council, the Governor shall in his discretion, after consultation with the Speaker or the President, as the case may be, make rules—

(a) for regulating the procedure of, and the conduct of business in, the Chamber in relation to any matter which affects the discharge of his functions in so far as he is by or under this Act required to act in his discretion or to exercise his individual judgment;

(b) for securing the timely completion of financial business;

(c) for prohibiting the discussion of or the asking of questions on, any matter connected with any Indian

State unless the Governor in his discretion is satisfied that the matter affects the interests of the Provincial Government or of a British subject ordinarily resident in the Province, and has given his consent to the matter being discussed, or to the question being asked;

(d) for prohibiting, save with the consent of the Governor in his discretion—

(i) the discussion of or the asking of questions on any matter connected with relations between His Majesty or the Governor-General and any foreign State or Prince; or

(ii) the discussion, except in relation to estimates of expenditure, of or the asking of questions on, any matters connected with the tribal areas or arising out of or affecting the administration of an excluded area; or

(iii) the discussion of, or the asking of questions on, the personal conduct of the Ruler of any Indian State or of a member of the ruling family thereof;

and, if and in so far as any rule so made by the Governor is inconsistent with any rule made by a Chamber, the rule made by the Governor shall prevail].

(2) In a Province having a Legislative Council the Governor, after consultation with the Speaker and the President, may make rules as to the procedure with respect to joint sittings of, and communications between, the two Chambers.

The said rules shall make such provision for the purposes specified in the proviso to the preceding sub-section as the Governor in his discretion may think fit.

(3) Until rules are made under this section the rules of procedure and standing orders in force immediately before the commencement of this part of this Act with respect to the Legislative Council of the Province, shall have effect in relation to the Legislature of the Province, subject to such

modifications and adaptations as may be made therein by the Governor acting in his discretion.

(4) At a joint sitting of two Chambers the President of the Legislative Council, or in his absence such person as may be determined by rulss of procedure made under this section, shall preside.

[85. All proceedings in the legislature of a Province shall be conducted in the English language.

Provided that the rules of procedure of the Chamber or Chambers, and the rules, if any, with respect to join sittings, shall provide for enabling persons unacquainted, or not sufficiently acquainted, with the English language to use another language].

86. (1) No discussion shall take place in a Provincial Legislature with respect to the conduct of any judge of the Federal Court or of a High Court in the discharge of his duties,

In this sub-section the reference to an High Court shall be construed as including a reference to a court in a Federated State which is a High Court for any of the purposes of Part IX of this Act,

(2) If the Governor in his discretion certifies that the discussion of a Bill introduced or proposed to be introduced in the Provincial Legislature, or of any specified clause of a Bill or of any amendment moved or proposed to be moved to a Bill, would affect the discharge of his special responsibility for the prevention of any grave menace to the peace or tranquility of the Province or any part thereof, he may in his discretion direct that no proceedings, or no further proceedings, shall be taken in relation to the Bill, clause or amendment, and effect shall be given to the direction]

87. (1) the validity of any proceedings in a Provincial Legislature shall not be called in question on the ground of any alleged irregularity of procedure.

(2) No officer or other member of a Provincial Legislature in whom powers are vested by or under this Act for regulating procedure or the conduct of business, or for maintaining order, in the Legislature shall be subject to the jurisdiction of any court in respect of the exercise by him of those powers.

CHAPTER IV
LEGISLATIVE POWERS OF GOVERNOR

88. (1) If at any time when the Legislature of a Province is not in session the Governor is satisfied that circumstances which render it necessary for him to take immediate action, he may promulgate such ordinances as the circumstances appear to him to require:

[Provided that the Governor—

(a) shall exercise his individual judgment as respects the promulgation of any ordinance under this section, if—

(i) a Bill containing the same provisions would under this Act have required his or the Governor-General's previous sanction to the introduction thereof into the Legislature; or

(ii) an Act of the Provincial Legislature containing the same provisions would under this Act have been invalid unless, having been reserved for the consideration of the Governor-General or for the signification of His Majesty's pleasure, it had received the assent of the Governor-General or of His Majesty; and

(b) shall without instructions from the Governor-General acting in his discretion, promulgate any such ordinance if—

(i) a Bill containing the same provisions would under this Act have required the Governor-General's previous sanction for the introduction thereof.into the Legislature; or

(ii) he would have deemed it necessary to reserve a Bill containing the same provisions for the consideration of the Governor-General; or

(iii) an Act of the Provincial Legislature containing the same provisions would under this Act have been invalid unless, having been reserved for the consideration of the Governor-General or for the signification of His Majesty's pleasure, it had received the assent of the Governor-General or of His Majesty.]

(2) An ordinance promulgated under this section shall have the same force and effect as an Act of the Provincial Legislature assented to by the Governor but every such ordinance—

(a) shall be laid before the Provincial Legislature and shall cease to operate at the expiration of six weeks from the reassembly of the Legislature, or if a resolution disapproving it is passed by the Legislative Assembly and agreed to by the Legislative Council, if any, upon the passing of the resolution or, as the case may be, on the resolution being agreed to by the Council;

(b) shall be subject to the provisions of this Act relating to the power of His Majesty to disallow Acts as if it were an Act of the Provincial Legislature assented to by the Governor; and

(c) may be withdrawn at any time by the Governor.

(3) If and so far as an ordinance under this section makes any provision which would not be valid if enacted in an Act of the Provincial Legislature assented to by the Governor, it shall be void.

[Provided that, for the purposes of the provisions of this Act relating tn the effect of an Act of a Provincial Legislature which is repugnant to an Act of the Federal Legislature or an existing Indian Law with respect to a matter enumerated in the Concurrent Legislative List an ordinance promulgated under this section in pursuance of instructions from the Governor-General acting in his discretion shall be cleaned to be an Act of the Provincial Legislature which has been reserved for the consideration of the Governor-General and assented to by him].

89. (1) If at any time the Governor of a Province is satisfied that circumstances exist which render it necessary for him to take immediate action for the purpose of enabling him satisfactorily to discharge his functions in so far as he is

by or under this Act required in the exercise thereof to act in his discretion, or to exercise his individual judgment, he may promulgate such ordinances as in his opinion the circumstances of the case require.

(2) An ordinance promulgated under this section shall continue in operation for such period not exceeding six months as may be specified therein, but may by a subsequent ordinance be extended for a further period not exceeding six months.

(3) An ordinance promulgated under this section shall have the same force and effect as an Act of the Provincial Legislature assented to by the Governor but every such ordinance—

(a) shall be subject to the provisions of this Act relating to the power of His Majesty to disallow Acts as if it were an Act of the Provincial Legislature;

(b) may be withdrawn at any time by the Governor; and

(c) if it is an ordinance extending a previous ordinance for a further period, shall be communicated forthwith through the Governor-General to the Secretary of State and shall be laid by him before each House of Parliament.

(4) If and so far as an ordinance under this section makes any provision which would not be valid if enacted in an Act of the Provincial Legislature, it shall be void:

Provided that for the purposes of the provisions of this Act relating to the effect of an Act of a Provincial Legislature which is repugnant to an Art of the Federal Legislature, [or an existing Indian Law with respect to a mailer enumerated in the Concurrent Legislative List], an ordinance promulgated under this section shall be deemed to be an Act of the Provincial Legislature which has been reserved for the consideration of the Governor-General and assented to by him.

(5) the functions of the Governor under this section shall be exercised by him in discretion but he shall not exercise any of his powers thereunder except with the concurrence of the Governor-General in his discretion:

Provided that, if it appears to the Governor that it is impracticable to obtain in time the concurrence of the Governor-General, he may promulgate as ordinance without the concurrence of the Governor-General, but in that case the Governor- General in his discretion may direct the Governor to withdraw the ordinance and the ordinance shall be withdrawn accordingly.

90. (1) If at any time it appears to the Governor that, for the purpose of enabling him satisfactorily to discharge his functions in so far as he is by or under this Act required in the exercise thereof to act in his discretion or to exercise his individual judgment, it is essential that provision should be made by legislation, he may by message to the Chamber or Chambers of the Legislature explain the circumstances which in his opinion render legislation essential, and either—

(a) enact forthwith as a Governor's Act a Bill containing such provisions as he considers necessary; or

(b) attach to his message a draft of the Bill which he considers necessary.

(2) Where the Governor takes such action as is mentioned in paragraph (b) of the preceding sub-section, he may, at any time after the expiration of one month, enact, as a Governor's Act, the Bill proposed by him to the Chamber or Chambers either in the form of the draft communicated to them, or with such amendments as he deems necessary, but before so doing he shall consider any address which may have been presented to him within the said period by the Chamber or either of the Chambers with reference to the Bill or to amendments suggested to be made therein.

(3) A Governor's Art shall have the same force and effect, and shall be subject to disallowance in the same manner as an Act of the Provincial Legislature assented to by the Governor and, if and, so far as it makes any provision which would not be valid if enacted in an Act of that Legislature, shall be void:

Provided that, for the purposes of the provisions of this Act relating to the effect of an Act of a Provincial Legislature which is repugnant to an Act of the Federal Legislature [for an existing Indian Law with respect to a matter enumerated in the Concurrent Legislative List], a Goveinor's Act shall be deemed to be an Act reserved for the consideration of the Governor-General and assented to by him.

(4) Every Governor's Act shall be communicated forthwith through the Governor-General to the Secretary of State and shall be laid by him before each House of Parliament.

(5) The functions of the Governor under this section shall be exercised by him in his d'scretion, but he shall not exercise any of his powers thereunder except with the concurrence of the Governor-General in his discretion.

CHAPTER V
EXCLUDED AREAS AND PARTIALLY EXCLUDED AREAS

91. (1) In this Act the expressions "excluded areas" and partially "excluded area mean respectively such areas as His Majesty may by Order in Coouncil declare to be excluded areas or partially excluded areas.

The Secretary of State shall lay the draft of the Order which it is proposed to recommend His Majesty to make under this sub-section before Parliament within six months from the passing of this Act.

(2) His Majesty may at any time by order in Council—

(a) direct that the whole or any specified part of an excluded area shall become, or become part of, a partially excluded area;

(b) direct that the whole or any specified part of a partially excluded area shall cease to be a partially excluded area or a part of such an area;

(c) alter, but only by way of rectification of boundaries, and excluded or partially excluded area;

(d) on any alteration of the boundaries of a Province, or the creation of a new Province, declare any territory not previously in any Province to be, or to form part of, an excluded area or a partially excluded area, and any such Order may contain such incidental and consequential provisions as appear to His Majesty to be necessary and proper, but save as aforesaid the Order in Council made under sub-seciion (1) of this section shall not be varied by any subsequent Order.

92 (1) The executive authority of a Province extends to excluded and partially excluded areas [herein, but notwithstanding anything in this Act, no Act of the Federal Legislature, shall apply to an excluded area or a partially excluded area, unless the Governor by public notification so directs; and the Governor in giving such a direction with respect to any Act may direct that the Act shall in its application to the areas, or to any special part thereof, have effect subject to such exceptions or modifications as he thinks.

(2) The Governor may make regulations for the peace and good government of any area in a Province which is for the time being an excluded area, or a partially excluded areas, and any regulations so made may repeal or amend any Act of the Federal Legislature or of the Provincial Legislature, or any existing Indian law, which is for the time being applicable to the area in question.

Regulations made under this sub-section shall be submitted! forthwith to the Governor-General and until assented to by him in his discretion shall have no effect, [and the provisions of this Part of this Act with respect to the power of His Majesty to disallow Acts shall apply in relation to any such regulations assented to by the Governor-General as they apply in relation to Acts of a Provincial Legislature assented to by him].

(3) The Governor shall, as respects any area in a Province which is for the time being an excluded area, exercise his functions in his discretion].

CHAPTER VI
PROVISIONS IN CASE OF FAILURE OF CONSTITUTIONAL MACHINERY

93. (1) If at any time the Governor of a Province is satisfied that a situation has arisen in which the government of the Province cannot be carried on in accordance with the provisions of this Act, he may by Proclamation—

(a) declare that his functions shall, to such extent as may be specified in the Proclamation, be exercised by him in his discretion;

(b) assume to himself all or any of the powers vested in or exercisable by any Provincial body or authority;

and any such Proclamation may contain such incidental and consequential provisions as may appear to him to be necessary or desirable for giving effect to the objects of the Proclamation, including provisions for suspending in whole or in part the operation of any provisions of this Act relating to any Provincial body or authority:

Provided that nothing in this sub-section shall authorise the Governor to assume to himself any of the powers vested in or exercisable by a High Court, or to suspend, either in whole or in part, the operation of any provisions of this Act relating to High Courts.

(2) Any such Proclamation may be revoked or varied by a subsequent Proclamation.

(3) A Proclamation under this section—

(a) shall be communicated forthwith to the Secretary of State and shall be laid by him before each House of Parliament;

(b) unless it is a Proclamation revoking a previous Proclamation shall cease to operate at the expiration of six months;

Provided that, if and so often as a resolution approving the continuance in force of such a Proclamation is passed by both Houses of Parliament, the Proclamation shall, unless revoked, continue in force for a further period of twelve months from the date on which under this subsection it would otherwise have ceased to operate, but no such Proclamation shall in any case remain in force for more than three years.

(4) If the Governor by a Proclamation under this section, assumes to himself any power of the Provincial Legislature to make laws, any law made by him in the exercise of that power shall, subject to the terms thereof, continue to have

effect until two years have elapsed from the date on which the Proclamation ceases to have effect, unless sooner repealed or re-enacted by Act of the appropriate Legislature, and any reference in this Act to Provincial Acts, Provincial laws, or Acts or laws of a Provincial Legislature shall be construed as including a reference to such a law.

(5) The functions of the Governor under this section shall be exercised by him in his discretion and no Proclamation shall be made by a Governor under this section without the concurrence of the Governor-General in his discretion.

PART IV
THE CHIEF COMMISSIONERS' PROVINCES

94. (1) The following shall be the Chief Commissioners' Provinces, that is to say, the heretofore existing Chief Commissioners Provinces of [British Baluchistan] Delhi, Ajmer-Menvara, Coorg and the Andaman and Nicober Islands, the area known as Panth Piploda, and such other Chief Commissiones Provinces as may be created under this Act.

[(2) Aden shall cease to be part of India].

(3) A Chief Commissioner's Province shall be administered by the Governor-General acting, to such extent as he thinks fit, through a Chief Commissioner to be appointed by him in his discretion.

95. (1) In directing and controlling the administration of British Baluchistan, the Govemor-Genenl shall act in his discretion.

(2) The executive authority of the Federation extends to British Baluchistan as it extends 10 other Chief Commissioner's Provinces, but notwithstanding anything in this Act, no Act of the Federal Legislature shall apply to British Baluchistan unless the Governor-General in his discretion by public notification so directs, and the Governor-General in giving such a direction with respect to any Act may direct that the Act shall in its application. to the Province, or to any specified part thereof, have effect subject to such exceptions or modifications as he thinks fit.

(3) The Governor-General may in his discretion make regulations for the peace and good government of British. Baluchistan, and any regulations so may made repeal or amend any Act

of the Federal Legislature or any existing Indian law which is for the time being applicable to the Province and, when promulgated by the Governor- General, shall have the same force and effect as an Act of the Federal Legislature which applies to the Province.

The provisions of Part II of this Act relating to the power of His Majesty to disallow Acts shall apply in relation to any such regulations as they apply in relation to Acts of the federal Legislature assented to by the Governor- General.]

96. The provisions of sub-section (3) of the last preceding section shall apply in relation to the Andaman and Nicober Islands as they apply in relation to British Baluchistan.

97. Until other provision is made by [His Majesty in Council], the constitution, powers and functions of the Coorg Legislative Council, and the arrangements with respect to revenues collected in Coorg and expenses in respect of Coorg, shall continue Unchanged.

98. The provisions of Part III of this Act with respect to police rules and with respect to crimes of violence intended to overthrow the government, including the provisions thereof relating to the non- disclosure of certain records and information, shall apply in relation to Chief Commissioners' Provinces as they apply in relation to Governor's Provinces with the substitution for references to the Governor and the Chamber or Chambers of the Provincial Legislature of references to the Governor-General and the Chamber of the Federal Legislature.

PART V
LEGISLATIVE POWERS

CHAPTER I.
DISTRIBUTION OF POWERS

99. (1) Subject to the provisions of this Act, the Federal Legislature may make laws [for the whole or any part of British India or for any Federated State] and a Provincial Legislature may make laws for the Province or for any part thereof.

[(2) Without prejudice to the generality of the powers conferred by the preceding sub-section, no Federal law shall, on the ground that it would have extra territorial operation, be deemed to be invalid in so far as it applies—

(a) to British subjects and servants of the Crown in any part of India or

(b) to British subjects who are domiciled in any part of India wherever they may be; or

(c) to, or to persons on, ships or aircraft registered in British India or any Federated State wherever they may be; or

(d) in the case of a law with respect to a matter accepted in Ihe Instrument of Accession of a Federated State as a matter with respect to which the Federal Legislature may make laws for that State, to subjects of that State wherever they may be; or

(e) in the case of a law for the regulation or discipline of a naval, military, or air force raised in British India, to member of, and persons attached to, employed with or following, that force, whenever they may be.]

100. (1) Notwithstanding anything in the two next succeeding sub sections, the Federal Legislature has and a Provincial Legislature has not, power to make laws with respect to any of the matters enumerated in List I in the Seventh Schedule to this Act (hereinafter called the "Federal Legislative List").

(2) Notwithstanding anything in the next succeeding sub-section, the Federal Legislature, and, subject to the-preceding sub-section, a Provincial Legislature also, have power to make laws with respect to any of the matters enumerated in List III in the said Schedule (hereinafter) called the "Concurrent Legislative List").

(3) Subject to the two preceding sub-sections the Provincial Legislature has, and the Federal Legislature has not, power to make laws for a Province or any part thereof with respect to any of the matters enumerated in List II in the said Schedule (hereinafter called the "Provincial Legislative List").

(4) The Federal Legislature has power to make laws with respect to matters enumerated in the Provincial legislative List except for a Province or any part thereof.

101. Nothing in this Act shall be constructed as empowering the Federal Legislature to make laws for a Federated State otherwise than in accordance with the Instrument of Accessions of that State and any limitation contained therein.

102. (1) Notwithstanding anything in the preceding sections of this chapter, the Federal Legislature shall, if the Governor-General has in his discretion declared by Proclamation (in this Act referred to as a "Proclamation (in this Act referred to as a "Proclamation of Emergency") that a grave emergency exists whereby the security of India is threatened, whether by war or internal disturbance, have power to make laws for a Province or any part thereof with respect to any of the natters enumerated in the Provincial Legislative List [or to make laws, whether or not, for a Province or any part thereof, with respect to any matter not enumedated in any of the lists in the Seventh Schedule to this Act]

Provided that no Bill or amendment for the purposes aforesaid shall be introduced or moved without the previous sanction of the Governor-Genera! in his discretion, and the Governor-General shall not give his sanction unless it appears to him that the provision proposed to be made is a proper provision in view of the nature of the emergency.

(2) Nothing in this section shall restrict the power of a Provincial Legislature to make any law which under this Act it has power to make, but if any provision of a Provincial law in repugnant to any provision of a Federal law which the Federal Legislature has under this section power to make, the Federal law, whether passed before or after the Provincial law, shall prevail, and the Provincial law shall to the extent of the repugnancy, but so long only as the Federal law continues to have effect, be void.

[(3) A Proclamation of Emergency—

(a) may be revoked by a subsequent Proclamation;

(b) shall be communicated forthwith to the Secretary of State and shall be laid by him befcre each House of Parliament; and

(c) shall cease to operate at the expiration of six months, unless before the expiration of that period it has been approved by Resolutions of both Houses of Parliament.]

(4) A law made by the Federal Legislature which that Legislature would not but for the issue of a Proclamation of Emergency have been competent to make [shall, to the extent of the incompetency, cease to have effect] on the expiration of a period of six months after the Proclamation has ceased to operate, except as respects things done or omitted to be done before the expiration of the said period.

[(5) A Proclamation of Emergency declaring that the security of India is threatened by war or by internal disturbance may be made before the actual occurrence of war or of any such disturbance if the Governor-General in his discretion is satisfied that there is imminent danger thereof,]

103. If it appears to the Legislature of two or more Provinces to be desirable that any of the matters enumerated in the Provincial Legislative List should be regulated in those Provinces by Act of the Federal Legislature, to pass an Act for regulating that matter accordingly, but any Act so passed may, as respects any Province to which it applies, be amended or repealed by an Act of the Legislature of that Province.

104. (1) The Governor-General may by public notification empower either the Federal Legislature or a Provincial Legislature to enact a law with respect to any mattter not enumerated in any of the Lists in the Seventh Schedule to this Act, including a law imposing a tax not mentioned in any such list, and the executive authority of the Federation or of the Province, as the case may be, shall extend to the administration of any law so made, unless the Governor-General otherwise directs.

(2) In the discharge of his functions under this section the Governor-General shall act in his discretion.]

[105. (1) Without prejudice to the provisions of this Act with respect to the legislative powers of the Federal Legislature, provision may be made by Act of that Legislature for applying Naval Discipline Act to the Indian naval forces and, so long as provision for that purpose is made either by an Act of the Federal Legislature or by an existing

Indian law, the Naval Discipline Act as so applied shall have effect as if references therein to His Majesty's navy and His Majesty's ships included references to His Majesty's Indian navy and the ships thereof, subject however:—

(a) in the application of the said Act to the forces and ships of the Indian navy and to the trial court martial of officers and men belonging thereto, to such modifications and adaptations, if any, as may be, or may have been, made by the Act of the Federal or Indian Legislature to adapt the said Act to the circumstances of India, including such adaptations as may be, or may have been, so made for the purpose of authorising or requiring anything which under the said Act is to be done by or to the Admiralty, or the Secretary of the Admiralty, to be done by or to the Governor-General, or some person authorised to act on his behalf; and

(b) in the application of the said Act to the forces and ships of His Majesty's navy other than those of the Indian navy, to such modifications and adaptations as may be made, or may have been made under section sixty-six of the Govern ment of India Act, by His Majesty in Council for the purpose of regulating the relations of those forces and ships to the forces and the ships of the Indian navy.

(2) Notwithstanding anything in this Act or in any Act of any Legislature in India, where any forces and ships of the Indian navy have been placed at the disposal of the Admiralty, the Naval Discipline Act shall have effect as if references therein to His Majesty's navy and his Majesty's ships included references to His Majesty's Indian navy and the ships thereof, with-cut any such modifications or adaptations as aforesaid.

106. (1) The Federal Legislature shall not by reason only of the entry in the Federal Legislative List relating to the implementing of treaties and agreements with other countries have power to make any law for any Province except with the previous consent of the Governor, or for a Federated State except with the previous consent of the Ruler thereof.

(2) So much of any law as is valid only by virtue of any such entry as aforesaid may be repealed by the Federal Legislature and may, on the treaty or agreement in question ceasing to have effect, be repealed as respects any Province or State by a law of that Province or State.

(3) Nothing in this section applies in relation to any law which the Federal Legislature has power to make for a Province or as the case may be, a Federated State, by virtue of any other entry in the Federal or the Concurrent Legislative List as well as by virtue of the said entry.

107. (1) If any provision of a Provincial law is repugnant to any provision of a Federal law which the Federal Legislature is competent to enact or to any provision of an existing Indian law with respect to one of the matters enumerated in the Concurrent Legislative List, then, subject to the provisions of this section, the Federal law, whether passed before or after the Provincial law, or as the case may be, the existing Indian law, shall prevail and the Provincial law shall, to the extent of the repugnancy, be void.

(2) Where a Provincial law with respect to one of the matters enumerated in the Concurrent Legislative List contains any provision repugnant to the provisions of an earlier Federal law or an existing Indian law with respect to that matter, then, if the Provincial law, having been reserved for the consideration of the Governor-General [or for the signification, of His Majesty's pleasure] has received the assent of the Governor-General or for the signification of His Majesty's pleasure has received the assent of the Governor-General or of His Majesty the Provincial law shall in that Province prevail, but nevertheless the Federal Legislature may at any time enact further legislation with respect to the same matter.

Provided that no Bill or amendment for making any provision repugnant to any Provincial law, which, having been so reserved has received the assent of the Governor-General or of His Majesty, shall be introduced or moved in either Chamber of the Federal Legislature without the previous sanction of the Governor-General in his discretion.

(3) If any provision of a law of a Federated State is repugnant to a Federal law which extends to that State, the Federal law, whether passed before or after the law of the State, shall prevail and the law of the State shall, to the extent of the repugnancy be void,

CHAPTER II

RESTRICTIONS ON LEGISLATIVE POWERS

[108. (1) Unless the Governor-General in_his discretion thinks fit to give his previous sanction there shall not be introduced into, or moved in either Chamber or the Federal Legislature, any Bill or amendment which—

(a) repeals, amends or is repugnant to any provisions of any Act of Parliament extending to British India; or

(b) repeals, amends or is repugnant to any Governor-General's or Governor's Act, or any ordinance promulgated in his discretion by the Governor-General or a Governor; or

(c) affects matters as respects which the Governor-General is, by or under this Act, required to act in his discretion; or

(d) repeals, amends or affects any Act relating to any police force; or

(e) affects the procedure for criminal proceedings in which European British subjects are concerned; or

(f) subjects persons not resident in British India to greater taxation than persons resident in British India or subjects companies wholly controlled and managed therein; or .

(g) affecfs the grant of relief from any Federal tax on income in respect of income taxed or taxable in the United Kingdom.

(2) Unless the Governor-General in his discretion thinks fit to give his previous sanction, there shall not be introduced into, or moved in, a Chamber of a Provincial Legislature any Bill or amendment which—

(a) repeals, amends, or is repugnant to any provisions of any Act of Parliament extending to British India; or

(b) repeals, amends or is repugnant to any Governor-General's Act, of any ordinance promulgated in his discretion by the Governor-General; or

(c) affects matters as respects which the Governor-General is by or under this Act, required to act in his discretion; or

(d) affects the procedure for criminal proceedings in which European British subjects are concerned;

and unless the Governor of the Province in his discretion thinks fit to give his previous sanction, there shall not be introduced or moved any Bill or amendment which—

(i) repeals, amends or is repugnant to any Governor's Act, or any ordinance promulgated in his discretion by the Governor; or

(ii) repeals, amends or affects any Act relating to any police force.

(3) Nothing in this section affects the operation of any other provision on this Act which requires the previous sanction of the Governor-General or of a Governor to the introduction of any Bill or the moving of any amendment].

109. (1) Where under any provision of this Act the previous sanction or recommendation of the Governor-General or of a Governor is required to the introduction or passing of a Bill or the moving of an amendment, the giving of the sanction or recommendation shall not be construed as precluding him from exercising subsequently in regard to the Bill in question any powers conferred upon him by this Act with respect to the withholding of assent to or the reservation of Bills.

(2) No Act of the Federal Legislature or a Provincial Legislature, and no provision in any such Act, shall be invalid by reason only that some previous sanction or recommendation was not given, if assent to that Act was given—

(a) where the previous sanction or recommendation required was that of the Governor, either by the Governor, [by the Governor-General], [or by His

Majesty]; (b) where the previous sanction or recommendation required was that of the Governor-General, either by Governor-General or by His Majesty.

[110. Nothing in this Act shall be taken—

(a) to affect the power of Parliament to legislate for British India, or any part thereof; or

(b) to empower the Federal Legislature, or any Provincial Legislature—

(i) to make any law affecting the Sovereign or the Royal Family, or the Succession to the Crown, or the sovereignty, dominion or suzerainty of the Crown in any part of India, or the law of British nationality, or the Army Act, the Air Force Act, or the Naval Discipline Act, or the law of Prize courts; or

(ii) except in so far as is expressly permitted by any subsequent provisions of this Act, to make any law amending any provision of this Act, or any Order in Council made thereunder, or any rules made under this Act by the Secretary of State, or by the Governor-General or a Governor in his discretion, or in the exercise of his individual judgment; or

(iii) except in so far as is expressly permiited by any subsequent provision of this Act, to make any law derogating from any prerogative right of His Majesty to grant special leave to appeal from any court].

CHAPTER III

Provisions with Respects to Discrimination, Etc.

111. (1) Subject to the provisions of this chapter, a British subject domiciled in the United Kingdom shall be exempt from the operation of so much of any Federal or Provincial law as—

(a) imposes any restriction on the right of entry into British India; or

(b) imposes by reference to place of birth, race, descent, language, religion, domicile, residence or duration, of residence, any disability, liability, restriction or condition in regard to travel, residence, the acquisition, holding, or disposal of property, the holding of public office, or the carrying on of any occupation, trade, business or profession:

Provided that no person shall by virtue of this sub-section be entitled to exemption from such restriction, condition, liability or disability as aforesaid if and so long as British subjects domiciled in British India are by or under the law of the United Kingdom subject in the United Kingdom to a like restriction, condition, liability, or disability imposed in regard to the same subject matter by reference to the same principle of distinction.

(2) For the purposes of the preceding sub-section, a provision, whether of the law of British India or of the law of the United Kingdom, empowering any public authority to impose quarantine regulations, or to exclude or deport individuals, wherever domiciled who appear to that authority to be undesirable persons, shall not be deemed to be a restriction on the right of entry.

(3) Notwithstanding anything in this section, if the Governor-General or, as the case may be, the Governor of any Province, by public notification certifies that for the prevention of any grave menace to the peace or tranquillity of any part of India or, as the case may be, of any part of the Province, or for the purpose of combating crimes of violence intended to overthrow the Government, it is expedient that the operation of the provisions of subsection (1) of this section should be wholly or partially suspended in relation to any law, then while the notification is in force the operation of those provisions shall be suspended accordingly.

The functions of the Governor-General and a Governor under this sub-section shall be exercised by him in his discretion.

112. (1) No Federal or Provincial law which imposes any liability to taxation discriminate against British subjects domiciled in the United Kingdom or Burma or companies incorporated, whether before or after the passing of this Act, by or under the laws of the United Kingdom or Burma, and any law passed or made in contravention of this section shall, to the extent of the contravention, be invalid.

(2) Without prejudice to the generality of the foregoing provisions, a law shall be deemed to be such as to discriminate against such persons or companies as aforesaid if it would result in any of the being liable tg greater taxation than that to which they would be liable if domiciled in British India or incorporated, by or under the laws of British India, as the case may be.

(3) For the purposes of this section a company incorporated before the commencement of Part III of this Act under any existing Indian law and registered thereunder in Burma shall be deemed to be a company incorporated by or under the laws of Burma.

113. (1) Subject to the following provisions of this chapter, a company incorporated, whether before or after the passing Act, by or under the laws of the United Kingdom, and the members of the governing body of any such company and the holders of its shares, stock, debentures, debenture stock or bonds, and its officers, agenls, and servants, shall be deemed to comply with so much of any Federal or Provincial law as imposes in regard to companies earning on or proposing to carry on business in British India requirements or conditions relating to or connected with—

(a) the place of incorporation of a company or the situation of its registered office, or the currency in which its capital or loan capital is expressed; or

(b) the place of birth, race, descent, language, religion, domicile, residence or duration of residence, of members of the governing body of a company or of the holders of its shares, stock, debentures, debentures stock or bonds, or of its officers, agents or servants;

Provided that no company or person shall by virtue of this section be deemed to comply with any such requirement or condition as aforesaid if and so long as a like requirement or condition is imposed by or under the law of the United Kingdom in regard to companies incorporated by or under the laws of British India and carrying on or proposing to carry on business in the United Kingdom.

(2) If and in so far as any total or partial exemption from, or preferential treatment in respect of, taxation imposed on companies by or under any Federal or Provincial law depends on compliance with conditions as to any of the matters mentioned in sub-section (1) of this section, any company incorporated by or under the laws of the United Kingdom carrying on business in British India shall be deemed to satisfy those conditions and be entitled to the exemption or preferential treatment accordingly, so long as the taxation imposed by or under the laws of the United Kingdom on companies incorporated by or under the laws of British India and carrying on business in the United Kingdom does not depend on compliance with conditions as to any of the matters so mentioned.

114. (1) Subject to the following provisions of this chapter, a British subject domiciled in the United Kingdom shall be deemed to comply with so much of any Federal or Provincial law as imposes in regard to companies incorporated or proposed to be incorporated, whether before or after the passing of this Act, by or under the laws of British India, any requirements or conditions relating to, or connected with, the place of birth, race, descent, language, religion, domicile, residence or duration of residence of members of the governing body of a company, or of the holders of its shares, stock, debentures, debenture stock or bonds or of its officers, agents or servants;

Provided that no person shall by virtue of this section be deemed to comply with any such requirement or condition as aforesaid if and so long as a like requirement or condition is imposed by or under the law of the United Kingdom in regard to companies incorporated or proposed to be incorporated by or under the laws of the United Kingdom on British subjects domiciled in British India.

(2) If and in so far as, in the case of any such companies as aforesaid, any total or partial exemption from, or preferential treatment in respect of, taxation imposed by or under any Federal or Provincial law depends on compliance with conditions as to any of the matters aforesaid, then, so far as regards such members of its governing body and such

of the holders of its shares, stock, debentures, debenture stock or bonds, and such of its officers, agents, and servants, as are British subjects domiciled in the United Kingdom, any such company shall be deemed to satisfy those conditions and be entitled to the exemption or preferential treatment accordingly, so long as the taxation imposed, by or under the laws of the United Kingdom on companies incorporated by or under those laws does not, as regards such of the members of a company's governing body, or such of the holders of its shares, stock, debentures, debenture stock or bonds, or such of its officers, agents, or servants, as are British subjects domiciled in British India, depend on compliance with conditions as to any of the matters aforesaid.

(3) For the purposes of this section, but not for the purposes of any other provision of this chapter, a company incorporated before the commencement of Part III of this Act under any existing Indian law and registered thereunder in Burma, shall be deemed to be a company incorporated by or under the laws of British India.

115. (1) No ship registered in the United Kingdom shall be subjected by or under any Federal or Provincial law to any treatment affecting either the ship herself, or her master, officers, crew, passengers cargo which is discriminatory in favour of ships registered in British India, except in so far as ships registered in the United Kingdom.

(2) This section shall apply in relation to aircraft as it applies in relation to ships.

(3) The provisions of this section are in addition to and not in derogation of the provisions of any of the preceding sections of this chapter.

116. (1) Notwithstanding anything in any Act of the Federal Legislature or of a Provincial Legislature, companies incorporated Whether before or after the passing of this Act, by or under the laws of the united Kingdom and carrying on business in India shall be eligible for any grant, bounty or subsidy payable out of the revenues of the Federation or of a Province for the encouragement of any

trade or industry to the same extent as companies incorporated by or under the laws of British India are eligible therefor:

Provided that this sub-section shall not apply in relation to any grant bounty or subsidy for the encouragement of any trade or industry, if and so long as under the laws of British India and carrying on business in the United Kingdom are not equally eligible with companies incorporated by or under the laws of the United Kingdom for the benefit of any grant, bounty or subsidy payable out of public moneys in the United Kingdom for the encouragement of the same trade or industry.

(2) Notwithstanding anything in this chapter, an Act of the Federal Legislature or of a Provincial Legislature may, require, in the case of a company which at the date of the passing of that Act was not engaged ia British India in that branch of trade or industry which it is the purpose of the grant, bounty or subsidy to encourage, that the company shall not be eligible for any grant, bounty or subsidy under the Act unless and until

(a) the company is incorporated by or under the laws of British India or, if the Act so provides, is incorporated by or under the laws of British India or of a Federal State; and

(b) such proportion, not exceeding one half, of the members of its governing body as the Act may prescribe, are British subjects domiciled in India or, if the Act so provides, are either British subjects domiciled in India or subjects of a Federated State; an

(c) the company gives such reasonable facilities as may be so prescribed for the training of British subjects domiciled in India or, if the Act so provides, of British subjects domiciled in India or subjects of a Federated State.

(3) For the purposes of this section a company incorporated by or under the laws of the United

Kingdom shall be deemed to be carrying on business in India if it owns ships which habitually trade to and from parts in India.

117. The foregoing provisions of this chapter shall apply in relation to any ordinance order by Iaw, rule or regulation passed or made after the passing of this Act and having by virtue of any existing Indian law, or of any law of the Federal at any Provincial legislature, the force of law as they apply in relation to Federal and Provincial laws, but, save as aforesaid, nothing in those provisions shall affect the operation of any existing Indian law.

118. (1) If after the establishment of the Federation a convention is made between His Majesty's Government in the United Kingdom and the Federal Government whereby similarity of treatment is assured in the United Kingdom to British subjects domiciled in British India and to companies incorporated by or under the laws of British India and in British India to British subjects domiciled in the United Kingdom and to companies incorporated by or under the laws of the United Kingdom, respectivtly, in respect of the matters, or any of the matters, with regard to which provision is made in the preceding sections of this chapter, His Majesty may, if he is satisfied that all necessary legislation has been enacted both in the United Kingdom and in India for the purpose of giving effect to the convention, by Order in council declare that the purpose of those sections are to such extent as may be specified in the Order sufficiently fulfilled by that convention and legislation, and while any such Order is in force, the operation of those sections shall that extent be suspended.

(2) An Order in Council under this section shall cease to have effect if and when the convention to which it relates expires or is terminated by either party thereto.

119. (1) No Bill or amendment which prescribes, or empowers any authority to prescribe, the professional or technical qualifications which are to be requisite for any purpose in British India or which imposes, or empowers any authority to impose, by reference to any professional or technical qualification, and disability, liability, restriction or condition

in regard to the practising of any profession, the carrying on of any occupation, trade or business, or the holding of any office in British India, shall be introduced or moved in either Chamber of the Federal Legislature without the previous sanction of the Governor-General in his discretion, or in a Chamber of a Provincial Legislature without this previous sanction of the Governor in his discretion.

(2) The Governor-General or a Governor shall not give his sanction for the purposes of the preceding sub-section unless he is satisfied that the proposed legislation is so framed as to secure that no person who, immediately before the coming into operation of any disability, liability, or condition to be imposed by or under that legislation, was lawfully practising any profession, carrying on any occupation, trade, or business, or holding any office in British India shall, except in so far as may be necessary in the interests of the public, be debarred from continuing to practise that profession, carry on that occupation trade or business, or hold that office, or from doing anything in the course of that profession, occupation, trade or business, or in the discharge of the duties of that office which he could lawfully have done if that disability, liability, restriction or condition had not come into operation.

(3) All regulation made under the provisions of any Federal or Provincial law which prescribe the professional or technical qualifications which are to be requisite for any purpose in British India or impose, by reference to any professional or technical qualification, any disability, liability, restriction or condition in regard to the practising of any profession, the earning on of any occupation, trade or business, or the holding of any office in British India, shall, not less than four months before they are expressed to come into operation, be published in such manner as may be required by general or special directions of the Governor-General, or, as the case may be, the Governor, and, if within two months from the date of the publication complaint is made to the Governor-General or, as the case may be, the Governor that the regulations or any of them will operate unfairly as

against any class of persons affected thereby, the Governor-General or Governor, if he is of opinion that the complaint is well founded, may, at any time before the regulations are expressed to come into operation, by public notification disallow the regulations or any of them.

In this sub-section the expression "regulations" includes rules, byelaws, orders and ordinances.

In the discharge of his functions under this sub-section the Govemor-Gcneral or a Governor shall exercise his individual judgment.

(4) If the Governor-General exercising his individual judgment by public notification directs that the provisions of the last preceding sub-section shall apply in relation to any existing Indian law, those provisions shall apply in relation to that law accordingly, and the functions which under those provisions are to be performed in relation to a Federal law by the Governor-General and in relation to a Provincial law by the Governor shall, in relation to that existing Indian law, be performed, according as may be directed by the notification, by the Governor-General exercing his individual judgment, by the Governor exercising his individual judgment or partly by the one and partly by the other of them.

120. (1) So long as the condition set out in sub-section (3) of this section continues to be fulfilled, a British subject domiciled ib the United Kingdom or India who, by virtue of a medical diploma granted to him in the United Kingdom, is, or is entitled to be, registered in the United Kingdom as a qualified medical practitioner shall not by or under any existing Indian law or any law of the Federal or any Provincial Legislature, be excluded from practising medicine, surgery or midwifery in British India, or in any part thereof, or from being registered as qualified so to do, on any ground other than the ground that the diploma held by him does not furnish a sufficient guarantee of his possession of the requisite knowledge and skill for the practice of medicine, surgery and midwifery, and he shall not he so excluded on that ground unless a law of the Federation or of the province, as the case may be, makes provision for securing—

(a) that no proposal for excluding the holders of any particular diploma from practice or registration shall become operative until the expiration of twelve months after notice thereof has been given to the Governor-General and to the University or other body granting that diploma; and

(b) that such a proposal shall not become operative or, as the case may be, shall cease to operate, if the Privy Council on an application made to them under the next succeeding sub-section determine that the diploma in question ought to be recognised as furnishing such a sufficient guarantee as a foresaid.

(2) If any University or other body in the United Kingdom which grants a medical diploma, or any British subject who holds such a diploma, is aggrieved by the proposal to exclude holders of that diploma from practice or registration in British India, that body or person may make an application to the Privy Council, and the Privy Council after giving to such authorities and persons both in British India and in the United Kingdom as they think fit an Opportunity of tendering evidence or submitting representation in writing, shall determine whether the diploma in question does or does not furnish a sufficient guarantee of the possession of the requisite knowledge and skill for the practice of medicine, surgery and midwifery, and shall notify their determination to the Governor-General, who shall communicate it to such authorities, and cause it to be published in such manner, as he thinks fit.

(3) The condition referred to in sub-section (1) of this section is that British subjects domiciled in India who hold a medical diploma granted after examination in British India shall not be excluded from practising Medicine, surgery or midwifery in the United Kingdom or from being registered therein as qualified medical practitioners, except on the ground that diploma does not furnish a sufficient guarantee of the possession of the requisite knowledge and skill for the practice of medicine, surgery and midwifery, and shall only be excluded on that ground so long as the law cf the

United Kingdom makes provision for enabling any question as to the sufficiency of that diploma to be referred to and decided by the Privy council.

(4) A medical practitioner entitled to practise or to be registered in British India by virtue of a diploma granted in the United Kingdom, or in the United Kingdom by virtue of a diploma granted in British India, shall not in the practice of his profession be subjected to any liability, disability, restriction or condition to which persons entitled to practise by virtue of diplomas granted in the other country are not subject.

(5) The foregoing provisions of this section shall, subject to the modifications hereinafter mentioned, apply in relation to British subjects domiciled in Burma who, by virtue of medical diplomas granted to them in Burma or the United Kingdom, are, or are entitled to be, registered in the United Kingdom as qualified medical practitioners as they apply in relation to British subjects domiciled in the United Kingdom who, by virtue of Medical diplomas granted in the United Kingdom, are or are entilled to be, registered in the United Kingdom as qualified medical practitioners.

The said modifications are as follows, that is to say,—

(a) sub-section (3) shall not apply and the reference in sub-section (l)to the condition set ou:t therein shall be deemed to be omitted;

(b) any reference in sub-section (2) or sub-section (4) to the united Kingdom shall be construed as a reference to Burma.

(6) nothing in this section shall be construed as affecting any power of any recognised authority in the United Kingdom or British India to suspend or debar any person from practice on the ground of disconduct, or to remove any person from a register on the ground.

(7) In this section the expression "diploma" includes any certificate, degree, fellowship, or other document or status granted to persons passing examinations.

121. A person whoholds a commission from His Majesty as a medical officer in the Indian Medical Service or any other branch to His

Majesty's forces and is on the active list shall by virtue of that commission be deemed to be qualified to practise medicine, surgery and midwifery in British India, and be entitled to be registered in British India or any part thereof as so qualified.

PART VI
ADMINISTRATIVE RELATIONS BETWEEN FEDERATION, PROVINCES AND STATES

General

122. (1) the executive authority of every Province and Federated State shall be so exercised as to secure respect for the laws of the Federal Legislature which apply in that Province or State.

(2) The reference in sub-section (1) of this section to laws of the Federal Legislature shall, in relation to any Province, include a reference to any existing Indian law applying in that Province.

(3) Without prejudice to any of the other provisions of this Part of this Act, in the exercise of the executive authority of the Federation in any Province or Federated State regard shall be had to the interests of that Province or State.

123. (1) The Governor-General may direct the Governor of any Province to discharge as his agent, either generally or in any particular case, such functions in and in relation to the tribal areas as may be specified in the direction.

(2) If in any particular case it appears to the Governor-General necessary or convenient so to do, he may direct the Governor of any Province to discharge as his agent such functions in relation to defence, external affairs, or ecclesiastical affairs as may be specified in the direction.

(3) In the discharge of any such functions the Governor shall act in his direction.

124. (1) notwithstanding anything in this Act, the Governor-General may, with the consent of the Government of a Province or the Ruler of [a Federated] State, entrust either conditionally or unconditionally to that Government or Ruler, or to their respective officers, functions in relation to any matter to which the executive authority of the [Federation] extends

(2) An Act of the [Federal] Legislature may, notwithstanding that it relates to a matter with respect to which a Provincial Legislature has no power to make laws, confer powers an impose duties [or authorise the conferring of powers and the imposition of duties] upon a Province or officers and authorities thereof.

(3) An Act of the [Federal] Legislature which extends to [Federated] State may confer powers and impose duties [or authorise the conferring of powers and the imposition of duties] upon the State or officers and authorities thereof to be designated for the purpose by the Ruler.

(4) Where by virtue of this section powers and duties have been conferred or imposed upon a Province or [Federated] State or officers or authorities thereof, there shall be paid by the [Federation] to the Province or State such sum as may be agreed, or, in default of agreement, as may be determind by an arbitrator appointed by the Chief Justice of India, in respect of any extra costs of administration incurred by the Province or State in connection with the exercise of those powers and duties.

125. (1) notwithstanding anything in this Act, agreements may, and, if provision has been made in that behalf by the Instrument of Accession of the State, shall, be made between the Governor-General and the Ruler of [a Federated] State for the exercise by the Ruler or his officers of functions in relation to the administration in his State of any law of the [Federal Legislature] which applies therein.

(2) An agreement made under this section shall contain provisions enabling the Governor-General in his discretion to satisfy himself by inspection or otherwise, that the administration of the law to which the agreement relates is carried out in accordance with the policy of the [Federal] Government and, if he is not satisfied, the Governor-General acting in his discretion, may issue such directions to the Ruler as he thinks fit.

126. (1) The executive authority of every Province shall be so exercised as not to impede or prejudice the exercise of the executive authority of the [Federation] shail ex-tend to the

giving of such directions to a Province as may appear to the [Fcderal] Government to be necessary for that purpose.

(2) The executive authority of the [Federation] shall also extend to the giving of directions to a Province as to the carrying into execution therein of any Act of the [Fedcral] Legislature which relates to a matter specified in Part II of the Concurrent Legislative List and authorises the giving of such directions:

Provided that a Bill or amendment which proposes to authorise the giving of any such directions as aforesaid shall not be introduced into or moved in either Chamber of the [Fcderal] Legislature with the previous sanction of the Governor-General in his discretion.

(3) 'Ihe cxecutive authority of the [Federation] shall also extend to the giving of directions to a Province as to the construction and maintenance of means of communication declared in the direction to be of military importance:

Provided that nothing in this sub-section shall be taken as restricting the power of the Federation to construct and maintain means of communication as part of its functions with respect to naval, military and air force works.

[(4) If it appears to the Governor-General that in any Province effect has not been given to any direction given under this section, the Governor-General, acting in his discretion, may issue as orders to the Governor of that Province either the directions previously given or those directions modified in such manner as the Governor-General thinks proper].

[(5) Without prejudice to his powers under the last preceding sub-section, the Governor-General, acting in his discretion, may at any time issue orders to the Governor of a Province as to the manner in which the executive authority thereof is to be exercised for the purpose of preventing any grave menance to the peace or tranquillity of India or of any part thereof].

[126-A. Where a proclamation of Emergency is in operation whereby the Governor General has declared that the security of India is threatened by war—

(a) the executive authority of the [Federation] shall extend to the giving of directions to a Province as to the manner in which the executive authority thereof is to be exercised, and any directions so given shall for the purposes of the last preceding section be deemed to be directions given thereunder;

(b) any power of the [Federal] Legislature to make laws for a Province with respect to any matter shall include power to have laws as respects a Province conferring powers and imposing duties, or authorising ihe conferring of powers and the imposition of duties, upon the Federation or officers and authorities of the [Federation] as respects that matter, notwithstandmg that it is one with respect to which the Provincial Legislature also has power to make laws:

Provided that no Bill or amendment which, as respects a Province, confers powers or imposes duties, or authorises the conferring of powers or he imposition of duties, upon the [Federation] or upon officers or authorities of the [Federation] in relation to such a matter as aforesaid shall be introduced or moved without the previous sanction of the Govemor-General in his discretion, and the Governor-General shall not give his sanction unless it appears to him that the provision proposed to be made is a proper provision in view of the nature of the emergency].

127. The [Federation] may, if it deems it necessary to acquire any land situate in a Province for any purpose connected with a matter with respect to which the [Federal] Legislature has power to make laws, require the Province to acquire the land on behalf, and at the expense, of the [Federation] or, if the land belongs to the Province, to transfer it to the [Federation] on such terms as may be agreed or, in default of agreement, as may be determined by an arbitrator appointed by the Chief Justice of India.

128. (1) The executive authority of every [Federated] State shall be so exercised as not to impede or prejudice the exercise of the executive authority of the [Federation] so far as it is exercisable in the State by virtue of a law of the [Federal] Legislature which applies therein.

(2) If it appears to the Governor-General that the Ruler of any [Federated] State has in any way failed to fulfil his

obligations under the preceding sub-section the Governor-General, acting in his discretion, may after considering any representations made to him by the Ruler issue such directions to the Ruler as he thinks fit:

Provided that, if any question arises under this section as to whether the executive authority of the [Federation] is exercisable in a State with respect to any matter or as to the extent to which it is so exercisable, the question may, at the instance either of the [Federation] or the Ruler, be referred to the Federal Court for determination by that Court in the exercise of its original jurisdiction under this Act.

Broadcasting

129. (1) The [Federal] Government shall not unreasonably refuse to entrust to the Government of any Province or the Ruler of any [Federated] State such functions with respect to broadcasting as may be necessary to enable that Government or Ruler—

(a) to construct and use transmitters in the Province or State;

(b) to regulate, and impose fees in respect of, the construction and use of transmitters and the use of receiving apparatus in the Province or State:

Provided that nothing in this sub-section shall be construed as requiring the [Federal] Government to entrust to any such Government or Ruler any control over the use of transmitters constructed or maintained by the [Federal] Govenment or by persons authorised by the [Federal] Government, or over he use of receiving apparatus by persons so authorised.

(2) Any functions so entrusted to a Government or Ruler shall be exercised subject to such conditions as may be imposed by the [Federal] Government, including, notwithstanding anything in this Act, any conditions regulating the matter broadcast by, or by authority of, the Government or Ruler.

(3) Any [Federal] laws which may be passed with respect lo broadcasting shall be such as to secure that effect can be given to the foregoing provisions of this section.

(4) If any question arises under this section whether any conditions imposed on any such Government or Ruler are lawfully imposed, or whether any refusal by the [Federal] Government to entrust functions is unreasonable, the question shall be determined by [the Governor-General in his discretion].

(5) Nothing in this section shall be construed as restricting the powers conferred the Govcrnor-General by this Act for the prevention of any grave menace to the peace or tranquillity of India or any part thereof, [or as prohibiting the imposition on Governments or Rulers of such conditions regulating matter broadcast as appear to be necessary to enable the Governor-General to discharge his functions in so far as he is by or under this Act required in the exercise thereof to act in his discretion or to exercise his individual judgment].

Interference with Water Supplies.

130. If it appears to the Government of any Governor's Province or to the Ruler of any [Federated] State that the interests of that Province or State, or of any of the inhabitants thereof, in the water from any natural source of supply in any Governor's or Chief Commissioner's Province or [Federated] State, have been, or are likely to be, affected prejudicially by—

(a) any executive action or legislation taken or passed, or proposed to be taken or passed; or

(b) the failure of any authority to exercise any of their powers .... with respect to the use, distribution or control of water from that source the Government or Ruler may complain to the Governor-General.

131. (1) If the Governor- General receives such a complaint as aforesaid, he shall, unless he is of opinion that the issues involved are not of sufficient importance to warrant such action, appoint Commission consisting of such persons having special knowledge and experience in irrigation, engineering, administration, finance or law, as he thinks fit, and request that Commission to investigate in accordance with such instruction as he may give to them, and to report to him on, the matters to which the complaint relates, or such of those matters as he may reffer to them.

(2) A Commission so appointed shall investigate the matters referred to them and present to the Govenor-General a report setting out the facts as found by them and making such recommendations as they think proper.

(3) If it appears to the Governor-General upon consideration of the Commissioner's report that anything therein contained requires explanation, or that he needs guidance upon any point not originally referred by him to the Commission, he may again refer the matter to the Commission for further investigation and a further report.

(4) For the purpose of assisting a Commission appointed under this section in investigating any matters referred to them, the [Federal] Court, if requested by the Commission so to do, shall make such orders and issue such letters of request for the purposes of the proceedings of the Commission as they may make or issue in the exercise of the jurisdiction of the Court.

(5) After considering any report made to him by the Commission, the Governor-General shall give such decision and make such order, if any, in the matter of the complaint as he may deem proper:

[Provided that if, before the Governor-Genera! has given any decision, the Government of any Province or the Ruler of any State affected request him so to do, he shall refer the matter to His Majesty in Council and His Majesty in Council may give such decision and make such order, if any, in the matter as he deems proper].

(6) Effect shall be given in any Province or State affected to any order made under this section by His Majesty in Council or the Governor-General, and any Act of a Provincial Legislature or of a State which is repugnant to the order shall, to the extent of the repugnancy, be void.

(7) Subject as hereinafter provided the Governor-General, on application made to him by the Government of any Province, or the Ruler of any State affected may at any time, if after a reference to, and report from, a Commission appointed as aforesaid he considers it proper so to do, vary any decision or order given or made under this section:

[Provided that, Where the application relates to a decision or order of His Majesty in Council and in any other case if the Government of any Province or the Ruler of any State affected requested him so to do, the Governor-General shall refer the matter to His Majesty in Council, and His Majesty in Council may, if he considers proper so to do, vary the decision or order.

(8) An order made by [His Majesty in Council or] the Governor-General under this section may contain directions as to the Government or persons by whom the expenses of the Commission and any costs incurred by any Province, State or persons in appearing before the Commission are to be paid, and may fix the amount of any expenses or costs to be so paid, and so far as it relates to expenses or costs, may be enforced as if it were an order made by the Federal Court.

[(9) The functions of the Governor- General under this section shall be exercised by him in his discretion].

132. If it appears to the Governor-General that the interests of any Chief Commissioner's Province, or of any of the inhabitants of such a Province, in the water from any natural source of supply in any Governor's Province or [Federated] State have been or are likely to be affected prejudicially by–

(a) any executive action or legislation taken or passed or proposed to be taken or passed; or

(b) the failure of any authority to exercise any of their powers, ... with respect to the use, distribution or conlrol of water from that source, he may, if he in his discretion thinks fit, refer the matter to a Commission appointed in accordance with the provisions of the last preceeding section and thereupon those provisions shall apply as if the Chief Commssioner's Province were a Governor's Province and as if a complaint with respect to the matter had been made by the Government of that Province to the Governor-General.

133. Notwithstanding anything in this Act, neither the Federal Court nor any other Court shall have jurisdiction to entertain any action or suit in respect of any matter if action in respect of that matter might have been taken under any of the three last preceding

sections by the Government of a Province, the Ruler of a State, or the Governor- General.

134. The provisions contained in this Part of this Act with respect to interference with water- supplies shall not apply in relation to any Federated State [the Ruler whereof] has declare in his Instrument of Accession that those provisions are [not] to apply in relation to his State.

Inter-Provincial Co-operation.

135. If at any time it appears to [His Majesty upon the consideration of representations addressed to him by] the Governor-General that the public interests would be served by the establishment of the Inter-Provicial Council charged with the duty of—

(a) inquiring into and advising upon disputes which may have arisen between Provinces;

(b) investigating and discussing subjects in which some or all of the Provinces, or the Federation and one or more of the Provinces, have a common interest; or

(c) making recommendations for the better co-ordination of policy and action with respect to that subject,..................it shall be lawful for [His Majesty in Council] to establish such a Council, and to define the nature of the duties to be performed by it and its organisation and procedure.

PART VII

FINANCE, PROPERTY, CONTRACTS AND SUITS

CHAPTER I

FINANCE

Distribution of Revenues between the Federation and the Federal Units.

136. Subject to the following provisions of this chapter with respect to the assignment of the whole or part of the net proceeds of certain taxes and duties to Provinces and federated states, [and subject to the provisions of this Act with respect to the Federal Railway Authority], the expression "revenues of the Federation" includes all revenues and public moneys raised or received by the Federation, and the expression "revenues of the Province" includes all revenues and public moneys raised or received by a Province.

137. Duties in respect of succession io property other than agricultural land,estate duty in respect of property other than agricultural land, such stamp duties as are mentioned in the Federal Legislative List, terminal taxes on goods or passengers carried by railway, or air, and taxes on railway fares and freights, shall be levied and collected by the [Federation] but the net prceeds in any financial year of any such duty or tax, except in so far as those proceeds represent proceeds attributable to Chief Commissioners' Provinces, shall not form part of the revenues of the [Federation] but shall be assigned to the Provinces and to the (Federated] States, if any, within which that duty or tax is leviable in that year, and shall be distributed among the Provinces and those States in accordance with such principles of distribution as may be formulated by Act of the [Federal] Legislature:

Provided that the [Federal] Legislature may at any time increase any said duties or taxes by a surcharge for [Federal] purposes and the whole proceeds of any such surcharge shall form part of the revenues of the [Federation].

138. (1) Taxes on income other than agricultural income shall be levied and collected by the Federation, but a prescribed percentage of the net proceeds in any financial year of any such tax, except in so far as those proceeds represent proceeds attributable to Chief Commissioners' Provinces or to taxes payable in respect of [Federal] emoluments, shall not form part of the revenues of the [Federation], but shall be assigned to the Provinces and to the [Federated] States, if any, within which that tax is leviable in that year, and shall be distributed among the provinces and those States in such manner as may be prescribed:

Provided that—

(a) the percentage originally prescribed under this sub-section shall not be increased by any [subsequent Order in Council].

(b) the [Federal] Legislature may at any time increase the said taxes by a surcharge for [Federal] purposes and the whole proceeds of any such surcharge shall form part of the revenues of the [Federation].

[For the purpose of this sub-section in each financial year [one percent., or] such [other] percentage as may be prescribed, of so much of the net proceeds of taxes on income as does not represent the net proceeds of taxes payable in respect of [Federal] emoluments shall be deemed to represent proceeds attributable to the Chief Commissioners' Provinces].

(2) Notwithstanding anything in the preceding sub-section, the [Federation] may retain out of the moneys assigned by that sub-section to Province and State —

(a) in each year of a prescribed period such sum as may be prescribed [or, if it is so prescribed, the whole of those moneys] ; and

(b) in each year of a further prescribed period a sum less than that retained in the preceding year by an amount, being the same amount in each year, so calculated that the sum to be retained in the last year of the period will be equal to the amount of each such annual reduction:

Provided that—

(i) neither of the periods originally prescribed shall be reduced by any subsequent Order in Council;

(ii) the Governor-General in his discretion may in any year of the second prescribed period direct that the sum to be retained by the [Federation] in that year shall be the sum retained in the preceding year, and that the second prescribed period shall be correspondingly extended, but he shall not give any such direction except after consultation with such representatives of [Federal], Provincial and State interest as he may think desirable, nor shall be give any such direction unless he is satisfied that the maintenance of the financial stability of the [Federal] Government requires him so to do.

(3) Where an Act of the [Federal] Legislature imposes a surcharge for [Federal] purposes under this section, the Act shall provide for the payment by each [Federated] State in which taxes on income are not leviable by such basis as may be prescribed with a view to securing that the contribution shall be the equivalent, as near as may be, of the net proceeds which it is estimated would result from the surcharge if it were leviable in that State, and the State shall become liable to pay that contribution accordingly.

(4) In this section —

"taxes on income" does not include a corporation tax;

"prescribed" means prescribed by [His Majesty in Council]; and

"Federal emoluments" includes all emoluments and pensions payable out of the revenues of the [Federation] or of the Federal Railway Authority in respect of which income-tax is chargeable.

[139. (1) Corporation tax shall not be levied by the Federation in any Federated State until ten years have elapsed from the establishment of the federation.

(2) Any Federal law providing for the levying of corporation tax shall contain provisions enabling the Ruler of any Federated State in which the tax would otherwise be leviable to elect that the tax shall not be levied in the State, but that in lieu thereof there shall be paid by the State to the revenues of the Federation a contribution as near as may be equivalent to the net proceeds which it is estimated would result from the tax if it were levied in the State.

(3) Where the Ruler of a State so elects as aforesaid, the officers of the Federation shall not call for any information or returns from any corporation in the State, but it shall be the duty of the Ruler thereof to cause to be supplied to the Auditor-General of India such information as the Auditor-General may reasonably require to enable the amount of any such contribution to be determined.

If the Ruler of a State is dissatisfied with the determination as to the amount of the contribution payable by his State in any financial year, he may appeal to the Federal Court, and if he establishes to the satisfaction of that Court that the amount determined is excessive, the Court shall reduce the amount accordingly and no appeal shall lie from the decision of the Court on the appeal].

140. (1) Duties on salt, Federal duties of excise and export duties shall be levied and collected by the Federation, but, if an Act of the Federal Legislature so provides, there shall be paid out of the revenues of the Federation to the Provinces and to the Federated States, if any, to which the Act imposing the duty extends, sums equivalent to the whole or any part of the net proceeds of that duty, and those sums shall be distributed among the Provinces and those States in accordance with such principles of distribution as may be formulated by the Act.

(2) Notwithstanding anything in the preceding sub-section, [one half, or such greater proportion as His Majesty in Council may determine], of the net proceeds in each year of any export duty on jute products shall not form part of the revenues of the Federation, but shall be assigned to the Provinces or Federated States in which jute is grown in proportion to the respective amounts of jute grown therein.

141. (1) No Bill or amendment which imposes or varies any tax or duty in which provinces are interested or which varies the meaning of the expression "agricultural income" as defined for the purposes of the enactments relating to Indian incometax, or which affects the principles on which under any of the foregoing provisions if this chapter moneys are or may be attributable to Provinces or States, or which imposes any such Federal surcharge as is mentioned in the foregoing provisions of this chapter, shall be introduced or moved in either Chamber of the Federal Legislature except with the previous sanction of the Governor-General in his discretion.

(2) The Governor-General shall not give his sanction to the introduction of any Bill or the moving it any amendment imposing in any year any such Federal surcharge as aforesaid

unless he is satisfied that all practicable econimies and all practicable measures for otherwise increasing the proceeds of Federal taxation or the portion thereof retainable by the Federation would not result in the balancing of Federal receipts and expenditure on account in that year.

(3) In this section the expression ''tax or duty in which Provinces are interested" means —

(a) a tax or duty the whole or part of the net proceeds whereof are assigned to any Province; or

(b) a tax or duty by reference to the net proceeds whereof sums are for the time being payable out of the revenues of the Federation to any Provinces.

142. Such sums as may be prescribed by [His Majesty in Council] shall be charged on the revenues of the Federation in each year as grants-in-aid of the revenue of such Provinces as His Majesty may determine to be in need of assistance, and different sums may be prescribed for different Provinces:

Provided that, Except in the case of the North-West Frontier Province, No grant fixed under this section shall be increased by a subsequent Order, unless all address has been presented to the Governor-General by both Chambers of the Federal Legislature for submission to [His Majesty] praying that the increase may be made.

[142–A.(1) Notwithstanding anything in section one hundred of this Act, no Provincial law relating to taxes for the benefit of a Province or of a municipality, district board, local board or other Iocal authority therein in respect of professions, trades, calling or employments shall be invalid on the ground that it relates to a tax on income.

(2) The total amount payable in respect of any one person to the Province or to any one municipality, district board, local board, or other local authority in the Province by way of taxes on professions, trades, callings and employments shall not, after the thirty-first day of March nineteen undred and thirty-nine, exceed fifty rupees per annum:

Provided that, if in the financial year ending with that date there was in force in the case of any Province or any such municipality, board or authority a tax in professions, trades callings or employments the rate, or the maximum rate, of which exceeded fifty rupees per annum, the preceding provisions of this sub-section shall, unless for the time being provision to the contrary is made by a law of the Federal Legislature, have effect in relation to that Province, municipality, board or authority as if for the reference to fifty rupees per annum there were substituted a reference to that rate or maximum rate, or such lower rate, if any (being a rate greater than fifty rupees per annum), as may for the time being be fixed by a law of the Federal legislature; and any law of the Federal legislature made for any of the purposes of this proviso may be made either generally or in relation to any specified Provinces, municipalities, boards or authorities.

(3) The fact that the Provincial Legislature has power to make laws as aforesaid with respect to taxes on professions, trades, callings and employments, the generality of the entry in the Federal legislative List relating to taxes on income].

143. (1) Nothing in the foregoing provisions of this chapter affects any duties or taxes levied in any Federated State otherwise than by virtue of an Act of the Federal Legislature applying in the State.

[(1A) Nothing in the foregoing provisions of this chapter authorizes the levy of any duty or tax by the Dominion in any Acceding State unless provision in that behalf is made in the Instrument of Accession of that State.]

(2) Any taxes, duties, cesses or fees which, immediately before the commencement of Part III of this Act, were being lawfully levied by any Provincial Government, municipality or other local authority or body for the purposes of the Province, municipality, district or other local area under a law in force on the first day of January, nineteen hundred and thirty-five, may notwithstanding that those taxes, duties, cesses or fees are mentioned in the Federal Legislative List, continue to be levied and to be applied to the same purposes until provision to the contrary is made by the Federal Legislature.

144. (1) In the foregoing provisions of this chapter "net proceeds" means in relation to any tax or duty the proceeds thereof reduced by the cost of collection, and for the purposes of those provisions the net proceeds of any tax or duty, or of any part of any tax or duty, in or attributable to any area shall be ascertained and certified by the Auditor-General of India, whose certificates shall be final.

(2) Subject as aforesaid, and to any other express provision of this chapter, an Act of the Federal legislature may, in any case where under this Part of this Act the proceeds of any duty or tax are, or may be, assigned to any Province or State, or a contribution is, or may be, made to the revenues of the Federation by any State, provide for the manner in which the proceeds of any duty or tax and the amount of any contribution are to be calculated, for the times in each year and the manner at and in which any payments are to be made, for the making of adjustments between one financial year and another, and for any other incidental or ancillary matters.

The Crown and the States

145. There shall be paid to His Majesty by the Federation in each year the sums stated by His Majesty's Representative for the exercise of the functions of the Crown in its relations with Indian States to be required, whether on revenue account or otherwise, for the discharge of those functions, including the making of any payments in respect of any customary allowances to members of the family or servants of any former Ruler of any territories in India.

146. All cash contributions and payments in aspect of loans and other payments due from or by any Indian State which, if this Act had not been passed, would have formed part of the revenue of India, shall be received by His Majesty, and shall if His Majesty has so directed, be placed at the disposal of the Federation, but nothing in this Act shall derogate from the right of His Majesty, if he think fit so to do, to remit at any time the whole or any part of any such contributions or payments.

147. (1) Subject to the provisions of sub-section (3) of this section His Majesty may, in signifymg his acceptance of the

Instrument of Accession of a State, agree to remit over a period not exceeding twenty years from the date of the accession of the State to the Federation any cash contributions payable by that State.

(2) Subject as aforesaid, where any territories have been voluntarily ceded to the Crown by a Federated State before the passing of this Act—

(a) in return for specific military guarantees, or

(b) in return for the discharge of the State from obligations to provide military assistance, there shall, if His Majesty, in signifying his acceptance of the Instrument of Accession of that State, so directs be paid to that State, but in the first mentioned case on condition that the said guarantees are waived, such sums as in the opinion of His Majesty ought to be paid in respect of any such cession as aforesaid.

(3) Notwithstanding anything in this section —

(a) every such agreement or direction as aforesaid shall be such as to secure that no such remission or payment shall be made by virtue of the agreement or direction until the Provinces have begun to receive moneys under the section of this chapter relating to taxes on income, and, in the case of a remission, that the remission shall be complete before the expiration of twenty years from the date of the accession to ihe Federation of the State in question, or before the end of the second prescribed period referred to in sub-section (2) of the said section, whichever first occurs; and

(b) no contribution shall be remitted by virtue of any such agreement save in so far as it exceeds the value of any privilege or imnunity enjoyed by the State; and

(c) in fixing the amount of any payments in respect of ceded territories, account shall be taken of the value of any such privilege or immunity.

(4) This section shall apply in the case of any cash contributions the liability for which has before the passing of this Act

been discharged by payment of a capital sum or sums, and accordingly His Majesty may agree that the capital sum or sums so paid shall be repaid either by instalments or Otherwise, and such repayments shall be deemed to be remissions for the purposes of this section.

(5) In this chapter "cash contributions" means—

(a) periodical contributions in acknowledgment of the suzerainty of His Majesty, including contributions payable in connection with, any arrangement for the aid and protection of a State by His Majesty, and contributions in commutation of any obligation of a state to provide military assistance to His Majesty, or in respect of the maintenance by His-Majesty of a special force for service in connection with a State, or in respect of the maintenance of local military forces or police or in respect of the expenses of an agent;

(b) periodical contributions fixed on the creation or restoration of a State, or on a re-grant or increase of territory, including annual payments for grants of land on perpetual tenure or for equalisation of the value of exchanged territory;

(c) periodical contributions formerly payable to another State but now payable to His Majesty by right of conquest, assignment or lapse.

(6) In this chapter "privilege or immunity" means any such right, privilege, advantage or immunity of a financial character as is hereinafter mentioned, that is to say—

(a) rights, privileges or advantages in respect of, or connected with, the levying of sea customs or the production and sale of untaxed salt;

(b) sums receivable in respect of the abandonment or surrender of the light to levy internal customs duties, or to produce or manufacture salt, or to tax salt or other commodities or goods in transit, or sums receivable in lieu of grants of free salt;

(c) the annual value to the Ruler of any privilege or territory granted in respect of the abandonment or surrender of any such right as is mentioned in the last preceding paragraph;

(d) Privileges in respect of free service stamps or the free carriage of State mails on government business:

(e) the privilege of entry free from customs duties of goods imported by sea and transported in bond to the State in question; and

(f) the right to issue currency notes, not being a right, privilege, advantage or immunity surrendered upon the accession of the State, or one which, in the opinion of His Mnjesty, for any other reason ought not to be taken into account for the purposes of this chapter.

(7) An Instrument of Accession of a State shall not be deemed to be suitable for acceptance by His Majesty, unless it contains such particulars as appear to His Majesty to be necessary to enable due effect to be given to the provisions of this and the next but one succeeding sections, and in particular provision for determining from time to time the value to be attributed for the purposes of those provisions to any privilege or immunity the value of which is fluctuating or uncertain.

148. Any payments made under the last preceding section and any payments heretofore made to any State by the Governor-General in Council or by any Local Government undet any agreements made with that State before the passing of this Act, shall be charged on the revenues of the Federation or on the revenues of the corresponding Province under this Act, as the case may be.

149. Where under the foregoing provisions of this chapter there is made in any year by the Federation to a Federated State any payment or distribution of, or calculated by reference to, the net proceeds of any duty or tax, the value in and for that year of any privilege or immunity enjoyed by that State in respect of any former or existing source of revenue from a similar duty or tax or from goods of the same kind, being a privilege or immunity which has not been otherwise taken into account shall, if and

in so far as the Act of the Federal Legislature under which the payment or distribution is made so provides, be set off against the payment or distribution.

Miscellaneous Financial Provisions

150. (1) No burden shall be imposed on the revenues of the Federation or the Provinces except for the purposes of [India] or some part of [India].

(2) Subject as aforesaid, the Federation or a Province may make grants for any purpose, nothwithstanding that the purpose is not one with respect to which the Federal or the Provincial Legislature, as the case may be, may make laws.

151. (1) Rules may be made by the Governor-General and by the Governor of a Province for the purpose of securing that all moneys received on account of the revenues of the Federation or of the Province, as the case may be, shall, with such exceptions, if any as may be specified in the rules, be paid into the public account of the Federation or of the Province, and the rules so made may prescribe, or authorise some person to prescribe, the procedure to be followed in respect of the payment of money into the said account, the withdrawal with or ancillary to the matters aforesaid.

[(2) In the exercise of his powers under this section the Governor-General or a Governor shall exercise his individual judgment]

152. (1) The functions of the Governor-General with respects to the following matters shall be exercised by him in his discretion, that is to say

(a) the appointment and removal from office of the Governor and Deputy Governors of the Reserve Bank of India, the approval of their terms of office;

(b) the appointment of an officiating Governor or Deputy Governor of the Bank;

(c) the supersession of the Central Board of the Bank and any action consequent therein; and

(d) the liquidation of the Bank.

(e) In nominating directors of the Reserve Bank of India and in removing from office any director nominated by him, the Governor-General shall exercise his individual judgment.

153. No Bill or amendment which affects the coinage or currency of the Federation or the constitution or functions of Reserve Bank of India shall be introduced into or moved in [either Chamber] of the Federal legislature without the previous sanction of the Governor-General in his discretion.

154. Property vested in His Majesty for purposes of the government of the Federation shall, save in so far as any Federal law may otherwise provide, be exempt from taxes imposed by, or by any authority within, a Province or Federated State:

Provided until any Federal law otherwise provides, any property so vested which was immediately before the commencement of Part III of this Act liable, or treated as liable, to any such tax, shall, so long as that tax continues, continue to be liable, or to be treated as liable, thereto.

[154-A. Save in so far as any Federal law may otherwise provide, no Provincial law or law of a Federated State shall impose, or authorise the imposition of, a tax on the consumption or sale of electricity (whether by a Government or other persons) which is —

(a) consumed by the Federal Government, or sold to the Federal Government for consumption by that Government; or

(b) consumed in the construction, maintenance or operation of a Federal Railway by [the Federal Railway Authority or] a railway company operating that railway, or sold to [that authority or] any such railway company for consumption in the construction, maintenance or operation of a Federal Railway; and any such law imposing, or authorising the imposition of a tax on the sale of electricity shall secure that the price of electricity sold to the Federal Government for consumption by that Government, or to the Federal Railway Authority or any such railway company as aforesaid for consumption in the construction, maintenance or operation of a Federal Railway, shall be less by the amount of the tax than the price charged to other consumers of a substantial quantity of electricity.]

155. (1) Subject as hereinafter provided, the Government of a province and the Ruler of a Federated State shall not be liable to Federal taxation in respect of lands or buildings situate in [British] India or income accruing, arising or received in British India;

Provided that—

(a) where a trade or business of any kind is carried on by or on behalf of the Government of a Province in any part of British India outside that Province or by a Ruler in any part of British India, nothing in this sub-section shall exempt that Government or Ruler from any Federal taxation in respect of that trade or business, or any operations connected therewith, or any income arising in connection therewith, or any property occupied for the purposes thereof;

(b) nothing in this subsection shall exempt a Ruler from any Federal taxation in respect of any lands, buildings or income being his personal property or personal income.

(2) Nothing in this Act affects any exemption from taxation enjoyed as of right at the passing of this Act by the Ruler of an Indian State in respect of any Indian Government securities issued before that date.

156. Where under the provisions of this Act the expenses of any court or commission, or the pesion payable to or in respect of a person who has served under the Crown in India, are charged on the revenues of the Federation or the revenues of a Province, then if—

(a) in the case of a charge on the revenues of the Federation the court or commission serves any of the separate needs of a Province, or the person has served wholly or in part in connection with the affairs of a Province; or

(b) in the case of charge on the revenues of a Province, the court or commission serves any of the separate needs of the Federation or another Province, or the person has served wholly or in part in connection with the affairs of the Federation or another Province, there shall be charged on and paid out of the revenues of the Province or, as the case may be, the revenues of the federation or of the other Province, such contribution in respect of the expenses or pension as may agreed, or as may in default of agreement be determined by an arbitrator to be appointed by the Chief Justice of India.

157. (1) The Federation and every Province shall secure that there are from time to time in the hands of the Secretary of State sufficient moneys to enable him to make such payments as he may have to make in respect of liability which falls to be met out of the revenues of the Federation or of the Province as the case may be.

(2) Without prejudice to their obligations under the preceding sub-section, the Federation and every Province shall secure that there are from time to time in the hands of the Secretary of State and the High Commissioner sufficient moneys to enable payment to be made of all pensions payable out of the revenues of the Federation or the Province, as the case may be, in the United Kingdom or through officers accounting to the Secretary of State or the High Commissioner.

158. (1) His Majesty in Council may take such provision as may appear to him to be necessary or proper for defining and regulating the relations between the monetary systems of India and Burma and for purposes connected with or ancillary to those purposes, and in particular, but without prejudice to the generality of this section, such provision as may appear to His Majesty to be neccsssry or proper for the purpose of giving eftect to any arrangements with respect to the said matters made before the commencement of Part III of this Act with the approval of the Secretary of State by the Governor of Burma in Council with the Governor-General in Council or any other persons.

(2) Any sums required by an Order under this section to be paid by the Federation shall be charged on the revenues of the Federation.

159. His Majesty in Council may make provision for the grant of relief from any Federal tax on income taxed or taxable in Burma.

160. With a view to preventing undue disturbance of trade between India and Burma in the period immediately following the separation of India and Burma and with a view to safeguarding the economic interests of Burma during that period, His Majesty may be Order in Council give such directions as he thinks fit for those purposes with respect to the duties which are, while the Order is in force, to be levied on goods imported into or exported from India or Burma and with respect to ancillary and related matters.

Appendix–III

The Manipur State Constitution Act, 1947*

Chapter III
The Executive

10. Council of Ministers:

(a) Subject to the provisions of this Act and subject also to the provisions of the Rules for the Administration of the Manipur State the Executive Authority of the State is delegated to and shall vest in the Council of Ministers.

(b) Where under this Act or the Rules for the Administration of the State, it is requisite that the approval of the Maharajah shall be taken to any measure, the Chief Minister shall seek the approval of the Maharajah in person or in writing and shall obtain the Maharajah's orders thereon. Should in any case the Maharajah's approval be withheld, the Maharajah shall be pleased to inform the Chief Minister in person or in writing and to communicate his reason for withholding such approval in writing to the Council.

Chapter IV
The State Assembly

17. There shall be constituted a State Assembly. The Assembly shall be elected for a period of three years and shall comprise Representatives freely elected by the people on an adult franchise and on the principle of Joint Electorate. Elections shall be in such manner and by such franchise as may be laid down under the Rules for the elections to the State Assembly provided always that the representatives returnable from General, Hill and

* Extract from *Manipur State Constitution Act, 1947* (Imphal: State Press, 1947).

Mahamadan Constituencies shall be in the ratios of 30:18:3 respectively with an additional two seats for the Representatives of Educational and Commercial Interests.

18. The StateAssembly may debate all matters concerning the Government and well being of the State which, in the opinion of five Members of the Assembly, it is in the public interest to debate. The Assembly shall tender such advice to the Council of Ministers in any matter in which a majority of the Members present, are agreed on the advice which shall be tendered provided that no matter touching the Maharajah's Prerogative shall be debated and provided that the Maharajah may on the advice of the Council, veto debates on any matter where such course shall in the public interest be necessary.
19. The State Assembly shall not tender advice to the Council on any matter which is of primary concern to the Hill People unless such advice has the support of a majority of the Hill Representatives in the Assembly.
20. Subject to the provisions of this Act, the Assembly may make Rules for regulating its proceedings and the conduct of Business.
21. Where in any case it is required to pass a vote of no confidence against a Minister of the Council for his individual acts, a motion of no confidence, signed by not less than ten Members of the Assembly and laying out in detail, the facts giving rise to the motion, may with the permission of the Speaker of the Assembly be moved. If such motion shall receive the support of at least 75 per cent of the Members present and voting, it shall be forwarded through the Chief Minister to the Maharajah, who, unless there appear strong and valid reasons to the contrary which shall be recorded in writing, shall after consultation with the Chief Minister require the Minister against whom the motion has been passed to resign.
22. Where in any case the State Council or the Maharajah is in the special circumstances of any case unable to accept the advice of the Assembly, the Maharajah or the State Council as the case may be, shall communicate in writing the reasons which have led to such course and shall give facilities for personal discussion of the matter with a representative or representatives deputed by the Assembly.
23. Subject to the provisions of this Act and to the Rules framed under it for the disposal of the Assembly Business, there shall

be Freedom of Speech in the Assembly and no Member shall be liable to any proceedings in any court in respect of any speech or vote given by him in the Assembly or a committee thereof and no person shall be liable in respect of any publication by or under the authority of the Assembly of any report, paper, vote or proceedings.

24. No Member of the Assembly shall be liable to arrest or detention in prison under a Civil Process:-

(a) If he is a member of the Assembly, during the continuance of the Assembly,

(b) If he is a member of any Committee of the Assembly, during the continuance of the meeting of the Committee.

25. The elected Ministers, the Speaker, Deputy Speaker and Members of the Assembly shall receive such emoluments as may be determined from time to time by the Assembly.

Chapter V
The Law Making Authority

26. The Law Making Authority in the State shall consist of the Maharajah in Council in Collaboration with the State Assembly acting under Section 18, above.

27. When the Council or the Assembly consider that a law should be enacted the Council shall cause a bill to be drafted, which shall be laid before the Assembly and a reasonable time shall be given for consideration thereof. The Council shall then cause to be made such alterations or amendments as may be deemed necessary in the light of the advice tendered by the Assembly and the Chief Minister shall submit the Bill in its final form for the assent of the Maharajah.

28. On the receipt of the Maharajah's Assent the Bill shall be published in the State Gazette and shall become an Act having the force of Law.

29. Should the Maharajah in any case withhold his Assent to a Bill, that Bill shall lapse as if it had not been passed. If the Assent of the Maharajah is not forthcoming within one calendar month of the Bill being submitted to him he shall be deemed to have withheld his Assent.

30. Where the Assent of the Maharajah to any Bill is withheld, the Council may cause the self-same Bill to be introduced in the next

session of the Assembly and if passed without amendment by a 75 per cent majority of the Assembly, the Bill shall be certified over the Seal of the Council and shall become Law.

31. Nothing in this Chapter shall be deemed to derogate from the absolute right of the Maharajah-in-Council to promulgate, in emergency cases, orders having the forces of law without previous reference to the Assembly where the public interest in their opinion demands that such order shall be promulgated provided that the first opportunity shall be taken of laying the order before the Assembly for consideration. Any such order shall not have the force of law for a period of more than six months.

Chapter VI
Finance

32. The Revenue of the State and such other receipts as may accrue from whatever source, less such reasonable percentage of the total real Revenue as may be reserved for the Civil List, are placed at the disposal of the Council for expenditure on the Government of the State in the manner prescribed by the State Account Rules saving that in every year a sum representing not less than 17½ per cent of the average real revenue of the State for the preceding three years shall be allocated for expenditure on the welfare and administration of the Hill people.

33. The Minister in charge of Finance shall prepare an Annual Budget showing the estimated receipts and expenditure for the ensuing year classified under the prescribed heads of account and shall submit it to the Assembly within fifteen days of its meeting for the Budget Session along with a statement of account for the previous year.

34. The Assembly shall after considering the budget, submit it with their recommendation to the Council, who, having made such modification as may be deemed necessary shall submit it to the Maharajah for approval. Where any delay occurs in the granting of Assent to the Budget by the Maharajah and where such Assent has not been obtained by the first day of the financial year, provisional affect shall be given to the Budget as passed by the Assembly and funds shall be drawn against its provisions as if it had received Assent.

35. The Maharajah's Civil List shall be fixed at a figure equal to 10 per cent of the real revenues of the State over the preceding three years, provided that no extraordinary revenues shall be

taken into account when determining this amount and provided that no State revenue in excess of Rs. twenty lakhs shall be taken into account in any one year. The appropriation to the Maharajah's Civil List shall be non-votable and shall not be the subject of debate in the Assembly.

36. No tax whatsoever shall be shown in the budget and no tax shall be collected by any officer of the State or by any person unless such tax has been imposed by due process of Law.

Chapter VII
Hill People

38. The Council shall be responsible for the welfare and the good administration of the Hill People of the State and shall provide such funds for this purpose as may, subject to the provision of Section 32 above, be deemed necessary, provided that the Local Authorities in the Hills shall exercise such powers of Local self Government as may be laid down in the Manipur State Hill (Administration) Regulation, 1947.

Chapter IX
The Judicature

(A) There shall be a complete separation of the Judiciary from the Executive.

Chapter X
Fundamental Rights and Duties of Citizenship

44. All citizens shall be equal before the law. Titles and other privileges of birth shall not be recognized in the eyes of law.

45. The liberty of the individual shall be guaranteed. No person may be subjected to any judicial interrogation or placed under arrest or be in any other way deprived of his liberty, save as provided by law.

46. No person shall be tried save by a competent Court.

47. No person may be tried except by a competent Court who shall give all opportunity to such person to defend himself by all legal means.

48. All penalties shall be as determined by law.

49. Capital punishment may not be inflicted for purely political crimes.

50. No citizen may be banished from the State, expelled from one part of the country to another, and obliged to reside in a specified place save in such cases as may be expressly determined by law.

51. Every dwelling shall be inviolable save under express provision of law.

52. There shall be guaranteed to all people, Justice, Social, Economic and Political; equality of status, of opportunity and before the law; freedom of thought, expression of belief, faith, worship, vocation, association, and action, subject to law and public morality.

53. The practice of Arts and Sciences shall be unrestricted and shall enjoy the protection and support of the State.

54. Without any prejudice to the communities concerned, public institution shall be opened to all citizens of the State.

55. (a) All Officials of the State or of a Local government shall be answerable before the law for their individual and unlawful actions.

(b) Where damage is caused to an individual by the act of an official of the State or an official of a Local Government, such individual may sue the State before the Chief Court and may seek redress save where such damage has been caused by a bona fide act of a State servant in pursuance of a policy duly laid down by a Competent Authority.

Chapter XI
General Clauses

56. Any provision of this Act may be subject to amendment by the Maharajah-in-Council provided that such amendment is laid before the Assembly and receives the support of at least 80 per cent of the members of the State Assembly present and voting, when such amendment is debated

57. Where in any case circumstances arise which prevent the proper operation in law or in spirit of this Constitution Act, the Council may at their discretion refer the matter for decision to such authority outside the State as may be decided hereafter and the decision of that authority shall be binding.

58. The Court Language of the State shall be Manipuri or English.

Sd/-
(Bodh Chandra Singh)
Maharajah of Manipur

Appendix–IV

The Manipur State Hill Peoples (Administration) Regulation 1947*

Whereas, it is expedient to consolidate and amend the law governing the administration of the Manipur State Hill Peoples ; now therefore the Maharaja of Manipur is pleased to make the following Regulation :-

Chapter 1. General

Title, Extent, Commencement and Repeal

1. (a) This regulation may be called the Manipur State Hill Peoples (Administration) Regulation 1947.

(b) It shall apply to all the Hill Peoples of the Manipur State.

(c) It shall come into force on such date as the Maharaja may appoint and all previous rules of administration which are in conflict with this regulation shall be deemed to be repealed.

Definition

2. In this Regulation except where the contrary appears from the context :-

(a) "Chief Court" shall mean the Chief Court of the Manipur State as constituted under the Manipur State Courts Act 1947 for the trial of cases or suits to which Hill men are a party.

(b) "Heinous Offence" shall mean and include any of the following:— Murder, Culpable Homicide, Causing Grievous Hurt, Rape, Kidnapping or Abducting in order to subject

* Extract from *Manipur State constitution Act, 1947.*

to slavery, Disposing or Buying of persons as slaves, Habitual dealing in slaves, Dacoity, Robbery, Rioting, House breaking Mischief by Fire, or any explosive substance, any offence under Chapter VI or XII of the Indian Penal Code, any offence punishable under the Arms Act and any attempt to commit or abetment of any of the above offences.

(c) "Pleader" shall include a Mukhtar or any professional Agent.

(d) "Sub Divisional Officer" shall mean the Officer appointed to be in executive charge of a Sub Division.

(e) "Circle Officer" shall mean the Officer appointed to be in executive charge of a Circle.

(f) "Circle Bench' shall mean the Circle Officer sitting with two or more members of the Elected Circle Council selected by him at his discretion for the trial of any given case.

Responsibility for Administration in the Hills.

3. The responsibility for the administration of the Hill Peoples is vested in the Maharaja in Council and shall be exercised in accordance with the Constitution Act of the State and the provisions of this Regulation as amended from time to time.

CHAPTER VI
General

34. The Chief Court may from time to time issue licenses to legal practitioners for practice in the State Courts and may make rules and regulations regarding such practitioners. The Chief Court may further appoint and make rules for the practice of petition – writers.

35. (a) The Courts of Criminal and Civil Judicature in the State shall be as given in Schedules I and II to this Act, and in consultation with the Chief Court, the State Council may revise the Schedules as may be deemed necessary from time to time.

(b) The appointment of Judges and Magistrates shall be governed by the Manipur State Administration and Appointment Board Rules.

(c) The Chief Court shall have power to invest the Judicial Officers and benches with the powers provided for in this Act.

36. Nothing contained in this Act shall be deemed to limit or bar the full and unqualified exercise of His Highness's pleasure in calling for the records of any civil or criminal case decided by any of the State Courts whenever in His Highness's opinion there has been a breach of law of custom or usage having the force of law and advising the Court to take such action as he may deem suitable.

37. The existing law and practice as far as they are not modified by this Act shall continue to be in force in regard to both Civil and Criminal Courts.

FIRST SCHEDULE

Criminal Courts

1. Chief Court in the Criminal side which shall also exercise the power of a Court of Session under this Act.
2. Two Courts of First Class Magistrate.
3. Two Courts of Second Class Magistrate.
4. Thirteen Courts of the Village Panchayets.

SECOND SCHEDULE

1. Chief Court is the civil side which shall also exercise the powers of a Court a District Judge.
2. Two Courts of Munsiffs.
3. Thirteen Courts of the Village Panchayats.
4. Appointments to all executive posts in the Hill Administration shall be made in accordance with the Rules for the Manipur State Appointments Board excepting where specific provision shall be made for such appointment in this Regulation.

CHAPTER II

Local Authorities

5. For the purpose of administration all villages to which this Regulation applies shall be grouped into Circles and Sub-Divisions as provided in Schedule I to the Regulation.

6. In each village of 20 tax paying houses or over, there shall be constituted a Village Authority which shall be nominated in accordance with the custom of the village and shall consist of the Chief or Khullakpa of the village with his council of elders,

if any. The village authority so nominated shall be formally recognized by the Sub-Divisional Officer who shall be the final authority in all matters concerning the appointment and constitution of a village authority saving that an appeal shall lie to the Minister in charge of Hill Administration from the decision of the Sub-Divisional Officer in such matters.

7. In each circle there shall be constituted a Circle Authority which shall comprise the Circle Officer and a Council of five Members elected by the Village authorities falling within the Circle. The Circle Authority so constituted shall be formally recognized by the Sub-Divisional Officer who shall be the final authority in all matters concerning the election and constitution of the Circle Authority saving that an appeal shall lie to the Minister in charge of Hill Administration from the decision of the Sub-Divisional Officer in such matters.

8. In each Sub-Division there shall be a Sub-Divisional Officer who shall exercise general executive control over the local authorities in the Sub-Division under the orders of the Minister in charge of Hill Administration.

Elections

9. (i) Elections to Circle Authorities shall be held triennially in the first week of November. The Sub-Divisional Officer acting through the Circle Officer shall be responsible for carrying out the elections within each Circle. In all Electorate matters the decision of the Minister in charge of Hill Administration shall be final.

(ii) In the election of the Circle Authority no village of under 20-tax paying houses at the house counting immediately prior to the election, shall be eligible to vote. In villages with houses in excess of this number the following votes may be recorded :—

20-50 Tax paying houses ... ... One vote.

51-100 Tax paying houses ... ... Two votes.

101-200 Tax paying houses ... ... Three votes.

In villages with more than 200 tax paying houses, one additional vote may be recorded for every 100 houses in excess of 200.

CHAPTER III
Executive Powers and Responsibilities

10. Subject to the provisions of this Regulation, the Minister of the State Council for the Hill Administration shall be responsible for the Administration of the Hill Peoples under this Regulation saving that in any matter concerning the exercise of executive functions in regard to Law and Order under this Regulation, the Levy, Assessment of Collection of any tax on houses, on land or on the produce of land, the settlement of any disputes regarding land or the produce of land and any questions regarding the ownership of land, the recommendation in writing of the Circle Authority concerned shall first be obtained and no decision of the Council which runs contrary to this recommendation shall have the force of Law unless it is supported by both the Hill Ministers on the Council.

11. The Minister in charge of Hill Administration may delegate such powers and functions to the Sub-Divisional Officer and to the Circle Officers as may seem suitable saving that such delegation shall not derogate from his general responsibility under Section 10 above.

12. Notwithstanding the provisions of Section 10 above, the Circle Authorities shall, subject to the specific provisions of this Regulation, exercise powers as under:—

    (a) Subject to general supervision by the State Educational Department the Circle Authority shall be responsible for the administration of Lower and Upper Primary Education within the Circle. Middle English and Higher Education shall be administered by the State Education Department.

    (b) Subject to general supervision by the State Public Works Department, the Circle Authority shall be responsible for the construction and maintenance of all public buildings of Katcha or semi Katcha type and the maintenance of Pucca Buildings within the circle. The construction and maintenance of iron and all major bridges and all Pucca Buildings shall be the responsibility of the State Public Work Department.

    (c) The State Medical Department shall be responsible for the provision of Medical facilities in the Hills and for the administration of Hill Dispensaries and Hospitals, saving that all measures for the betterment of the Public Health and for the control of disease shall be carried out in collaboration with the Circle Authority and that the Circle Authority shall have a special responsibility for the encouragement of personal hygiene and the provision of clean water supplies.

(d) Administration of all State Reserved Forests or Mahals shall be the responsibility of the State Forest Department who shall operate in collaboration with the Circle Authority in that area in which the Reserved Forest lies. No new era shall be demarcated as Forest Reserve without prior consultation with the Circle Authority concerned who shall be given an opportunity to record in writing any objection they may have to the formation of such reserve.

The Circle Authority shall have a special responsibility for the preservation of timber in the open reserves and no timber shall be cut from such reserves without a permit from the Circle Authority who shall levy such fees for the issue of such permits as may be laid down by the State Council from time to time.

It shall further be the special responsibility of the Circle Authority to check wasteful and unnecessary firing of the Hill sides and to reduce the areas under Jhum Cultivation to the minimum.

(e) Subject to the general supervision of the State Agricultural Department, the Circle Authority shall be responsible for the encouragement of better means of agriculture in the Circle, the introduction of improved seeds and the spread of wet rice and terraced cultivation with a consequent reduction of Jhuming. It shall be the particular responsibility of the Circle Authority to ensure that Jhum land once relinquished shall not in any circumstances revert to Jhum cultivation.

(f) Subject to such Rules and Regulations as may be issued by the State Council, the Circle Authority shall be responsible for the maintenance of land Records within the Circle and for the assessment and collection of such taxes on the land or other immovable property as may be levied from time to time. It shall be the responsibility of the Circle Officer to ensure that all such collections are accounted for in a correct manner and are credited to the State Account in accordance with the State Account Rules.

13. Where any specific responsibility in vested in the Circle Authority under the provisions of Section 12 above, the Circle Authority shall have full power to determine how such responsibility shall be carried out and shall issue such orders in this regard as it may consider necessary, saving that in any case where such orders run contrary to Public policy or are likely to lead to breach of the peace of a break-down in the administration, the State Council may require the Minister in charge of Hill Administration to intervene and revoke the order issued by the Circle Authority.

CHAPTER IV. A

Law and Justice and the Maintenance of Public Order

14. The Circle Authorities shall be responsible for the maintenance of Law and Order within the Circle and shall exercise this authority wherever such authorities exist.

15. (a) The ordinary duties of the Police in respect of crime shall be discharged by the Village Authorities where such exist and by the Circle Authority where there is no Village Authority. They shall maintain peace and order within their jurisdiction.

    (b) The Village Authorities shall not be deemed to be Police for the purpose of Section 162 of the Code of Criminal Procedure 1898.

    (c) The Village Authorities shall watch and report on any vagrant or any bad or suspicious character found within their jurisdiction and may apprehend any such person if they have reasonable grounds for suspecting that he has committed or is about to commit an offence and shall hand him over to the Circle Officer without delay.

16. On the commission of any heinous offence within their jurisdiction, the inhabitants of the village shall at once, if possible, apprehend the offender and hand him over with a report on the crime to the

Circle Officer. If the culprit is not apprehended the Village Authority shall proceed to the scene of the occurrence and having enquired into it shall forward a report to the Circle Officer.

17. It shall be the duty of the Village Authority to report to the Circle Officer as soon as is possible all Crimes, Violent Death and Serious Accidents occurring within its jurisdiction and all occurrences whether within or beyond that jurisdiction which come to their knowledge and are likely to affect the Public Peace; and to arrest and to deliver of offenders as soon as may be, to the court having jurisdiction to try them.

18. The Village Authority may pursue beyond their jurisdiction any offender or vagrant or any bad character or suspicious character whom they consider it necessary to apprehend under the provision of Sub Section (c) of section 15. They shall not however ordinarily arrest the offender or such person without informing the Village Authority within whose jurisdiction he is found, and inviting their assistance, but may do so if there is reasonable apprehension that he may otherwise escape.

19. When the Village Authority is unable to arrest an offender, they may apply to the Circle Officer or a Head Lambu for assistance.

20. (a) All inhabitants of the Areas, or any person, to which or to whom this regulation applies are bound to aid the Village Authority when required to do so, for the maintenance of order or apprehending offenders and are liable to a fine for failing to give such assistance.

    (b) Such fine if imposed by a Village Authority shall not exceed Rs. 200/- , if imposed by a Circle Authority shall not exceed Rs. 500/-.

    (c) An appeal shall lie from an order passed by a Village Authority under Sub Section (b) to the Circle Authority provided the fine imposed is not less than Rs. 20/- and from such a fine passed by a Circle Authority to the Hill Bench at Imphal provided the fine imposed is not less than Rs. 100/-.

    (d) If it should appear in any case arising under Sub Section (a) above, that a whole community is to blame and that particular offenders cannot be discovered, the matter may at the discretion of the Sub-Divisional Officer be submitted to the Hill Bench at Imphal who shall consider the case and may impose a fine not exceeding Rs. 5,000/- on the community. An appeal against such order may lie to the Chief Court whose decision shall be final.

(e) Any fine levied under Sub Section (b) or (d) of this Section may be recovered by distraint of the property of the persons or person on whom it is imposed.

21. Without prejudice to any punishment to which he may be liable under any other law, a member of a Village Authority shall, for any misconduct in the exercise of his functions under this chapter, but punishable with a fine which may extend to Rs. 1000/- or with imprisonment of either description for a term which may extend to six months, on conviction by the Circle Authority. An appeal shall lie against any order passed under this section to the Hill Bench at Imphal, whose decision shall be final.

22. The Chief Court may at any time call for the proceedings in any matter arising under Sections 20 and 21 where it appears that grave injustice has been done and may modify or set aside an order passed by a Village Authority under Section 20 (b) or an order original or appellate passed by a Circle Authority or the Hill Bench under either of these Sections.

CHAPTER IV. B
Hill Courts and Criminal Proceedings

23. Criminal Justice shall be administered by the Court of the Village Authority, the Court of the Circle Authority, the Hill Bench at Imphal and the Chief Court of the Manipur State as constituted for the trial of Hill cases under the Manipur State Courts Act 1947. In any area for which there is no Village Authority, Original Criminal Powers shall be exercised by the Circle Bench of that area provided always that the Chief of Elders of any village may try any case which it is customary for them to try and may pass such sentence as in customary. 24. The Court of a Village Authority shall try any case involving any of the under mentioned offence in which the person or persons accused is or are resident within their jurisdiction.

(a) Theft including theft in a building.

(b) Mischief not being mischief by fire or any explosive substance.

(c) Cattle theft and illegal slaughter of cattle.

(d) Simple Hurt.

(e) Assault or using criminal forces. 25. The Circle Bench shall exercise the powers of a Magistrate of the first class as defined in the Criminal Procedure Code and shall comprise the Circle Officer and any two members of the Circle Council.

26. The Hill Bench at Imphal shall exercise the powers of a Sessions Court under the Criminal Procedure Code and shall comprise a bench of which a judge of the Chief Court shall be chairman sitting with two Hill men as Judges.

27. A Village Authority may impose a fine not exceeding Rs. 200/- for any offence which they are competent to try and may also award payment in restitution or compensation to the extent of the injury sustained. Such fines and payments may be enforced by distraint of the property of the offender.

Where a Village Authority is of the opinion that the sentence they are competent to pass is insufficient in the circumstances of the case they shall without a further delay produce the offender before the Circle Authority who shall hear the evidence and pass sentence.

28. The Hill Bench may order compensation to be paid to any person in a Criminal Case out of the proceeds of fines imposed in the Case.

29. The Village Authorities shall decide all cases in open Darbar in the presence of at least three witness who shall be independent, the complainant and the accused. They are empowered to order the attendance of all the foregoing and of the witness to be examined in the case and to impose a fine not exceeding Rs. 100/- on any person failing to attend when so ordered.

30. If any person on whom a fine has been imposed by a Village Authority fails to deposit the amount at once or within such further time as the Village Authority may allow, that Authority shall send him to the Circle Officer to be a dealt with in such

manner as he may deem fit unless the accused person gives notice to appeal against such decision and appeal is permissible under this Regulation.

31. Any person aggrieved by the decision of a Village Authority may appeal within fifteen days to the Circle Bench who on the receipt of the appeal shall try the case **de novo**, provided always that no appeal shall lie in any case where the sentence imposed is the payment of a fine of Rs. 20/- or less.

32. An appeal shall lie from an original or appellate order of the Circle Bench to the Hill Bench provided always that no appeal shall lie from an original order in which the sentence involved is a fine of Rs. 100/- or less or a term of imprisonment of one month or less.

33. An appeal shall lie to the Chief Court of the State from a sentence of the Hill Bench imposing imprisonment for any term exceeding one year, or a fine exceeding Rs. 500/- or from an order imposing a sentence of death or transportation for life. In all other cases no appeal shall lie from an order of the Hill Bench saving that in any case where a person other than a Hill man is party, an appeal shall lie from a sentence of imprisonment or a fine exceeding Rs. 100/-

34. All appeals under Sections 32 and 33 above, must be presented within 30 days from the date of the order appealed against, excluding the time taken in obtaining a copy of the order, provided that an appeal from a sentence of death shall be preferred within seven days from the date of sentence excluding the time taken in obtaining a copy of the order. The Hill Bench shall on passing a sentence of death, inform the person sentenced, of the above provision.

35. The Hill Bench or the Circle Bench may call for the proceedings of any subordinate Court and may reduce, enhance or cancel any sentence passed or may remand the case for retrial if in the opinion of the Hill Bench or the Circle Bench gross injustice has been done. The Chief Court may in any case where they consider gross injustice has been done, exercise the same power with regard to a sentence passed by the Hill Bench. The Minister in charge of Hill Administration may also require the Chief Court

to call for any proceedings and pass such orders as may be deemed necessary in review.

36. When final orders involving the death sentence have been passed by the Chief Court, a petition of Mercy may lie to the Maharaja who shall take the advice of the Council as to the orders which shall be passed thereon. Final orders of any death sentence shall be subject to confirmation by His Excellency the Agent to the Crown Representative as laid down in section 12 of the Manipur State Courts Act. On rejection of such petition the sentence of death shall be executed at the Manipur State Jail in accordance with the rules and procedure in force in the State from time to time.

37. The Chief Court, the Hill Bench and the Circle Bench shall be guided in regard to procedure by the principles of the Code of Criminal Procedure 1898 so far as they are applicable to the circumstances of the tribes and consistent with the principles of this Regulation. The chief exceptions are:—

(a) Verbal orders or notice shall only be requisite in any case except when a regular Lambu is employed or when the person concerned is not a resident of, or not present in the Tribal Area at the time, but orders of summons shall in every case be for a fixed day and the order shall be made known to the person concerned or to some adult member of his family, or failing this, shall be openly proclaimed at the place he was last known to be, in time to allow him if he sees fit to appear.

(b) The proceedings of the Village Authorities need not be recorded in writing, but the Hill Bench and the Circle Bench may require the Village Authorities to report their proceedings in any way which appears suitable.

(c) There shall be no preliminary enquires by Lambus unless a Sub Divisional Officer, a Circle Officer or the Hill Bench sees fit to direct one.

(d) Recognisance to appear shall not be taken unless it appears necessary to the Circle Officer or the Hill Bench.

(e) Proceedings before the Circle Bench or the Hill Bench may be in English or Manipuri.

38. No pleader shall allowed to appear in any case before a Circle Bench of Village Authority and may only appear before the Hill Bench with the permission of that Bench.

CHAPTER IV. C
Civil Courts and Proceedings

39. Civil Justice shall be administered by the Chief Court, the Hill Bench, the Circle Bench and the Village Authorities.

40. The Village Authorities may try suits the value of which does not exceed Rs. 500/- in which both the parties reside within their jurisdiction. The Village Authority may appoint one or more assessors to assist them in coming to a decision and when they do so shall record, but shall not be bound by, the opinion of such assessor or assessors.

41. (a) All suits tried by the Village Authority shall be decided in open Darbar in the presence of the parties and at least three independent witness.

(b) The Circle Officer may direct a Village Authority to report their proceedings in any case or class of case in any way which may appear to him to be suitable. Save as required by such direction no record of any proceeding need be maintained.

(c) After hearing the parties and their witness if any, the Village Authority shall pronounce a decision.

42. Any person aggrieved by the decision of a Village Authority may appeal to the Circle Bench provided that no appeal shall lie where the value of the suit does not exceed Rs. 35/-.

43. (a) Unless any party having a right of appeal against a decision of a Village Authority give notice when such decision is announced of his intention to appeal, the Village Authority shall carry out the decision forthwith and for such puropose may proceed by distraint of any property belonging to any person liable to pay any sum under the decision, unless such person furnishes security to the satisfaction of the Village Authority.

(b) If notice of intention to appeal is given, the Village Authority shall send the parties and witness to the Appellate Authority at once, and one of the members of the Village Authority or one of the independent witnesses shall accompany them.

44. The Circle Bench shall try all suits the value of which does not exceed Rs. 1,000/- in which both the parties reside within the Circle which do not fall within the competence of a Village Authority.

45. Any person aggrieved by the decision of a Circle Bench may appeal to the Hill Bench provided that no appeal shall lie where the value of the suit does not exceed Rs. 100/- .

46. The Hill Bench shall try all suits which do not fall within the competence of the Village Authority or the Circle Bench.

47. Any person aggrieved by the decision of the Hill Bench may appeal to the Chief Court provided that no appeal shall lie where the value of the suit does not exceed Rs. 1,000/-.

48. All Civil Courts operating under this Regulation shall have power to order attendance of the parties and witness and to levy a fine of up to Rs. 100/- against persons failing to attend when ordered to do so.

49. All Civil Courts shall have power to award cost as well as compensation which shall not exceed Rs. 100/-, to the defendants in any case brought against them where the case is found to be vexatious or unfounded.

50. In any case where it appears that a grave injustice has been done the Chief Court, the Hill Bench or a Circle Bench may on application by the aggrieved party, call for the records from the immediately subordinate court and may direct that a case shall be re-tried. In every such case the attention of the lower court shall be drawn to the defects in the case and advice shall be given on the action which requires to be taken: in the alternative a court exercising powers under the Section may amend or cancel the decree.

51. Every petition or application under Section 50 above, shall be accompanied by a copy of the order against which the application is made and shall be filed within 30 days of the date of such order excluding the time taken in procuring a copy of the order.

52. All Courts shall be guided by the spirit but shall not be bound by the letter, of the Code of Civil Procedure 1908, and shall follow the State Limitation Act.

53. (a) If any decree is modified or amended as a result of an appeal or an order under Section 50 above, the decree as so modified or amended shall for the purpose of execution be deemed to be the decree of the Original Court.

    (b) Decrees against persons resident beyond the jurisdiction of a court, if satisfaction cannot be obtained within that jurisdiction, shall be transferred for execution to a court having jurisdiction.

54. Houses, necessary clothing, cooking utensils or implements whereby the owner or his family subsist, shall not be attached, sold or transferred in execution of a decree, unless the house or other thing so exempted is the actual subject matter of the suit. Land may be sold or temporarily transferred where custom admits of individual rights in it being recognized.

55. No person shall be imprisoned for debt except when the Circle of Hill Bench is satisfied that h has made a fraudulent disposition or concealment of property. In such case the debtor may be detained for a period not exceeding six months.

56. No pleader shall be allowed to appear in any case before the Village Authorities of Circle Bench. The Chief Court and the Hill Bench may at their discretion allow a pleader to appear before them when hearing a case in which Hill men are involved.

CHAPTER IV. D
Evidence and General Provisions

57. (a) In Criminal Cases before the Circle and Hill Bench, oaths shall be administered to all witnesses.

    (b) In Civil suits before the Circle and Hill Benches oaths shall not be administered to the parties and witness unless either party so require of the court so determine.

    (c) When an oath is administered it shall be in the form in which the court considers most binding on the person making it.

    (d) In any case where the parties so elect, whether civil or criminal, decision shall be made by oath or ordeal and such decision shall be binding on the parties. Where any party refuses to take such oath or undergo such ordeal when challenged to do so, judgment may be passed against him without further proceedings.

58. The Circle and the Hill Benches shall be guided by the principles of the Indian Evidence Act 1872 in all Criminal Cases and Civil Suits but shall not be bound by the letter of that Act.

59. (a) All Civil Suits and Criminal Proceedings to which both Hill men and Manipuris of the Valley are a party shall be tried by the Hill Bench as a Court of Original Jurisdiction.

(b) In all cases where the parties reside in different Circles the case shall be tried by the Circle Bench under whose jurisdiction the cause of action arises.

CHPTER IV. E

Case Regarding Land and Village Settlement

60. Where any dispute arises regarding the ownership of land or the right of cultivation over land, the Village Authority shall where the land in dispute falls within their jurisdiction and where both parties to the dispute resigned within their jurisdiction, take all steps necessary to effect a compromise between the parties. If compromise proves impossible or if the parties to the dispute reside within the jurisdiction of two or more Village Authority, the dispute shall be placed before the Circle Bench who shall decide the case.

61. (a) An appeal shall lie against any decision of the Circle Bench under Section 60 above, to the Sub Divisional Offer to the Hill Bench, whose decision shall be final.

(b) The Hill Bench may call for the proceedings of any Subordinate Court and may amend any decision of that courts if in the opinion of the Hill Bench gross injustice has been done.

62. Where the matter in dispute is in regard to the Settlement of a Village or in any case where Village Boundaries are involved, the case shall invariably be placed before the Circle Bench by the Village Authorities concerned. The Circle Bench shall enquire into the case and shall submit a report with their recommendations to the Sub Divisional Officer who shall pass orders thereon.

63. An appeal shall lie from an order passed by a Sub Divisional Officer under Section 62 above, to the Hill Bench.

64. No new settlement, nor the formation of any Machet shall be permitted without the authority in writing of the Sub Divisional

Officer. Any party aggrieved by the order of such authority may petition the Member in charge of Hill Administration for redress.

CHAPTER V
Financial Provisions

65. The Sub Divisional Officer shall in February of each year direct the Circle Officer to frame a budget for the Circle administration during the ensuing financial year in those matters which are the particular responsibility of the Circle Authority. Provision funds for all other matters shall be made in the budget of the State Department concerned by the Minister in charge of that Department in consultation with the Minister in charge of the Hill Administration. The Budgets for the Circle when complete shall be forwarded by the Sub Divisional Officer to the Minister in charge of all Hill Administration who shall pass them with his comments to the State Finance Department.

66. (a) On the Receipt side Revenue including all Judicial fines levied by the Circle Bench, proceeds from the sale of Courts fee stamps and all miscellaneous receipts.

(b) Where a fine is levied by a village Authority the customary village fine may be retained by the Authority and the balance shall be credited to the State Revenue.

67. On the Expenditure side shall be show all expenditure required for the administration of those subjects which are the particular responsibility of the Circle Authority and for the day to day administration of the Circle Head Quarters and staff provided that no provision shall be made for any item for which the approval of competent authority has not first been obtained.

68. The Sub Divisional Officer shall be competent to sanction expenditure on any item for which provision is made in the Circle Budget, but he may in no case sanction expenditure in excess of the Budget provision or re-appropriation from any head without the express sanction of the Minister in charge of Hill Administration according to Rule.

69. In all financial and account matters the principles laid down in the State Account Rules shall so far as is possible be followed. Accounts shall be maintained in accordance with instructions to be issued by the State Finance Department and shall be subject to Audit by the State Audit Officer.

70. All Bills for payments to be made by a Circle Officer shall be drawn by the Circle Officer and shall be submitted to the Minister in charge of Hill Administration through the Sub-Divisional Officer who shall be brought into the Circle Account and credit shall be made to the Treasury through the Sub-Divisional Officer who shall be held responsible for the full collection of such revenues within the Sub-Division.

71. The Budget for the Hill Administration shall be dealt with according to rule provided that in no financial year shall the total expenditure on Hill Administration under all heads fall below a figure equal to 17½ % of the average real revenues of the State for the immediately preceding three years.

72. A Circle Authority may, with the previous sanction of the Minister in charge of the Hill Administration, levy such local rate or cess within the circle as may seem suitable for the provision of funds for local improvement schemes subject to the proviso that the levy of such rate or cess shall not be made in such manner as to adversely

Appendix–V

Rules for the Administration of the Manipur State 1947

In supersession of all previous orders on this subject, His Highness the Maharajah of Manipur has been pleased to promulgate the following rules for the administration of the Manipur State.

These Rules shall be called "THE MANIPUR STATE ADMINISTRATION RULES".

1. They shall come into force the 1st july 1947 and shall override all previous rules.

2. Subject to the previous of these rules and subject also to such other direction as His Highness may be pleased to sanction hereafter, the Executive Authority of the State shall be exercised by the Manipur State Council, which shall consist of the Chief Minister as President of the Council, and six Ministers.

3. The Chief Minister and the Ministers of the Council shall be appointed by His Highness on such terms and condition as may be agreed upon.

4. The control of the Judiciary shall vest in the Chief Judge. The power and jurisdiction of the State Chief Courts subordinate thereto shall be governed by the Manipur State Courts Act. The Chief Judge shall be appointed or removed by His Highness acting on the advice of the Council. The Chief Judge shall not be a Minister of the Council but shall have a similar status and shall rank next below the Chief Minister in order of precedence. No Judge of the Chief Court shall be appointed by His Highness in Council on the advice of the Chief Judge.

5. Each Minister of the Council and the Chief Judge shall be responsible for the internal economy and the efficient working

of the Departments placed under him will be responsible for seeing that orders are carried out faithfully and without delay.

6. All matters relating to His Highness's Civil List and all matters affecting His Highness's personal prerogatives shall be the sole responsibility of His Highness.

   Note:- His Highness the Maharajah's personal prerogative shall for the purpose of this rule be taken to mean all matters relating to the privy purse which are the sole concern of His Highness as head of the Ruling Family, all matters which are his sole concern as Religious head of the Manipur Hindus and all Matters connected with Palace Ceremonial and the award of Titles to State subjects. His Highness's personal prerogative shall not however be taken to comprise any matter wherein the legitimate interest of the State Administration or a civil right sustainable in a court of law is involved.

7. The Chief Minister shall preside at meetings of the Council and in his absence the Senior Minister present should preside.

8. Cases intended for submission to the Council shall be sent to the Secretary to the Council with a note explaining the case by the Minister concerned. The Secretary shall then take the orders of the Chief Minister whether the case shall be:-

   (a) Circulated, or

   (b) Discussed in Council.

9. The business of the Council shall be disposed of (a) by the circulation of papers, (b) by discussion at a meeting of the Council.

10. All cases of the nature described in Appendix I to these Rules shall be circulated under the orders of the Chief Minister and shall be discussed in Council.

11. His Highness may direct that a particular case of whatever sort shall be circulated and taken at the meeting of the Council.

12. Notwithstanding anything contained in Rule 10 above, the Chief Minister may at any time either of his own motion or at the request of another Minister circulate any case for subsequent discussion in the Council.

13. When a case has been circulated under the provisions of Rules 10, 11 and 12 and if there is no difference of opinion among Ministers of the Council, orders may issue under the authority of the Chief Minister if the subject matter of the case is of such urgency that it is inexpedient to delay issue of orders pending a meeting of the Council. Such cases shall however be subsequently considered in Council so that the orders issued may be confirmed.

14. Not less than four Ministers shall constitute a quorum of the Council. The decision shall be by a majority of the votes and if the votes are equal the President, whether he be the Chief Minister or the Senior Minister, shall have a casting vote.

15. The Council will ordinarily meet once a week and it will be the duty of the Chief Minister to ensure that a list of all cases for discussion at the next meeting is submitted to His Highness and circulated to each Minister at least one day before the meeting is due to taken place. The Chief Minister may however summon an Extraordinary meeting at any time. His Highness will have the power of directing the Chief Minister to convene a special meeting of the Council on any matter of great urgency.

16. When any Minister differs from the opinion of the majority of the Council it shall be open to him to record his dissent and his reasons thereof.

17. Should the Chief Minister consider that any decision of the Council is prejudicial to the interest of the State or that for any reason it is undesirable that effect should be given to it, he may suspend action on the resolution, and forward it with a full statement of his reasons for the orders of His Highness.

18. A copy of the proceedings shall be submitted in duplicate by the Chief Minister to His Highness within a week of each meeting of the Council.

19. All orders or instruments made or executed by order of or on behalf of the Council shall be issued as by the order of His Highness. Action on all decisions of the Council shall be taken in the name of His Highness in Council. Orders passed by the Council which have to be issued by or order the authority of the Minister in charge and all communication to any outside authority shall be signed by the Chief Minister.

20. Cheques on the Treasury or Bank shall be signed by the Chief Minister or in his absence by an authority specially authorised by the Chief Minister in this regard.

21. The Chief Minister may call for the record of any case in order to scrutinise the orders issued by the Minister in charge.

22. His Highness may call from the Council for information in respect of any orders issued by them or by the Minister in charge.

23. The Chief Minister is empowered to pass orders on behalf of His Highness on any matter arising in any. Department except the Department dealing with His Highness's Civil List when on account of the urgency of the matter, or His Highness's absence from the State, it is necessary for him to do so. Such orders shall be reported to His Highness after issue. If any matter arises which is not of sufficient importance to require consideration by the Council as a whole but on which the orders of His Highness appear to be order of His Highness through the Chief Minister.

24. The Chief Minister and the Minister in their individual capacity shall have the following powers in regard to their own Departments:-

    (i) .Subject to the provision of the Appointments Board Rules, to appoint, promote, suspend, reduce, fine, dismiss, transfer and grant leave and pension to State Servants under his control whose maximum pay does not exceed Rs. 100/- p.m. in the case of the Chief Minister and Rs. 50/- p.m. in the case of the Minister, provided no infringement of the State Rules is involved. The Chief Minister may grant casual leave to the Ministers and the Chief Judge in accordance with rule.

    (ii) To remit fines imposed by himself or by subordinate officers.

    (iii) To sanction leases and contracts up to the value of Rs. 1,000/- and Rs. 500/- in the case of the Chief Minister and Ministers respectively.

    (iv) To hear appeals against the decisions of his subordinate officers.

    (v) To exercise such powers as may be specially delegated to him by the Departmental rules and laws in force in the State under proper authority.

(vi) To sanction any item of non-recurring expenditure within officers.

(vii) To sanction estimates of public works including additions and alterations and repairs provided the expenditure on Original Works does not exceed Rs. 5,000/- and provided further that provision for the work in question has been specially made in the sanctioned budget and the estimates have received administrative and technical sanction.

(viii) To sanction excess does not exceed five per cent of the original estimate and it was not due to the expenditure on a new service which was not approved by the proper authority.

(ix) To sanction re-appropriation of funds within a major head, subject to the conditions:-

(a) That without the previous consent of the State Finance Department, he may not (1) meet by re-appropriation expenditure which the Chief Minister/Minister is not empowered to sanction or expenditure other than contingent expenditure which is likely to involve further outlay in a future financial year and (2) transfer funds from the sub head "Pay of Establishment".

(b) That the total amount so re-appropriated does not exceed Rs. 1,000/- and Rs. 500/- in the case of the Chief Minister and the Ministers respectively, and

(c) That both the sub-heads are controlled by the Chief Minister of Ministers making re-appropriation.

(x) To write off any State debt or dues up to a maximum of Rs. 100/- in the case of the Chief Minister and Rs. 50/- in the case of Ministers and to write off the stock register articles up to the value of Rs. 100/- and Rs 50/- in the case of the Chief Minister and Ministers respectively.

(xi) To sanction advances of Tacavi up to the limit of sanctioned allotment and refunds of revenue under the Department Rules.

(xii) To sanction advances for department purpose within the budget allotment.

25. The Chief Minister or a Minister of the Council may with the previous approval of the Council ratify ant existing delegation and make any fresh delegation, of the powers conferred upon him in sub rule (ii), (vi), (vii), and (x) above to any subordinate authority.

26. The Revenue Minister shall have power to confirm the sale and settlement of land, to suspend land revenue on account of failure of crops of other calamity according to the rules and to write off the purchase price of land, the proceeds of which have not been realised.

Note:- Statements will be submitted to His Highness through the Council each half year indicating the amount of revenue suspended and sales of land effected during the period of six months preceding the 1st October and 1st of April respectively.

27. The Chief Minister shall exercise the power of a Minister in respect of the Council Secretariat.

28. The Council as a body shall exercise full executive authority in the State and shall be jointly responsible for their acts saving that the approval of His Highness shall be taken before orders are issued in the following matters:-

    (i) All matters connected with the Ruling family affecting the administrative budget.

    (ii) Agreement with Neighboring States or Provinces on matters relating to administration.

    (iii) Sanction of the annual Budget Estimates of the State duly prepared and passed by the State Council.

    (vi) Question relating to Taxation, Exports and Imports, alienation of Land or fisheries otherwise than in accordance with sanctioned Policy and the grant of free land and having the force of law.

    (vii) Important matters of State Policy.

    (viii) Grant of prospecting Licenses and mining leases for the extraction of minerals and the creation of Forest or other Reserves within the State.

    (ix) The creation or abolition of a post carrying a minimum pay of Rs. 150/- per **mensem** or above.

(x) The appointment of an official who is not a State subject to a post carrying a pay of more than Rs. 150/- per mensem.

(xi) Sanction of Leave or Casual Leave to the Chief Minister and the Chief Judge and arrangements for the disposal of their work during their absence.

In any such matter where special circumstances appear to His Highness to render this necessary, His Highness may on communicating the grounds for his decision to the Council, exercise a veto on the proposal submitted to him.

29. Subject to the general supervision of the Chief Minister the Chief Judge is authorised.

(a) Subject to the provisions of the Appointments Board Rules, to appoint, suspend, fine, discharge, dismiss and grant leave to State Servants under his control the maximum pay of whom is less than Rs. 75/- p.m.

(b) To remit fines imposed by himself or his predecessor in office or by subordinate officers.

(c) To permit expenditure within the sanctioned budget up to Rs. 100/- and

(d) To exercise such powers as may be specially delegated to him by Department Rules and Laws in the State.

30. The Heads of Department shall be as in the annexed schedule A which may be amended by His Highness from time to time in the public interest.

31. The distribution of the Department of the State among the Chief Minister and the other Ministers of the Council shall be as in the annexed Schedule B which may be amended by His Highness from time to time in the public interest.

Sd/-
(Bodh Chandra Singh)
Maharajah of Manipur

Appendix–VI

Proclamation of His Highness Maharaja Bodhachandra Singh on the Inaugural Function of the First Manipur State Assembly on October 18, 1948

Introduction

This is the first time I as a Representative of Manipur Crown and Monarchy, unbroken and safeguard with the blood of my forefathers for about two thousand years, address the first Assembly of Manipur State on this historic day following the modern practice and British style. I consider myself fortunate to see the birth of an Assembly in the State during my time and again I feel proud to be able to place on record and make it known to the rest of India that though painted otherwise abroad, my State for the first time in India has, just as the sun rises earlier in the east, taken the lead in the direction of democratic government, based on adult franchise and joint electorate in the line of which India is soon following. I take more pride in that though in countries like England, responsible government has been the outcome of blood of so many persons, there has been in my State no bloodshed since I took the initiative here.

The New Constitution

While I have been all along anxious to accord responsible government, I have been sincerely watching as to the practicability or impracticability of the Constitution Act. I now bring to the mind of the people that I had transferred my powers and responsibilities other than those of a constitutional Ruler to the State Council since 1st July, 1947 before the lapse of the British paramountcy and since then, I have already remained as a Constitutional Ruler. But most of the people innocent as they are, have been imputing to me the actions of the Council. My only earnest wish is to see a more prosperous Manipur. Though the literacy is below five per cent, you have had the best opportunities, as afforded by a responsible government to serve your country to the fullest extent you desire with toleration and concord to make Manipur, a greater Manipur.

Aim

Administratior and citizens of the State, in order that the integrity and separate entity of the State is preserved for ever as heretofore ensured by Pandit Jawaharlal Nehru, I wish to attach the highest measure of importance to detailing some account of what the State Manipur is—I mean the State and people, whom you now represent and on whose better administration you are now out to embark.

Historical Background

To begin with, I feel a sudden emotion in my heart—I mean the sweet reminiscences of the past history of Manipur. Let the patriots fight for today. I will see that yesterday shines once more before the people, ignorant of the beauty of yesterday. I am sure, a look back to the history of our land will at once inspire your mind towards greater and nobler deeds to prove your worth as worthy sons of worthy sons of worthy fathers.

Lo! the sweet and green valley with sweeter and greener hills all around along the easternmost part of India—a smiling land, all hailed by footprints of heroes and admired as the Switzerland of India by strangers. It is Manipur, a salubrious land of hoary antiquity— a land of gems. Geographically, it is singularly isolated from the rest of India. Strategically, nature impresses on her a stamp of unity by fully encircling her with lofty mountains and hills making it an impregnable fortress and bulwark of defence doing the sentinel for the millions in India. She was a star in the eastern political firmament of India. Strong nations of the world covet her natural position. Such is Manipur.

Read her political history from 24 A.D. She had her dominion over a wide area extending as far as the southern portion of China in the north, the gold mines in the Sibasagar valley, the river Chindwin in the east and south, and Chandrapore (Cachar) in the west. Her present area is 8,650 square miles plus 7,000 square miles of the Kabaw valley, including 7,900 square miles of the hills. Read the war operations of Maharaja Garibaniwaza in 1711, which shows how far the spirit of heroism and independence ran rampant in the veins of our forefather. Read the Treaty of Maharaja Gourashyam and Mr. Verelst of the East India Company at Chittagong on the 14th September, 1762, which shows the vast wealth and economic status of Manipur. Read the Treaty of Yandaboo, dated the 9th January, 1834 ratified between Maharaja Gambhir Singh and the Company. This treaty left for us a good heritage, namely the Kabaw valley of 7,000 square miles for which we now get from Burma Rs.6, 270 as annual tribute which according to the spirit of the terms of the Agreement, will cease when the area is reverted to our State. Maharaja Gambhir Singh died of disappointment for this loss of territory under duress. Sreejut Nara Singh's role in redeeming Manipur from Burma, when she was devastated and dismembered for 7 years was very great. Manipur was thus, by reason of her vast territories and economic resources, self-supporting as a self-contained unit. Her sphere of influence and mercantile activities was very wide. During the British rule, foreign goods gave a dulling effect to the indigenous products by dumping operations. Now is the best time to revive all these vanquished industries. Attempts are now being made to recover the losses of territories as in Cachar under duress.

Unity of Hill and Valley

All these times when Manipur was in the height of her power, Hill and Valley were one; and this oneness defended Manipur against all invasions and thus, she could maintain her independence upto 1891, when the rest of India had already been conquered by the British. British conquest of this land resulted from the slackened unity between the Valley and Hills. Now, since the withdrawal of British paramountcy after 56 years' rule, we have reinforced the union of Hill and Valley; and best opportunities have reached us in order to work hand-in-hand towards achieving the common object for progress and national prosperity. The relation has become one of complete understanding and active sympathy and it must be so, for Manipur is one and the hopes and aspirations of Hill and Valley are identical.

Manipur's Position in the Dominion of India

These are great days ; great destinies are gathering momentum; great ideas are occupying the hearts of men and great causes have aroused great enthusiasms and great sacrifices. Amid the interplay of world forces India comes out stronger than before and Manipur too as a component part is the same with the removal of artificial hedge between Hill and Valley. I believe the sons of Manipur will be alive to it. In the large galaxy of heroes in the imperishable roll of honour, there were and there are now and there will never cease to be, beloved Manipuri names testifying to the fact that our people would rather die unsullied than outlive the disgrace of surrender to any measure that work prejudicial to the preservation of the separate entity of the State, while fostering the good and cordial relations with the Dominion of India I am confident that the members of the Assembly will please see that this fair record is never breached.

State Finance Based on a Sound Economic Planning

A strong government means a government with a strong financial infrastructure. In order to ensure finance a well thought out economic planning is necessary. I lay special stress on it, for a totally unplanned economy is a totally unplanned nation. I invite your attention to the inevitability of this economic planning so that you may be prepared to cope with it before the State finance assumes threatening proportions. The inexhaustible sources of her economic potentialities are already there, as it is provided by nature. What is only wanting is the modus operandi *for increased productivity. The people will have to cultivate thriftiness, since the present rate of the flowing out of people's money in exchange of less important articles will jeopardize, at no distant date, the economic status of the individuals constituting the nations.*

If the entire area of the State is properly explored and the sources are tapped, there is every possibility of the State's one crore of rupees as annual income enabling us at the same time to produce all our requirements. Places like Jiribam and Moreh, if properly industrialized with the running of saw-mills, cotton mills, paper mills, etc. , will bring huge incomes to the State. Manipur has been declared the best place for installing hydroelectric power on commercial basis too. There should be industrial centres at strategic places—Hill and Valley—equipped with modern techniques and modern technology. I shall be glad to see Hill towns properly electrified, springing up. I desire that prior consideration be given to the construction of roads in the hills in order to facilitate communications. There are now only one lakh of 'Paris' of land thrown open to cultivation. There is tem times the space still available for agricultural operations. Plantation of betal-nut, tea and jute also may be introduced successfully in the now neglected but fertile soils. Export should outpace the import. During my long tours in the hills, I was deeply impressed with the yet surviving cottage industries which can stand any competition. The consequences of the war heavily told upon the raw materials. Charkha and handlooms have been the essential marriage gifts to our mothers and sisters. In redressing economic problems these should be developed. As regards the raw materials, eastern Kasom still stands a living testimony. Khaddar is not a new thing here, but rather—I should say—it originated from Manipur. The silk industry from cocoons is a long standing industry here. The Muga of Khurkhul remains unrivalled and unapproached in India. Rural reconstruction schemes be implemented in order to achieve all-round progress.

Education

Prior consideration should also be given to education. I wish to see at least a High School in each of the Tahsils and important centres in the hills with good communication. While pursuing our future educational policy, we should be prepared to select more practical courses to suit the mode of our national life. Indigenous science of medicine and treatment should also be promoted. Fine Arts also has received the appreciation of the world. It attracted the world-poet Rabindranath Tagore also, Sir Akbar Hydari, His Excellency, the Governor of Assam, also highly encouraged it.

Our Part in the Individual and Collective Responsibility for Frontier Protection and Defence of Manipur in Particular

Manipur should be made militarily strong as, in the contemporary world, militia is the noblest estate of mankind. In the history and accounts of 1874, written by Col. Johnstone, you will come across that

Manipuri nation constituted the best armies in the world. In January 1947, I apprised India Government through the Chamber of Princes, of the need for a strong Eastern Frontier protecting military installations in order to safeguard Manipur in particular and India as a whole, as a result of the withdrawal of British paramountcy from India and Burma. But India Government has not yet communicated their final plan in this matter.

Now as from today, you have joined responsible government. I feel it my duty to point out, in the interest of this country and Commonwealth that it should be our individual and collective responsibility to work out a scheme for frontier protection, in collaboration with the Central Government. The present situation calls for immediate action in this respect. Since we are sincere, I am confident that the Central Government will give us proper and timely assistance with subsidies and finance and equipment. In the meantime with what little finance, we have, we should raise our small force to an efficient standard as home-guard without further delay. The inherent warlike spirit of the Manipuris should be maintained for the noble cause of India. Peace here in Manipur will be a fine contribution to India Government, while they are moulding India's destiny to enable her to stand up as one of the most powerful nations in the world.

The paramount importance of the strategic location of Manipur for defence and security reasons of India deserves the careful attention of enlightened governments ; and we should be mindful of the benefits that we may render to our Dominion from her position, if we seriously depend on it.

Time is now roughly going on in the world and as such, it is a critical phase of Manipur too. Nevertheless, it is the best time for you to serve your mother country while she needs and to prove that you are her worthy sons. You are to show to the world and to your people, the achievements or progress of the welfare of the people under this new government with clear results of a change for the better. Otherwise, the name "Responsible government" may not be worth the name and the next step will be for the Constitutional Ruler to judge.

Our Guiding Principles

We should not forget that we are Manipuris, destined to live in Manipur and die in Manipur. Providence has bound our fates together indissolubly.

Leaders of the nation! While undertaking to finance economic planning—long and short—for the material progress of the country in the nearest future, I want to make it a watchword that the means of increasing the State revenues from other sources are devised without causing hardship or burden to the people. I expect that every one of you, as a part of his obligation, will take care to acquaint himself with the mode of life on hills too by studying the four walls of the territory of Manipur, he is now going to govern, Send students abroad to foreign lands that they may bring back knowledge with which they may do service to her, but they should not bring ideas and ways of life that do not always conform to the environment of Manipur.

I wish to see you all becoming great and noble not for your own sake but noble for the country—to make Manipur great, a greater Manipur to enable her to stand up with head erect among the nations, as she did in the past. Work that Manipur may prosper. Suffer that Manipur may rejoice. Unite that Manipur may be strong.

Do the right that you may be brave. Whether you use pen or tongue, let your hearts be pure; and your resolve, manly. The prosperity of a nation does not depend on the number of buildings, but it depends on the number of men of character—that is, radiant man of well-disciplined mould. I shall always remain aglow with splendour of destiny of our people.

In fine, I call upon you all to take this as your motto and to join with men in a fervent prayer for the well-being of our Motherland.

Appendix–VII

Manipur Merger Agreement*

Agreement made this twentyfirst day of September 1949 between the Governor-General of India and His Highness the Maharaja of Manipur.

WHEREAS in the best interests of the State of Manipur as well as of the Dominion of India it is desirable – to provide for the administration of the said State by or under the authority of the Dominion Government.

IT IS HEREBY AGREED as follows:-

Article 1

His Highness the Maharaja of Manipur hereby cedes to the Dominion Government full and exclusive authority, jurisdiction and powers far in to the governance of the State agrees to transfer the administration of the State to the Dominion government on the fifteenth day of October 1949 (herein-after referred to as "the said day").

As from the said day the Dominion Government will be Competent to exercise the said powers.

Article II

His Highness the Maharaja shall continue to enjoy the pernal rights, privileges, dignities, titles, authority over religious observances, customs, usages, rites and ceremonies and institutions incharge of the same in the State, which he would have enjoyed had this agreement not been made.

Article III

His Highness the Maharaja shall with effect from the said day be entitled to receive for his lifetime from the revenues of the State

* Ministry of States, *White Papers on Indian States.* (New Delhi: Government of India Press, 1950), Appendix XXXII, pp. 232-34.

annually for his Privy Purse the sum of Rupees three lakhs free of all taxes.

This amount is intended to cover all the expenses of the Ruler and his family, including expenses on account of his personal staff and armed guards, maintenance of his residences, marriages and other ceremonies, etc. and the allowances to the Ruler's relations who on the date of execution of this agreement were in receipt of such allowances from the revenues of the State, and will neither be increased nor reduced for any reason whatsoever.

The Government of India undertake that the said sum of Rupees three lakhs shall be paid to His Highness the Maharaja in four equal instalments in advance at the beginning of each quarter from the State treasury as may be specified by the Government of India.

Article IV

His Highness the Maharaja shall be entitled to the full ownership, use and enjoyment of all private properties (as distinct from State properties) belonging to him on the date of this agreement.

His Highness the Maharaja will furnish to the Dominion Government before the first January 1950 an inventory of all the immovable property, securities and cash balance held by him as such private property.

If any dispute arises as to whether any item of property is the private property of His Highness the Maharaja or State property, it shall be referred to a judicial Officer qualified to be appointed as a High Court Judge, and the decision of that officer shall be final and binding on both parties.

Provided the His Highness the Maharaja's right to the use of the residences known as "Redlands" and "Les Chatallettes" in Shillong, and the property in the town of Gauhati known as "Manipuri Basti" shall not be questioned.

Article V

All the members of His Highness's family shall be entitled to all the personal rights, privileges, dignities and titles enjoyed by them whether within or outside the territories of the State, immediately before the 15th August 1947.

Article VI

The Dominion Government guarantees the succession, according to law and custom, to the *gaddi* of the State and to His Highness the

Maharaja's personal rights, privileges, dignities, titles, authority over religious observances customs, usages, rites and ceremonies and institutions incharge of the same in the State.

Article VII

No enquiry shall be made by or under the authority of the Government, and no proceedings shall lie in any court in Manipur, against His Highness the Maharaja whether in a personal capacity or otherwise, in respect of anything done or omitted to be done by him or under his authority during the period of his administration of that State.

Article VIII

(1) The Government of India hereby guarantees *either* the continuance in service of the permanent members of the Public Service of Manipur on conditions which will be not less advantageous than those on which they were serving before the date on which the administration of Manipur is made over to the Government of India or the payment of reasonable compensation.

(2) The Government of India further guarantees the continuance of pensions and leave salaries sanctioned by His Highness the Maharaja to servants of the State who have retired or proceeded on leave preparatory to retirement, before the date on which the administration of Manipur is made over to the Government of India.

(3) The Government of India also undertake to make suitable provisions for the employment of authority and jurisdiction in such manner and through such agency as it may think it.

Manipur—is in the various branches of Public Services, and in every way encourage Manipuris to join them. They also undertake to preserve various laws, customs and conventions prevailing in the State pertaining to the social, economic and religious life of the people.

Article IX

Except with the previous sanction of the Government of India no proceedings, civil or criminal, shall be instituted against any person in respect of any act done or purporting to be done in the execution of this duties as a servant of the State before the day on which the administration is made over to the Government of India.

In confirmation whereof Mr Vapal Pangunni Menon Advisor to the Government of India in the Ministry of States, has appended his signature on behalf and with the authority of the Governor-General of India and His Highness Maharaj Bodh Chandra Singh, Maharaja of Manipur has appended his signature on behalf of himself, his heirs and successors.

Sd/-
(Bodh Chandra Singh)
Maharaja of Manipur

Sd/-
(SRI PRAKASA)
Governor of Assam
Shillong, September 21,1949.

Sd/-
(V.P. Menon)
Advisor to the
Government of India
Ministry of States

Bibliography

A. Private Papers

1. Nehru Memorial Museum and Library

Jawaharlal Nehru Papers

B. Other Unpublished Sources

(i) The Official Records of the Government of India, deposited at the National Archives India esp. Foreign and Political Department files, Home Department and Police Department, Political Branch Proceedings, 1916-45.

(ii) The All India Congress Committee files available at Nehru Memorial Museum and Library.

(iii) The All India State Peoples' Conference files available at Nehru Memorial Museum and Library.

(iv) Political Agent files available at Manipur Secretariat Library and Record Branch.

(v) Dominion Agent files available at Manipur Secretriat Library and Record Branch.

(vi) Durbar and Council records available at Manipur Secretariat Library and Record Branch.

(vii) Office Records Files available at Manipur State.

(viii) Congress Office at Imphal.

(ix) Private Office Records files collected from Elangbam Tompok Singh, the then Manipur State Congress.

C. Official Records

(i) Rules for the Management of the State of Manipur, 1916.

(ii) Reports of the Indian States Committee, 1928-29.

(iii) Memorandum on Indian States, 1940.

(iv) Minutes of the Meetings of the Manipur State Constitution

Making Committee with Recommendations for a State Constitution Act and a Hill Peoples Regulation, 5 May 1947.

(v) Manipur State Constitution Act, 1947.

(vi) The Manipur State Courts Act 1947 and the Manipur State Hill Peoples Regulation 1947.

(vii) The Manipur State Election Rules, 1948.

(viii) Minutes and Debates of the Assam Legislative Assembly, 1930-1946

(ix) Government of India Act, 1935.

(x) Government of India, Ministry of States, White Papers on Indian States, Delhi, Government of India Press, 1950.

(xi) Assam Legislative Debates, Vol. II Shillong: Assam Government Press, 1942.

II. Secondary Sources

A. Book and Monographs

1. Aitchison, C.U. *A Collection of Treaties, Engagements and Sanads Relating to India and Neighbouring Countries.* Calcutta: Central Publication Branch, 1931.
2. Alexander Mackenjie. *History of the Relations of the Government with the Hill Tribes of the North-Eastern Frontiers of Bengal.* Calcutta: Home Department Press, 1884.
3. Ali Abdul, *Notes on the Early History of Manipur.* Calcutta: Superintendent, Government Printing, 1923.
4. Ali, Alben and Eric Lambert, *Assam*, London: Geoffry Cumberlege, Oxford University Press, 1946.
5. *An Account of the Province of Assam and its Administration.* Shillong: The Assam Secretariat Printing Office, 1903.
6. Antrobus, H.A. *A History of The Assam Company.* Edinburgh: T. And A. Constable Ltd., 1957.
7. An Indian Mahomedan. *British India.* London: Issac Pitman & Sons, Ltd. 1926.
8. Anand, V.K. *Nagaland in Transition.* New Delhi: Associated Publishing House, 1967.
9. Ao, M. Alemchiba. *Brief Historical Account of Nagaland.* Kohima: Naga Institute of Culture, 1970.

10. Ao, Tajenyuba (ed.). *A History of Anglo-Naga Affairs*, 1832-1913.

11. Aung. Maunghtin. *A History of Burma*. London: Columbia University Press, 1961.

12. Banerjee, A.C. *The Eastern Frontier British India*, 1784-1826. Calcutta: A Mukherjee & Co. (P) Ltd.

13. Barua, B.K. A *Cultural History of Assam – Early Period,* Vol. 1. Assam: Shri B.N. Dutt Barooah, Lawyers' Book Stall, 1951.

14. Barker, A.J. *The March on Delhi*. London: Faber and Faber, 1963.

15. Barooah, Upendra Nath. *A Glimpse of Assam*. Jorhat: Upendra Nath Barooah, 1946.

16. Barkataki, Padma.*Hidden Facts from The Magic Land of Assam.* Calcutta: Satish Chandra Bhattacharji for ABC Publications, 1958.

17. Barua, Hem. *The Red River and The Blue Hill or The State of Assam*. Assam: Lawyers' Book Stall, 1954.

18. Barpujari, H.K. *Assam in the Days of the Company 1826-1858.* Gauhati: Lawyers Book Stall, 1963.

19. Banerjee, Anil Chandra, *The Eastern Frontier of British India, 1784-1826*. Calcutta: A Mukherjee and Co. Private Ltd., 1943.

20. Bhat, Sudhakar. *The Challenge of the North East.* Bombay: Popular Prakashan, 1975.

21. Brown, R. *Statistical Account of the Native State of Manipur and the Hill Territory under its Rule*. Calcutta: Office of the Superintendent of Government Printing, 1874.

22. Bruce, George. *The Burma Wars*. London: Mart-Davis, MacGibbon, 1973.

23. Butler, Major John. *Travels and Adventures in the Province of Assam-During A Residence of Fourteen Years*. London: Smith, Elder, And Co., 65, Cornhill, 1855.

24. Chakravarty Birendra Chandra. *British Relation with the Hill Tribes of Assam*. Calcutta; Firm K.L. Mukhopadhyay, 1964.

25. Chaliha (Comp.), Parag. *The Outlook on NEFA*. Assam: Assam Sahitya Sabha, 1955.

26. Chandna, Dev Raj. *Slavery in Ancient India*. New Delhi: People's Publishing House, Pvt. Ltd., 1960.

27. *Chief and Leading Officials and Personages in Manipur*, Shillong: The Assam Secretariat Press, 1914.
28. Clow, Sir Andrew. *Future Government of the Assam*. Shillong: 1945.
29. Crawford, C.G. *Administration Report, Manipur State, 1922-23*. Imphal: The State Printing Press, 1923.
30. _______, *Administration Report, Manipur State, 1923-24*. Imphal: The State Printing Press, 1924.
31. _______, *Administration Report, Manipur State, 1924-25*. Imphal: The State Printing Press, 1925.
32. _______, *Administration Report, Manipur State, 1925-26*. Imphal: The State Printing Press, 1926.
33. _______, *Administration Report, Manipur State, 1926-27*. Imphal: The State Printing Press, 1927.
34. Das, Durga. (Ed.). *Sardar Patel's Correspondence*, Vols. V,VI, VIII. Ahmedabad: 1974.
35. Das, Nagendra Narayan, *Sword of The East*, Shillong: Nepali Press, 1941.
36. Dalton, Edward 7. *Descriptive Ethnology of Bengal*, Calcutta: Office, Superintendent, Government Printing, 1872.
37. Desai, W.S. *A Pageant of Burma History*, New Delhi: Orient Longman, 1961.
38. Dube, S.C. *Tribal Situation in India*. Simla: Indian Institute of Advanced Study, Simla, 1972.
39. _______, (ed). *Tribal Heritage of India*, Vol. I. New Delhi: Vikas Publishing House, Pvt. Ltd. 1977.
40. Dunbar, Sir George. *Frontier*. London, 1932.
41. Edward, Michael. *The Last Year of British India*. London: Cox and Wyman Ltd.
42. Elwin, Verrier. *The Nagas in the Nineteenth Century*. Oxford: Oxford University Press, 1969.
43. _______, *A New Book of Tribal Fiction*. Shillong: North East Frontier Agency, 1970.
44. _______, *Nagaland*. Calcutta: Saraswaty Press, Ltd., 1961.
45. Evans, Geoffrey and Antony Baett-James. *Imphal*, London: Macmillan & Co. Ltd., 1962.

46. Frazer, R.W. *British India*. London: T. Fisher Unwin, 1896.
47. Furnivall, *Colonial Policy and Practice*. Cambridge; University Press, 1948.
48. Furer Haimendorf, C.V. *Naked Nagas*. Calcutta: Thacker Sprink & Co., Private Ltd., 1933.
49. Fyitche, A. *Burma Past and Present*, 2 Vols. London: Kegan & Paul, 1878.
50. Ghurya, G.S. *Scheduled Tribes*. Poona: Gokhale Institute of Politics and Economics, 1943.
51. Gimson, C. *Administration Report, Manipur State, 1918-1919*. Imphal: The State Printing Press, 1919.
52. _______, *Administration Report, Manipur State, 1919-1920*. Imphal: The State Printing Press, 1920.
53. Gogoi, Padmeswar. *The Tai and the Tai Kingdom*. Gauhati: Department of Publication, Gauhati University, 1968.
54. Gohain, Bikash Chandra. *Human Sacrifice and Head Hunting in North-Eastern India*. Gauhati: Lawyer Book Stall, 1977.
55. Grierson, G.A. (Ed.). *Linguistic Survey of India*, Vol. V. Calcutta: Government of India, 1903.
56. Grimwood, Ethel St. Clair. *My Three Years in Manipur and Escape from the Recent Mutiny*. London: Richard Bentley and Son-Publishers in Ordinary to Her Majesty the Queen, 1891.
57. Hall, D.G.E. *Burma*, London: Hutchinsons University Library, 1925.
58. Hamilton, Francis and others. *An Account of Assam*. Assam Government of Assam in the Department of Historical and Antiquarian Studies, Narayani Handiqui Historical Institute, 1940.
59. Henderson, Robert H. *Administration Report, Manipur State 1917-18*. Calcutta: Thacker, Sprink & Co., 1918.
60. Harvey, C.W.L. *Administration Report, Manipur State, 1930-31*. Imphal: The State Printing Press, 1932.
61. _______, *Administration Report, Manipur State, 1931-1932*. Imphal: The State Printing Press, 1932.
62. Higgins, J.C., *Administration Report, Manipur State, 1914-1915*. Calcutta: Thacker, Spink & Co., 1915.

63. _______, *Administration Report, Manipur State, 1915-1916*, Calcutta: Thacker, Spink & Co., 1916.
64. _______, *Administration Report, Manipur State, 1916-1917*. Calcutta: Thacker, Spink & Co., 1917.
65. Holdich, T.H. *India*. London: Oxford University Press.
66. Horam, Mashangthai, *Naga Polity*. New Delhi: B.R. Publishers Corporation, 1975.
67. _______, *Social and Cultural Life of Nagas: The Tangkhul Nagas*. New Delhi: B.R. Publishers Corporation, 1977.
68. Hudson, T.C. *The Metheis*. London: David Nutt, 1908.
69. Hunter, W.W. *The Imperial Gazetteer*, Vol. II. London: 1819.
70. Jesse, F. Tennyson. *The Story of Burma*. London: Macmillan & Co., Ltd., 1946.
71. Johri, Sitaram, *Where India China and Burma Meet*. Calcutta: Thacker, Spink & Co., Pvt. Ltd., 1933.
72. John Butler. *Sketch of Assam*. London: 1847.
73. Johnstone, James. *Manipur and the Naga Hills*. New Delhi: Vivek Publishing House, 1971.
74. John, M. 'Cosh. *Topography of Assam*. Delhi: Sanskaran Prakashak, 1975.
75. Kakati, Satis Chandra. *Discovery of Assam* Gauhati: Hiss Road, Ujan Bazar, 1954.
76. Kesne, H.C. *History of India*, II. Edinburgh: John Grant, 1906.
77. Lahiri, R.M. T*he Annexation of Assam*. Calcutta: Central Printers & Publishers Ltd., 1954.
78. Luther, P.N. *Nagaland from a Neighbourhood*. Gauhati: Tribune Press, 1975.
79. Lydall, Alfred. *The Rise and Expansion of the British Dominion in India*. London: John Murry, Albermarine Street, 1914.
80. Lydall, E.F. *Administration Report, Manipur State, 1939-1940*. Imphal: The State Printing Press, 1943.
81. _______, *Administration Report, Manipur State, 1940-1941*. Imphal: The State Printing Press, 1943.
82. _______, *Administration Report, Manipur State, 1943-1945*. Imphal: The State Printing Press, 1945.

83. Macmunn, George. *The Romance of the Indian Frontiers*. London: Jonathan Cape, Thirty Bedford Square, 1936.

84. Malcolm, H. *Travels in the Burman Empire*. Edinburgh, 1840.

85. Manipur: *List of Ruling Princes, Chiefs and Leading Personages*. Shillong: Assam Government Press, 1924.

86. Mankekar, D.R. *On the Slippery Slope in Nagaland*. Bombay: Manaktolas, 1967.

87. Marriott, Sir John A.R. *The English in India*. Oxford: The Clarendon Press, 1932.

88. Menon, V.P. *The Story of the Integration of the Indian States*, New Delhi: Orient Longmans Private Ltd., 1961.

89. McCall, A.G. *Administration Report, Manipur State, 1927-28*. Imphal: The State Printing Press, 1928.

90. _______, *Administration Report, Manipur State, 1928-1929*. Imphal: The State Printing Press, 1929.

91. _______, *Administration Report, Manipur State, 1929-1930*. Imphal: The State Printing Press, 1930.

92. _______, *Administration Report, Manipur State, 1930-1931*. Imphal: The State Printing Press, 1931.

93. Mills, A.J. Moffat. *Report on the Province of Assam*. Gauhati: 1853.

94. Millington, Powell. *On the Track of the Abor*. London: Smith, Elder & Co., 1912.

95. Moore, P.H. (Ed.). *Twenty Years in Assam, or Leaves from My Journal*. Calcutta: Baptist Mission Press, 1901.

96. Mullen, C.S. *Administration Report, Manipur State, 1920-1921*. Imphal: The State Printing Press, 1920.

97. _______, *Administration Report, Manipur State, 1921-1922*. Imphal: The State Printing Press, 1922.

98. Nath R.M. *The Background of Assamese Culture*. Assam: A.K. Nath, Mimora Ridge, Nogthymai, 1948.

99. Nehru Jawaharlal. *The Unity of India*. London: Lindslay Drummond, 2 Guilford Palace, 1948.

100. Nibedon, Nirmal. *Nagaland the Night of the Guerrillas*. New Delhi: Lanchers Publishers, 1978.

101. Nisbet, J. *Burma Under British Rule and Before*, 2 Vols. London: Westminster, Constable, 1901.

102. Pearson, F.F. *Administration Report, Manipur State, 1944-1945*. Imphal: The State Printing Press, 1946.

103. Pemberton, R. Boileau, *Report on the Eastern Frontier of British India*. Gauhati: Department of Historical Antiquarian Studies in Assam, 1966.

104. Phayre, A.P. *History of Burma*, London: 7A High Street, Wanstead, 1967.

105. Playne, Somerset, and others. B*engal and Assam, Behar and Orissa- Their History, People, Commerce, and Industrial Resources*. London: The Foreign and Colonial Compiling and Publishing Co., 1917.

106. *Physical and Political Geography of the Province of Assam*. Shillong: The Assam Secretariat Printing Office, 1896.

107. Rao, V. Venkata. *A Century of Tribal Politics in North East India, 1874-1974*. New Delhi: S. Chand & Company Ltd., 1976.

108. Rao B. R. Subha. *Nagaland.* Bombay: Educational Trust, 1976.

109. *Report on the Census of Assam for 1881*. Calcutta: Office of Superintendent of Government Printing, 1883.

110. *Report of the Indian Statutory Commission*, Vol. I. Calcutta: Government of India, Central Publication Branch, 1930.

111. *Report on the Administration of the Province and Assam for the Year 1881-82*. Shillong: Assam Secretariat Press, 1883.

112. Reid, Robert. *Years of Change in Bengal and Assam*. London: Ernest Benn Ltd., 1966.

113. _______, *History of the Frontier Areas Bordering on Assam, 1883-1941*. Shillong: The Assam Government Press, 1942.

114. Robertson, Thomas Campbell. *Political Incidents of the First Burmese War*. London: Richard Benley, 1853.

115. Robinson, William, *A Description Account of Assam: With a Sketch of the Local Geography, and a Concise History of the Tea-Plant of Assam: to which is Added, a Short Account of the Neighbouring Tribes Exhibiting Their History, Manners, and Customs*. London: Thomas Ostell & Co. 1841.

116. Rose, Leo. E. Margaret W. Fishers. *The North-East Frontier Agency*. California: Institute of International Studies, University of California, 1970.

117. Sarkar, Sourindranath. *Psycho-dynamics of Tribal Behaviour*. Calcutta: Bookland, 1965.

118. Scott, J.G. and Hardiman. *Gazetteer of Upper Burma*, 5 Vol. Rangoon, 1906.

119. _______._______, *Burma, A Handbook of Practical Information*, Edinburgh: Moring, 1906.

120. Shakespeare J. *The Lushei-Kuki Clans*. London: Macmillan, 1912.

121. _______, *History of the Assam Rifles*. London: Macmillan and Co. Ltd., 1929.

122. _______, *Manipur Under British Management 1891-1907*. Shillong: Assam Secretariat Printing Office, 1907.

123. Shakespeare, L. W. *History of Assam, Upper Burma and North-East Frontier*. London: 1914.

124. Sharma, Jagdish Saran (Ed). *India's Struggle For Freedom*, Vol. III. Delhi: S. Chand and Company, 1965.

125. Sharma, S. Gopendra. *Manipur a Decade of Progress*. Calcutta: Navana Printing Works Private Ltd., 1962.

126. Sharma, Sudesh K, *Union Territory*. Patiala: Chandi Publishers, 1968.

127. Shaw, William. *Notes on the Thadore Kukis*. London, 1929.

128. Singh, M.K. Priyabarata, *Administration Report. Manipur State, 1946-47*. Imphal: The State Printing Press, 1948.

129. Singh, Prakash, *Nagaland*. New Delhi: National Book Trust, 1972.

130. Soppitt, C.A. *A Short Account of the Kacha Naga Tribes*. Shillong, 1885.

131. Stewart, G.P. *Administration Report, Manipur State, 1932-1933*. Imphal: The State Printing Press, 1933.

132. _______, *Administration Report, Manipur State, 1933-1934*. Imphal: The State Printing Press, 1934.

133. _______, *Administration Report, Manipur State, 1934-1935*. Imphal: The State Printing Press, 1935.

134. Stracy, P.D. *Nagaland Nightmare*. New Delhi: Allied Publishers Private Limited, 1960.

135. Stewart, A.T.Q, *The Pagoda War*. London: Faber & Faber, 1972.

136. Symes, M. *An account of an Embassy to the Kingdom of Ava.* London, 1827.

137. Thomas, M.M. and R.W. Taylor, *Tribal Awakening*. Bangalore: Christian Institute for the Study of Religion and Society, 1965.

138. *The Cultural History of India*, Vol. I. Calcutta: The Ramkrishna Mission Institute of Culture, 1937.

139. *The Imperial Gazetteer of India*, Vol. IV. Oxford: 1901.

140. *The Imperial Gazetteer of India*, Vol. II. Oxford: 1908.

141. *The Imperial Gazetteer of India*, Vol. XVII. Oxford: 1908.

142. Thompson, Edward, *Rise and Fulfilment of British Rule in India.* London: Macmillan & Co. Ltd. 1934.

143. Tinker, Hugh. *The Union of Burma*. London: Oxford University Press, 1959.

144. Trant, T.A. *Two Years in Ava*, 1824-26. London: 1827.

145. Trager, Frank N., *Burma*. London: Pall Mall Press, 1966.

146. Trumball, Robert, *As I See India*. London: Cassell and Com. Ltd., 1957.

147. Tupper, Charles Lewis, *Our Indian Protectorate*. London: 1893.

148. Viscount Marsey, *The Viceroys and Governors-General of India.* London; 1947.

149. Ward, S.R. (Ed.), *Glimse of Assam*. Calcutta: Thomas S. Smith City Press, 1884.

150. Wilson, Horace Hayman, *Narrative of the Burmese War*. London, Win H. Allen, And Co., 1852.

151. Wheeler, J. Talboys, *A Short History of India*. London: Macmillan & Co., 1889.

152. White, W.A. *Political History of the Extraordinary Events Which Led to the Burmese War*. London: 1827.

153. Woodman, Dorothy, *The Making of Burma*. London: The Cresset Press, 1962.

154. Yule, H.A. (Comp.), *Narrative of the Mission to the Court of Ava in 1855*. London: Oxford University Press, 1968.

B. Newspapers and other Periodicals

1. In Britain

The Times (London)

2. In India (English Language only)
The Assam Tribune (Gauhati)
The Amrita Bazar Patrika (Calcutta)
The Bengalee (Calcutta)
The Citizens Voice (Kohima)
The Forward (Calcutta)
The Hindustan Standard (Calcutta)
The Indian Express (Bombay)
The Motherland (New Delhi)
The Naga News (Kohima)
The Nagaland Times (Kohima)
The Pioneer (Lucknow)
The Patriot (Delhi)
The Star of India (Calcutta)
The Tribune (Chandigarh)
The Young India (Shillong)331

3. In Manipur (Manipuri Language Only)
The Bhagyavati Patrika (Imphal)
The Daily Praja (Imphal)

4. The Indian Annual Register
N.N. Mitra (ed.),
An Annual Digest of Public Affairs in India 1919-40, (Calcutta)

Index

L

M

N

O

P

Q

R

S

W

Y

Z